The Godspell Experience

Stephen Nathan (right) as Jesus makes a point with his ventriloquist's dummy. Herb Braha and David Haskell respond. From a performance by the original *Godspell* cast in June 1971 at the Cherry Lane Theatre. (Photo by Kenn Duncan/©The New York Public Library)

The Godspell Experience
Inside a Transformative Musical

Carol de Giere

Foreword by Stephen Schwartz

Scene 1 Publishing
Bethel, Connecticut USA

The Godspell Experience: Inside a Transformative Musical
Copyright © 2014 by Carol de Giere

All rights reserved. No part of this book may be reproduced in any form, without written permission, except by a reviewer who wishes to quote brief passages in connection with a review.

Published in 2014 by Scene 1 Publishing
A division of Scene 1 Arts, LLC
10 Library Place #909
Bethel, CT 06801-0909

www.TheGodspellExperience.com
www.caroldegiere.com

Printed in the United States of America
Book cover by Jerry Dorris of Author Support
Inside book design by V. Paul Smith Jr.

Publisher's Cataloging-In-Publication Data
(Prepared by The Donohue Group, Inc.)

De Giere, Carol.
   The Godspell experience : inside a transformative musical / Carol de Giere ; foreword by Stephen Schwartz.

      pages : illustrations ; cm

      Companion website to book (www.TheGodspellExperience.com) provides additional material about Godspell, access to audio and video clips, and links to additional resources.
   Issued also as an ebook.
   Includes bibliographical references and index.
   ISBN: 978-0-9895660-0-1

   1. Schwartz, Stephen. Godspell. 2. Bible. Matthew--Drama--History and criticism. 3. Bible. Matthew--Songs and music--History and criticism. 4. Godspell (Motion picture) 5. Musicals--United States--History and criticism. I. Schwartz, Stephen. II. Title.

   ML410.S39 D44 2014
   782.1/4/0973

ISBN: 978-0-9895660-0-1

Contents

Foreword by Stephen Schwartz ix

Part I The Making of *Godspell* 1

1. The Lights Go Up 3
2. Tebelak and Schwartz: Theatrical Childhoods 7
3. An Eclectic Talent Gathering at CMU in the 1960s 15
4. The Turning Point: 1968 25
5. The College *Godspell* 35
6. Experiments in New York City 53
7. Enter Lansbury, Beruh, and Schwartz 69
8. An Off-Broadway Collaboration 77
9. Mishaps, Miracles, and a Completed New Musical 89
10. Long Live *Godspell* 105

Part II Understanding *Godspell*: Concepts and Colorful Details 121

11. Why Send in the Clown Characters? 125
12. What Holds *Godspell* Together? 131
13. The John/Judas Relationship Arc with Jesus 141
14. Symbol Wars, or Is Clown Makeup a Message? 145
15. Q & A: Is *Godspell*'s Comic Tone Spiritually Appropriate? (and Other Concerns) 151

Part III *Godspell*'s Score – Song by Song 163

16. Notes on the Score, Recordings, and Lyrics 165
17. *Godspell*'s "Prologue" and the War of Words 171
18. Prepare Ye: Solving the Problem of a One-Line Lyric . 179
19. "Save the People" – Is This What Jesus Wants? 183
20. The "Day by Day" Sing-Along 187

21. "Learn Your Lessons Well" – a Flexible Song 193
22. Bless the Lord My Burst of Energy 201
23. "All for the Best" – The Friendship Duet 207
24. "All Good Gifts" – *Godspell*'s Thanksgiving 213
25. "Light of the World" – Rhymes for Matthew 5:13–16 . 219
26. "Turn Back, O Man" – an Invitation to Act II 225
27. "Alas for You" – Song of Frustration 229
28. "By My Side" – Songwriters and the Pebble "Dare" . . 233
29. "We Beseech Thee" – Come Sing about Love 243
30. "On the Willows" – The Ballad of Psalm 137 249
31. "Finale" – Long Live God Counterpoint 253
32. "Beautiful City" – The Lasting Tribute 257

Part IV A *Godspell* Grab Bag **261**

33. *Godspell* Worldwide: The Stories Continue 263
34. The *Godspell* Commune Company 277
35. The *Godspell* Movie 281
36. The 2011 Broadway Revival 303
Epilogue: Reflections on *Godspell* as a
    Transformative Musical 313

Appendices

Appendix A: *Dramatics Magazine* 1975 interview with
    Schwartz and Tebelak 323
Appendix B: Credits for *Godspell* at CMU, Café La MaMa,
    and the Cherry Lane Theatre productions 335
Appendices C and D are posted on the book's website
    TheGodspellExperience.com
Appendix C: Where Are They Now?
Appendix D: The *Godspell* Costume Story

Notes 339
Bibliography and Resources for Further Information 345
Acknowledgments 348
Lyrics Permissions 350
Photography Credits 353
Index 355

A portrait of John-Michael Tebelak, who conceived *Godspell* and directed the early productions. He is wearing his signature outfit: overalls with embroidered ducks on the bib.

The Companion Website

www.TheGodspellExperience.com

Readers are invited to visit this book's companion website that provides additional material about *Godspell*, access to audio and video clips, a store, links to additional resources, and updates from the author. The website also includes two of the appendices for the book:

Appendix C: "Where Are They Now," with more of John-Michael Tebelak's biography and the lives of other key people mentioned

Appendix D: "The *Godspell* Costume Story," featuring original costume sketches and related details

About the Photographs in this Book

Many individuals contributed photos from their private collections. Rights holders provided others. Credits and courtesy notes are listed at the back of the book on the Photography Credits page, except when a photographer or rights holder preferred a listing with the image.

Foreword
by Stephen Schwartz

A Somewhat Hazy Recollection

I was spending the evening of my twenty-third birthday, March 6, 1971, at the Long Island home of my parents, along with my wife, Carole. It was not a particularly festive occasion, as my prospects for the future were not looking terribly bright. I had recently left my job as an A&R producer for RCA Records by mutual agreement (meaning I wasn't liking the job and they weren't liking the job I was doing), and that, coupled with the failure of *The Survival of Saint Joan*, a rock musical for which I had been musical supervisor, meant a precipitous drop in income from almost decent to none. Well, not quite none, since I still was receiving $25 a week for the title song for *Butterflies Are Free*, or more accurately, $22.50 after agent's commission. The situation wasn't entirely dire, since Carole was doing pretty well as an actress, but it was a little scary, and we were bemoaning the situation over birthday cake when the telephone rang. That telephone call changed my life.

On the line was Charles Haid, a talented director whom I had known at Carnegie Mellon University, where we had both been drama students. Charlie told me that he was serving as an associate producer for Edgar Lansbury and Joseph Beruh, who were interested in a show currently playing off-off-Broadway at the experimental Café La MaMa. The show was called *The Godspell*, and Edgar and Joe thought it had potential as a commercial musical and were looking for a composer. Edgar and Joe had heard some of my work several months before, when my agent, Shirley Bernstein, had taken me to audition for them the score to *Pippin* (in which they showed no interest whatsoever, hence my surprise that they had remembered me at all). To this day, I don't know how my name came up in discussions among them, but in any event, Charlie told me that the show had one more performance at La MaMa on the following (Sunday) night and asked if I would go to see it. Although Edgar adamantly denies it, I have always assumed that the reason they didn't call me until the night before closing was that they had approached every known composer in New York and been turned down by all of them, and finally in desperation, they were turning to that kid who had brought them the cockamamie musical about the son of Charlemagne. Whatever the truth, Carole and I were at Café La MaMa the following evening.

    I was astonished by what I saw. First of all, there was the pleasant surprise that I not only knew the conceiver and director of the show, John-Michael Tebelak, from Carnegie Mellon, but there were other friends of mine from school as cast members. But it was the show itself that really blew me away. A wildly imaginative re-telling of the Gospel of St. Matthew (with a little Luke and John thrown in for good measure), it was theatrically inventive, original, and above all, hilarious. Think about that for a moment: This story had been around for nearly two thousand years, and no one before had realized it could be funny. That's my definition of genius: the ability to imagine what others cannot until it is shown to them, at which time it seems obvious. (Another example of this, in my opinion, was Gregory Maguire realizing that the Wicked Witch of the West was a great protagonist for a novel.) And by funny, I don't mean satirical let's-make-fun-of-religion funny, I mean the humor that arises from human beings behaving according to human foibles. And then at the end, it was suddenly and unexpectedly moving and uplifting. So to my thinking, John-Michael had a genius idea, and I was only too happy to sign on and try to help him bring it to fruition.

Now let's face it: At this point in my career (or lack thereof), I would have been happy if I'd been offered *Bike Boys Meet Godzilla*. The fact that the show with which I got to make my New York musical theater debut was *Godspell* (we dropped the "The" from the title somewhere along the way) was nothing short of, well, miraculous. As Carol de Giere details in the following book, the score had to be written quickly–five weeks to be precise. But I had some advantages: For one thing, many of the songs were settings or adaptations of Episcopal hymns which John-Michael had selected and placed in the script. So the lyrics for many of the songs already existed, meaning I had to write only music for those. John-Michael had useful suggestions as to who should sing which song and vivid insights into what the feel of many of them should be (for instance, saying that he felt the music for "On the Willows" should be "oceanic"). I was also able to draw inspiration from many of the songwriters and groups I was listening to and enjoying at the time: Laura Nyro, James Taylor, Elton John, The Supremes, The Mamas and the Papas, etc., so that the score became a kind of pastiche of my favorite pop styles. Where lyrics were required, I often had text to draw from that John-Michael had found, including Biblical passages. In any event, the score was ready for our first day of rehearsal, and away we went.

The rehearsals passed in a kind of blur, but there was truly a quality of kids-putting-on-a-show-in-a-barn. We laughed a lot, fought a bit, but somehow managed to remain insulated from the usual pressures of putting on a new musical in New York. I give the producers a lot of credit for that, but our general naiveté and ignorance helped. It wasn't until we were about to start previews that one of our cast members, Jeffrey Mylett, pointed out that other people were actually going to see the show. I remember it coming as a shock.

Right before previews began, since anxiety was now mounting a bit, one of the producers, Joe Beruh, took me out to dinner to help calm me down. I will never forget what he said to me that night. I can still see where we were sitting and hear his voice. He told me that, having seen what we had in rehearsal, he was confident that we were going to be all right with the show. But then he spoke more quietly and leaned into me a little, and said, "But if you really do your jobs now during previews, if you really get this together, you're not going to believe what's going to happen."

Those are probably the most prescient words I've ever heard from a producer. Within a year, *Godspell* had become a worldwide phenomenon and an out-of-work twenty-three-year-old composer and lyricist had embarked on what has been a long and, I'm happy to say, ongoing career.

All these years later, it has been fascinating to me to read Carol de Giere's thoroughly researched and colorfully written book, which contains many details about the development of the show that I never knew before. Although unfortunately she was unable to speak to some of the original creators and participants, including most significantly John-Michael Tebelak, who died prematurely of a heart attack in 1985, as well as some of the male original cast members such as Jeffrey Mylett, Lamar Alford, and David Haskell, she has interviewed the seven living original cast members and many others involved with the creation of the show. She's even culled the recollections of John-Michael's sister. She has been able to record stories about the origins of the show before they are lost, to explore details about each song, and to answer many frequently asked questions.

Foreword

To this day, the strange experimental little show that began in the cinder-block Studio Theatre at Carnegie Mellon and traveled from off-off-Broadway to a tiny off-Broadway house to Broadway and international success, is still constantly playing in theaters, schools, churches, and other venues around the world. I feel lucky and proud to have been a part of it, and now feel lucky again to have this book to remind me how it all came to be.

Stephen Schwartz composed songs for *Godspell* and *Pippin* on this upright Sohmer piano that he now keeps in his basement.

Stephen Schwartz stands in front of the marquis for two of his Broadway musicals: the long-running show *Wicked* playing at the Gershwin Theatre and the revival of *Godspell* that was staged next door at the Circle in the Square Theatre (lower logo) from November 2011 to June 2012. (Photo by Jeremy Daniel)

PART I
The Making of *Godspell*

Original *Godspell* cast members perform "Bless the Lord" at the Cherry Lane Theatre. Front: Joanne Jonas. Second row, from left: Peggy Gordon, Sonia Manzano, Gilmer McCormick, Robin Lamont. On the platform, from left: Herb Braha, Stephen Nathan, Jeffrey Mylett, David Haskell. (Photo by Martha Swope/©The New York Public Library)

The Godspell Experience

Godspell's original cast approaches Biblical material with childlike playfulness. Facing forward: Lamar Alford, Gilmer McCormick, Stephen Nathan, Joanne Jonas. (Photo by Kenn Duncan/©The New York Public Library)

Chapter 1

The Lights Go Up

On opening night, May 17, 1971, a curtain could only metaphorically rise on the new Off-Broadway musical, *Godspell*, playing in New York City's Greenwich Village. No draping fabric covered the performing space because John-Michael Tebelak, who conceived and directed the show, wanted audiences to easily view the redbrick back wall of the Cherry Lane Theatre and the acting space he set off on three sides by a nine-foot-tall silvery metal chain link fence. This environment was his way of suggesting an abandoned playground, according to cast member Peggy Gordon. As childlike clown characters played with Biblical parables, they would, in Gordon's words, "rediscover this person, Jesus, through the innocent, unprejudiced prism of a child."

Five months earlier, Tebelak and other students at Carnegie Mellon University in Pittsburgh had introduced a rawer version (called *The Godspell*) with a different score. Along with playful parable enactments within a similar chain link fence environment, that four-performance production wove in a Beatitudes rap, pot smoking, and the actor playing Jesus singing "Oh God, I'm busted" before his Crucifixion scene. Carnegie audiences went wild for the bold and boundary-breaking creation.

Next, Ellen Stewart fit a two-week run of a slightly more refined version into the schedule at her experimental theater, Café La MaMa, in Manhattan's East Village. Then, for the Cherry Lane Theatre opening, a newly revamped *Godspell* integrated the first professional score by an unknown twenty-three-year-old composer, Stephen Schwartz. The song list that audiences would soon be raving about included a roof-raising gospel number, stirring choral numbers, rock ballads, a delightful soft-shoe piece, and the future pop hit "Day by Day."

Virtually everyone in the *Godspell* company was in their late teens or early twenties and, in varying degrees, new to New York City's commercial show business, so they were both wide-eyed and worried about the official opening. Music director Stephen Reinhardt remembers his concern that "the mentally overwrought critics were going to come down and tear it apart. You have to have your heart on your sleeve when you come to see *Godspell* in order to receive the full experience that it has to offer." Would anyone get it?

Sitting in the house with several theater critics that spring night, an enthusiastic audience frequently applauded the ten actors on stage as they sang, danced, tumbled, pantomimed, painted each other's faces, leapt, wept, and sometimes skipped up and down the center aisle.

To the producers' relief, *Godspell* worked its magic for many of the critics. One reviewer praised the "cheerful ebullient passion play" for being a children's masquerade party, carnival, circus, charades, vaudeville show, and revival meeting all in one. A New Jersey critic lauded its infectious joy and the "jubilation in their robust delivery of Schwartz's palm-smacking and widely ranging rock numbers."

With word-of-mouth buzz and positive reviews around town, it didn't so much matter what Clive Barnes wrote in his review for *The New York Times*. He captured part of the show's appeal in his comments published on May 18, 1971: "Innocence reigned like thunder at the Cherry Lane Theatre, where last night a new musical called *'Godspell'* opened." Yet he wasn't ready to give it a rave review. He closed his remarks by saying, "…there may well be those who will find freshness and originality here where I could discover only a naïve but fey frivolity."

Nonetheless, *Godspell* played on.

The show nourished its audiences because, while it was fun, it wasn't actually frivolous. Tebelak had conceived a multi-layered theatrical happening that allowed audiences to be entertained with comedic performances while they savored subtle meanings in the underlying story of community and compassion.

Cast member Gilmer McCormick remembers feeling that *Godspell* was an antidote for the times. "Don't forget, it was during the Vietnam War. I think people needed that kind of message. There was something about the good news of that message that suddenly you would find nuns and priests in the audience and they're saying, 'I can look at Jesus the man and I can rediscover the joy of this message. He didn't mean for us to sit around and mope.'"

Six weeks after it opened, when the colorfully costumed cast appeared on *The Today Show* and actor Robin Lamont led them in singing "Day by Day" in her hearty, folk-rock-suited voice, the new musical reached a receptive public. Lamont recalls, "When we came to the theater that night, the producers were jumping all around. They said, 'The phones are ringing off the hook!' From that moment, we were sold out almost every night, as a result of that appearance and word of mouth. It was delightful."

Schwartz remembers taking the subway from his Upper West Side apartment to Greenwich Village for performances and standing in the back of the theater. "It was so amazing to watch the audience, and there were all these celebrities coming down. I was twenty-three years old, watching my childhood dream come true. Needless to say, I went a lot."

How did he and his twenty-something colleagues launch a blockbuster musical with less than a year of preparation? Were they singularly talented? Did their theatrical training as teenagers make a difference? Were they driven by social transformations of the 1960s to fulfill a need of the times? Perhaps a combination of factors served them well.

In Tebelak's estimation, so much depended upon what happened beforehand. His remarks for a *Dramatics Magazine* interview explore this point: "I remember hearing of one playwright—I think he was in his mid forties before his first play was done—and someone asked, 'How long did it take you to write your play?' He said, 'Well, thirty-nine years to live, and I think, maybe three days to put it down on paper.'"

For Tebelak and his colleagues it had taken a bit longer than three days to develop *Godspell*, but the playwright's idea about essential background experience still holds: this new musical couldn't have emerged in isolation without the life adventures that came before it.

Part I of *The Godspell Experience* presents the story of how *Godspell* sprang to the stage on the basis of these experiences and with the aid of some inspired creativity.

Chapter 2

Tebelak and Schwartz: Theatrical Childhoods

John-Michael Tebelak

Godspell is the brainchild of someone who didn't fit a mold, even in childhood. "My mom would always say he was from another planet," recalls Trudy Tebelak Williams about her brother, John-Michael. "Living with him was one surprise after another."

There were unexpected little things, like his coming up with philosophical words in conversation as a child that his parents had never spoken. And then there was his consuming passion for the theater at a very young age.

John-Michael Tebelak was born September 17, 1949, in Akron, Ohio. Nine years later, after the family moved to the Cleveland area, he started working on local theater productions and found a world to which he'd be devoted for the rest of his life.

His sister, who was four years older than John-Michael, remembers him as an inquisitive, happy kid who had few inhibitions when it came to theatrical productions. She recalls, "My mom and I would go to a show, and she'd say, 'Trudy, isn't that the end table that used to be in the garage?'" He had brought it in for a prop. Once, when he was older, he borrowed a truck and just backed it up to the house to pick up what he needed for a set.

Tebelak's family heritage foreshadows the hint of vaudevillian sketch style within *Godspell*. His mother's parents, Tony and Margaret Brill, were involved with a chain of vaudeville houses back in the silent movie era. They didn't believe the newfangled "talkies" would ever take away their business. But when movies came to dominate entertainment, the Brills ended up working in rubber factories in Akron.

Their daughter, Genevieve Brill Tebelak, and her husband, John Tebelak, were schoolteachers. An inclination toward a theater career skipped this generation and emerged in full flower in Genevieve and John's son, John-Michael.

Although the Tebelaks were all focused on their own activities with work and education, they were a close-knit family. John-Michael and his mother had a strong bond, and he and his sister were in constant contact. She drove him to theaters and helped with makeup or other backstage activities.

John-Michael's father was sympathetic and encouraging. This impressed John-Michael's friend, Bill Phillips, who visited the home. "Here was John, a stalwart physical education teacher, while his son was tall, gangly, self-effacing, and definitely non-athletic. But to John's credit, he always made it work."

John-Michael's theater fascination proved fortunate, as he wasn't especially interested in traditional school subjects. Although Trudy enjoyed reading *Time* magazine before she entered first grade, her brother was oriented differently, showing signs of dyslexia and other academic challenges. The eventual outcome of nature and nurture was a boy with a singular focus. Trudy notes, "I guess all the passion that was lacking from reading and writing became like a pure light beam for theater."

Unlike most of his future colleagues for *Godspell*, Tebelak didn't gravitate to the dramatic stage in order to act, although he played a few parts in high school and elsewhere, and listed six roles on his professional resumé. Instead, the future M.F.A. degree recipient created a theater-oriented life by focusing on design and directing.

Starting at age nine, with the Berea Summer Theatre in the Cleveland suburb of Berea, Ohio, Tebelak began accumulating stagecraft experiences. By the summer of 1965, when he was 15 years old, he was proficient enough to serve as an assistant designer for several shows at the Cleveland Musicarnival, one of the first large tent theaters in America. When he was sixteen, he designed sets and costumes for a show at Cleveland State University, and after graduating from high school, he returned to the Berea Summer Theatre where he performed in *Little Mary Sunshine* and stage managed their production of *Carnival*.

His talents, experience, and school grades were strong enough that he was accepted into the highly respected B.F.A. program at Carnegie Mellon University in Pittsburgh, Pennsylvania. There he would meet songwriter Stephen Schwartz and most of the actors he would cast in *Godspell*.

Stephen Schwartz

Like Tebelak, Schwartz developed his musical theater chops throughout his youth. By the time he wrote the score for *Godspell*, he had already been immersed in musicals for over a decade.

Stephen Lawrence Schwartz was born on March 6, 1948, in New York City to Stan and Sheila Schwartz. Sheila was a music lover, and as a youngster her son listened as she played recordings from her Broadway musicals, folk, opera, and classical collections.

After several relocations, when Stephen was seven years old, the family (that by then also included a daughter, Marge) settled in the upper-middle-class suburb of Roslyn Heights on Long Island. Their next door neighbor was composer and pianist George Kleinsinger, who happened to be co-writing the Broadway-bound musical *Shinbone Alley* (based on Don Marquis' Archy and Mehitabel stories). Kleinsinger worked at home and sometimes would play a new tune for Stan and Sheila, with their son in attendance. "Steve," as he was then called, would pick out the tunes he just heard. Kleinsinger encouraged him, and told his parents that the boy had talent. Stan and Sheila bought an upright piano and started their son on piano lessons.

When *Shinbone Alley* opened in 1957, it was a flop, closing after only 49 performances. But for a music-loving nine-year-old boy, seeing his neighbor's show on stage was a life-changing experience. "From then on, that was my ambition—to write for the Broadway musical theater," Schwartz reflected later. "I think a lot of us get smitten and fall in love with theater the first time we see it; it certainly was true in my case."

From writing pieces for backyard puppet shows to songs for school events, his creativity couldn't be turned off. Sheila Schwartz recalls, "He was always fooling around at the piano. He really loved it, and so even when he was supposed to be practicing, he would play things that weren't assigned. Every once in a while I'd realize what he was doing and I'd say, 'Let's practice first; do that later.'"

After many years of private piano lessons, Stephen auditioned for and was accepted to Juilliard School of Music Preparatory Division in Manhattan, where he'd study performance, theory, and composition on weekends for four years.

In his spare time he studied the songwriting craft. "I used to go to the library and take out the scripts for musicals I hadn't seen," he recalls. "I would look at the lyrics and write tunes to them, then go listen to the cast album and hear what the composer had actually done." He even made up a dream list of imaginary names of shows he'd write and how long they would run on Broadway.

His parents never tried to dissuade their son from following an "impractical" dream of a career in the arts. They encouraged him by supporting his music lessons and taking him to Broadway musicals several times a year.

As with Tebelak's early life, his was another fortunate convergence of nature and nurture: young Schwartz came equipped with an acute sensitivity to music, and he benefited from an environment that fostered an accelerated artistic development.

For more on Schwartz's personal background and his remarkable theater and film career, see "Defying Gravity: The Creative Career of Stephen Schwartz, from Godspell to Wicked."

Because he had entered kindergarten early and advanced a grade in primary school, Schwartz was ready to graduate from high school at age sixteen. He applied to Carnegie Mellon University's drama school by submitting a play he had written, was accepted, and headed to Pittsburgh in the fall of 1964.

NOTE

Schwartz, Tebelak, and others started attending Carnegie when it was called the Carnegie Institute of Technology. In 1967, it merged with the Mellon Institute of Industrial Research to become Carnegie Mellon University. In this book I will simply refer to it as Carnegie Mellon University, or CMU.

The Godspell Experience

ABOVE: John-Michael Tebelak as a toddler. LEFT: The Tebelak family gathers in front of their home in Ohio. John-Michael stands in front of his sister Trudy, his father John, and his mother Genevieve. RIGHT: Tebelak in high school with his date.

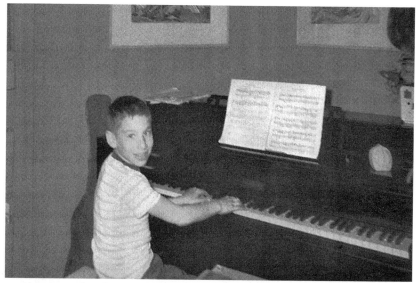

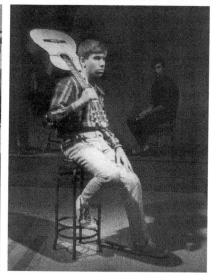

ABOVE: Stephen Schwartz, age 7, plays the family's Knabe upright. LEFT: Schwartz sits on Santa's lap. The Schwartz family celebrated an American-style Christmas as well as major Jewish holidays. RIGHT: Schwartz performs in a theater camp production of *Spoon River Anthology* in the early 1960s. He played guitar in the show. In high school, he joined the school drama club and acted in several shows.

Drama program classes at Carnegie Mellon University were generally held in the College of Fine Arts building, a space shared with music, visual arts, and architecture majors. "We were in a true arts community," recalls Stephen Nathan, a CMU student and future *Godspell* actor. "The art department at Carnegie was phenomenal. The music department was incredible. It was an extraordinary place."

CHAPTER 3

An Eclectic Talent Gathering at CMU in the 1960s

In the mid to late 1960s, Carnegie Mellon University's drama program drew together a diverse cadre of aspiring performers, directors, playwrights, and designers. They would eventually land acting, directing, or writing roles in *1776, Godspell, Grease, Pippin, Hill Street Blues, L.A. Law, NYPD Blue, Sesame Street,* and many other stage and television shows, as well as roles in films.

Stringent entrance requirements narrowed the freshman classes to a chosen few who excelled at CMU's auditions or submitted samples of their work. Each year the faculty chose a limited number of students to invite back to continue their studies, so enrollment became increasingly exclusive.

During their time together, the "Dramats," as students in the drama program were called, benefited from camaraderie. "The Dramats were a small, tightly-knit family," remembers Katie Hanley, who would appear several years later in the *Godspell* movie and stage productions. "I started my first day of classes as a hopeful freshman, honored to have been chosen to be a part of a gifted, elite group of actors. As we gathered in the auditorium for the first time, it was announced that we would be torn down, molded, and could expect only four or five of us to be able to endure it. My classmates became trench buddies, and it bonded us for life."

At the same time that *Godspell*'s creators were enrolled there, the idealistic and revolutionary 1960s spirit cast its own light over the era. As on other college and university campuses, colorfully adorned students in jeans tossed Frisbees between classes, while others slipped away to smoke pot or practice meditation. There were sit-ins and other protests against the Vietnam conflict. Many students moved off campus as soon as they were allowed and had no qualms about mixed gender housing. The youthful spirit of questioning assumptions of elders touched Schwartz, Tebelak, and others who would be involved in *Godspell*, and helped them take a fresh approach to a new musical with centuries-old religious content.

The mid to late 1960s brought shifts in the musical environment as well. Recording artists responded to the themes, challenges, and new freedoms of the decade. Trends in popular music shifted away from naive rock 'n' roll toward hard rock, singer-songwriter folk-rock, and protest songs. Message songs like "All You Need Is Love" (The Beatles) and "Let's Get Together" (The Youngbloods) represented ideals of the day.

Changes were rocking the dramatic arts. American theater educator Viola Spolin was one of many innovators challenging the old ways. Spolin developed theater games and exercises for stimulating the creativity of each actor contributing to a project. She and her son, Paul Sills, established trends and improvisational techniques that led to Chicago's The Second City comedy club and later, Paul Sills' Story Theatre and *Saturday Night Live*. Students at CMU were exposed to improvisation and similar techniques through the faculty and other contacts.

Still, young people needed to acclimate to traditional theater as well. The years that the acting and directing students spent at Carnegie Mellon University would help shape their future artistic endeavors.

Schwartz as a Drama Student

When Stephen Schwartz entered Carnegie in 1964, he started out as a playwriting major before switching to the directing program. That program allowed him to take classes in all aspects of theater. He once commented that his training in the dramatic arts was essential for his future artistic efforts. "I decided to go to drama school when I went to college, rather than majoring in music. I'd already studied music for ten years; I knew very little about theater. It turned out that, despite my having no acting talent, the four years of acting I took proved especially valuable. They helped teach me what actors need to make a scene or song work for them. I think everybody writing for theater should take acting." He says that while writing for musicals, "I try to become the character, think about what the character's action is (what he or she is trying to 'do' at that moment), and then express myself as that character would."

Schwartz also honed his musical writing skills outside of class, collaborating on four original musicals that were staged as part of the student-run Scotch 'n' Soda Club. His college friend, Colette Bablon, remembers listening to his newly composed works for the Scotch 'n' Soda productions. "There was a tiny cubicle of a rehearsal room in the College of Fine Arts building with a piano," Bablon recalls. "That's where he would play me his songs. I was amazed at what was coming from this kid. And the lyrics were really clever. He was very precocious."

Few others around him focused on musicals. There wasn't even a musical theater program at CMU at that time, but the composer was inspired by his love of the Broadway shows he had seen, such as *Fiddler on the Roof*, *Gypsy*, and *My Fair Lady*. He hoped he could write something new that would fit into the canon of beloved works.

As much as he liked tradition when it came to musical storytelling, he embraced change in other regards. About the experience of studying at CMU in the 1960s he has said, "In terms of liberation and 'doing your own thing,' Carnegie was the sixties squared—it was very extreme in that way and I found it very helpful." The spirit of doing your own thing freed him artistically to incorporate the styles he liked into his musical theater scores. He decided to draw from Motown, The Beatles, Simon and Garfunkel, and other popular recording groups, rather than restrict himself to the style of theater composers he admired like Richard Rodgers, Jerry Bock, Jule Styne, or Frederick Loewe. (More details are provided in Part III of this book.)

In spring 1968, Schwartz graduated from Carnegie Mellon University with a B.F.A. degree in directing. He met many of his future *Godspell* colleagues on campus but he wasn't involved with the show's earliest incarnations.

John-Michael Tebelak and Nina Faso at Carnegie

In 1966, John-Michael Tebelak entered Carnegie Mellon University's drama program where he would at first study design and technical production, and later would focus on directing. Settling into college life, he grew his hair long and started wearing what became his standard dress: blue denim overalls with yellow ducks embroidered on the bib. (He once revealed that he liked wearing oversized overalls because it made people laugh.)

Academically, he was fortunate to be in a program with Nina Faso, a petite, dark-haired freshman from Syracuse, New York, who would eventually become *Godspell*'s first professional stage manager, the director of numerous *Godspell* productions, and a friend and colleague of Stephen Schwartz.

Faso was not only experienced in the theater arts, but was proficient in the language skills that Tebelak lacked. She recalls, "He had a terrible time writing and reading. He was a painterly kind of person. He saw everything in pictures and music, and would only direct by hearing or speaking—he would rarely write anything down. So he became extremely dependent on me as a friend because I was in his classes and I could write things down. We shared a lot of work in college."

The support worked both ways. Faso admired her new friend's ideas. "If I had something I was working on that really needed a spark, I'd ask him what he thought. He was always a step ahead of everybody in the sense that he had a wonderful appreciation of what was going on in the theater world—all the new techniques."

Although he was connected with theater trends and had numerous friends, he also developed ways to disconnect. Faso notes, "The best way I can describe John-Michael is he was almost always either standing or sitting in a chair with a cigarette and a Coke in his hand. I'd never seen him play the piano or dance; he was always removed, always the watcher." He'd soon use his propensity to witness the world around him in service of his emerging role as a director.

Tebelak used some of his spare time to keep up with trends in music and culture. He enjoyed popular music, which influenced his choices for his theater work. The 1968 musical *Hair* brought rock music and "Age of Aquarius" sentiments to Broadway. It captured the expansive and playful mood of the times in a way that Tebelak loved. "I remember him listening to the *Hair* album on the record player in our apartment," says Bill Phillips, a graduate student in directing who at one point was Tebelak's off-campus apartment mate. "He played it over and over."

Among the faculty members who understood Tebelak's spirit was Leon Katz, a professor of playwriting. Katz recalls, "He didn't want to miss opportunities to experiment," referring to Tebelak's exploration of drug-induced psychedelic experiences as well as his enthusiasm for theatrical innovations. Katz later played an important role in helping Tebelak get the college version of *Godspell* off the ground.

The 1960s at CMU: Culture and Curriculum

One thing that attracted students to CMU in the first place was the minimal liberal arts requirements, which meant that students majoring in drama could focus on career-relevant subjects from the beginning of their undergraduate studies. Original *Godspell* cast member Robin Lamont says about her freshman year: "We took dancing, speech, fencing, voice, movement, and mime. Those were our 101 courses." It also meant, as they discovered, they could be recruited for stage crew activities and be working into the night preparing costumes or whatever was required of them.

Stephen Nathan, who would later play Jesus in post-college productions of *Godspell*, cherished the opportunities and freedom of his student days at CMU. "What I remember and relish even now is that I got to do plays all the time." He adds that another attraction was the pass/fail system. "We were terrible students because there were no grades. There was absolutely no inherent respect for authority."

Sonia Manzano, who grew up in an impoverished area of the Bronx, felt that the pass/fail system was ideal for her. Some of her academic skills, like writing, were weak, but she had trained as a performer at the High School of Performing Arts. She was granted a scholarship to Carnegie based on her audition. At CMU she especially loved the movement classes that helped her develop her own physical comedy style. Manzano was later cast in the college and New York versions of *Godspell* before she was recruited to play Maria on *Sesame Street*.

The pass/fail policy likely helped other students feel bolder about extracurricular creative activities. While their time was mostly structured with coursework, many students seized moments to mount or create shows on the side. In their free time, Tebelak and friends staged *A Funny Thing Happened on the Way to the Forum* in the student center. (Tebelak apparently performed well in the show as he sang "Everybody Ought to Have a Maid," hamming it up appropriately.) Future *Godspell* cast member Peggy Gordon wished that as an acting major, she could also minor in playwriting or music, but regulations prohibited it. So she wrote during her free time.

Gordon and several fellow students, including Jay Hamburger, spent some of their unscheduled hours planning for a summer traveling troupe they called the Open Players. They wrote their own plays for it, including Hamburger's play *Marigold and Elkin*. Gordon composed the music for "Marigold's Song," an excerpt (turned lyrics) from Hamburger's unfinished play. The Open Players project closed down before the summer, but "Marigold's Song" lived on. It eventually became *Godspell*'s "By My Side," which Gordon performed as part of the original Off-Broadway cast, along with fellow cast member Gilmer McCormick.

(Details about this song's evolution are included in the Song-by-Song section of this book.)

Actor Training

The changing values of the 1960s influenced the CMU drama department's instructional program. A few faculty members explored innovative techniques, while others adhered to the acting methods they had learned, or passed along specialized skills like mime, dance, and diction. The diversity of their approaches was both helpful and challenging for the undergraduates. Leon Katz remembers, "There was no uniform attitude to the faculty. We had five acting teachers. All of them were tremendously good and they loathed what one another was doing. Each one had a totally different conceptual training. The students were confused. They would go to [department chairman] Earle Gister and say, 'What are we supposed to believe? We're totally confused!' He said, 'Good, that's your training. You sort it out and find the thing that's right for you.'"

> *"The sixties was not a time when students would accept traditional training at face value. The whole idea was to explore as much as possible outside that framework, and they explored on their own terms."*
>
> —Leon Katz

What was right for them? No one was quite sure. Student actors gained experience with Shakespeare and with 18th and 19th century plays that were often performed in professional theaters around the country. Robin Lamont explains, "If you graduated from Carnegie you were expected to go into a repertory theater in a place like Seattle or Chicago and do all the classic plays, like do a lot of Shakespeare," and so the faculty geared the curriculum and opportunities in that direction, whether or not it was what the students wanted. Gilmer McCormick (known later for the *Godspell* stage play and movie) didn't feel the training was sufficient. "In those days the emphasis was on the classics. Their feeling was if you can do the classics you can do anything, which is absolutely not true."

For the most part, acting students were trained to memorize scripts and perform roles they had carefully studied, so their classroom experience didn't actually prepare them for working with someone like Tebelak, who liked spontaneity. Fortunately, the play instinct within them and their feeling of comfort on stage would carry them through.

The Directing Program

The directing program required students to train in every area of theater, from acting through the complete range of technical production procedures. Nina Faso reports, "We were carrying double loads: the acting program and the directing program. It was a very exhausting regimen."

For directing concepts, Tebelak looked to innovators. Faso remembers his fascination with Jerzy Grotowski's work. "Grotowski was a revolutionary Polish theater director whose theater would look almost like a boxing arena, with benches on both sides. Actors would sit on benches in sight of the audience, and when they had to do something, they just got up and became that character." Tebelak and his *Godspell* group would later use this approach with the enactment of parables, such as when a cast member would leap up to be the prodigal son, and another would step in as his father.

Among the faculty at CMU, one of the most influential for Tebelak was Word Baker, who was not primarily an academic, but rather was known for his successful direction of the Off-Broadway musical hit *The Fantasticks*. Baker and Tebelak would sometimes have drinks together and they became friends.

Andy Rohrer, an acting student whom Tebelak befriended and cast in *Godspell*, remembers how Professor Baker was an inspiration. "He was a Texas boy and not an intellectual; he was a showman, and spectacle was what he did well. I think he probably gave John-Michael license to explore spectacle and the physical expression of things."

Next, Tebelak needed opportunities to test his ideas and try out his training with actors. It helped that he had made friends with his fellow "Dramats," many of whom were willing to participate in his projects.

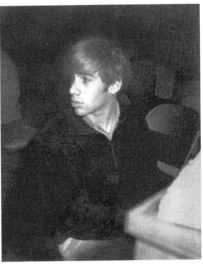

John-Michael Tebelak (date of photo unknown)

Stephen Schwartz at piano during a rehearsal for a college version of *Pippin*.

> *"College life was very different at that time, particularly at an art school like Carnegie....Back then people were much more interested in being bohemian. My whole freshman year I used to walk around in a cape. People were dressing up and behaving in very artsy ways at school...everybody had his or her own thing that they did. John-Michael wasn't any more eccentric than fifty percent of the other people who were there in the drama department."*
> —**Stephen Schwartz**

Chapter 4

The Turning Point: 1968

If there was a turning point year for the future of *Godspell* it was 1968. For one thing, although a minor detail, Tebelak helped make tissue-paper flowers for the set of Stephen Schwartz's senior directing project, the first act of Bock and Harnick's *The Apple Tree*. And so the future *Godspell* collaborators briefly worked together.

Most important were Tebelak's experiences during the summer and fall of 1968; they strongly impacted his confidence, style, and future casting ideas for *Godspell*.

As Carnegie's 1967–1968 academic year was coming to a close, Tebelak used his hometown connections to set up a summer stock program in Cleveland, Ohio. He discovered that no one was using the Huntington Playhouse, a theater created inside an old carriage barn on an estate that had been turned into a park. He made arrangements to open it up and invited actors from college to be in his "Limited in Company," to spend the summer living in the Playhouse and creating shows together.

At that point, Tebelak had performed in shows and designed for them, but had never yet been a director, let alone an artistic director. But he was still able to attract a talented troupe that included future *Godspell* cast members Stephen Nathan, Gilmer McCormick, and Jeffrey Mylett, as well as Nina Faso, Jay Hamburger, and several others.

Tebelak chose *MacBird!* as the first show and it became a precursor to his work on *Godspell* in the way he led the troupe. *MacBird!* was a controversial satire that had been playing at The Village Gate in New York City over the previous year. The story parodied Shakespeare's *Macbeth* but was recast in modern times.

Playwright Barbara Garson set Lyndon Johnson's steps to power after the Kennedy assassination in a parallel with *Macbeth*'s murderous power reach in Shakespeare's tale. (According to one report, she didn't necessarily believe Johnson was involved in the Kennedy assassination but wanted to explore the theme of 'things are not always what they seem.')

To enhance the show, Tebelak appropriated music from The Beatles' "Sergeant Pepper's Lonely Hearts Club Band," changing the lyrics to make it "Lyndon Johnson's Lonely Hearts Club Band." He invited the Quinn brothers—three brothers from Cleveland who were friends of his family—to be the show's band. It was a role they would reprise for the La MaMa version of *Godspell* three years later.

By directing an innovative play in a venue that was under his control, Tebelak had a chance to follow his instincts for staging. For example, for *MacBird!* he put the band on the stage at the edge of the actors' space—something that was rarely done at that point in stage productions but that he would use again for *Godspell*. Also, for one scene, Tebelak had Stephen Nathan walk through the audience singing while a strobe light flashed. Strobe lights were in vogue in nightclubs and dance halls at the time, but theatrical use was unusual. Tebelak liked the effect enough to repeat it several years later during a segment of "All for the Best" in *Godspell*.

The costume preparation for the show foreshadowed things to come. "No costume cost more than about twenty-five cents," says Carla Meyer, another member of the 1968 summer stock troupe who later played in the Boston production of *Godspell* and became a dialect coach for Hollywood. "Personally, I think John-Michael thrived in making do. It charged his creativity to not have everything at his fingertips, and I think that fed everybody. It was all from our own stuff. This went into the ethos of *Godspell*."

MacBird! was an instant hit and it sold out immediately after the reviews came out. "John-Michael was the darling of the critics in Cleveland," recalls Bill Phillips. This might have gone unnoticed by Carnegie Mellon University faculty except that directing teacher "Larry" [Lawrence] Carra was also in Cleveland that summer directing *Hamlet* at the Great Lakes Shakespeare Festival. Phillips notes, "While the *Hamlet* production was successful, it was *MacBird!* with its innovation that became the theatrical sensation of Cleveland. This put Carra on notice that here was a talent unlike any he had seen before."

The group went on to perform Tebelak's version of *Marat/Sade*, which had been directed by Peter Brook in London, New York, and on film. In Brook's stage play and film, a group of mental patients perform a play for members of the French aristocracy. Some of the actors in the play-within-the-play wore clown outfits. A wire fence surrounded their stage. Tebelak would eventually make these elements central to his concept for *Godspell*.

Jay Hamburger was impressed with Tebelak's adaptations. "That was the first real hint that he was onto something. He was a wizard. He would keep an eye on the way other theatrical productions were done, filter that, and throw in his own ideas. And he knew who to hire. He had very good people working with him, so he was dealing with extraordinarily talented and trained people."

Directorial Style and Skill

The 1968 experiences helped eighteen-year-old Tebelak clarify his interest in directing, and he continued to seek out models and methods, particularly ones that encouraged a director to be a facilitator rather than an authoritarian figure. "What I liked about John-Michael was he was easy to act for," says Jay Hamburger. "In rehearsal I remember having the freedom to try stuff. He wouldn't be overbearing or terribly judgmental. Eventually, he would make the decisions, but he would have enough insight to know who you were and allow you the freedom to go with that."

According to Faso, Tebelak adored Peter Brook's book, *The Empty Space* (Penguin, 1968). Brook looked to theater as a way of waking humanity to a fuller, more immediate knowledge of itself, and so he wanted shows to be provocative in some way. To aid a director's process in giving shows an immediacy that would stimulate the audience, Brook advised them against preparing all blocking and details in advance of rehearsals, but rather to let things evolve more fluidly.

Tebelak even liked having dialogue be developed quickly or on the spot through group participation. According to Leon Katz, he took inspiration from a branch of theater that advocated this kind of spontaneity. "It works extremely well, but it takes a very smart organizer to finally get a production out of it," says Professor Katz.

Whatever the challenges, it was obvious to his peers that the more creative styles of script development and directing suited Tebelak. "He allowed actors to really improvise," says Hamburger, "and then he helped to shape that improvisation. As long as John-Michael put the right pieces together and let the right pieces work, I think basically he was in cream. It just flowed. He worked in a very open-ended way."

This directorial bent came in handy when things went wrong, as they did with *An Italian Straw Hat*, another Limited in Company show that summer of 1968. The first problem was that few people wanted to see a traditional 19th century comedy. The group went from full houses every night with *MacBird!* to only about a dozen people attending *An Italian Straw Hat*. A creative solution spontaneously arose through a response to an actor's memory problem, and Tebelak let it flow.

Stephen Nathan remembers how the show became more appealing: "I'm in the middle of a scene with somebody else, and I gave him his cue and he looked at me blankly. I said another line and he just kept looking at me blankly, and he finally said, 'It's your line!' I said, 'No it's not,' and that was the start of the chaos." Nathan started winging it from that moment on, making up lines and voices, with the others joining in. "I would come out in different costumes, and everybody started to improvise this comedy that was not working when it was done in a reverential way, but seemed to be vastly entertaining when we were just screwing around. To John-Michael's credit, he said, 'All right, fine.' And then we started to get more and more people coming to see what chaos this group of actors was going to cause on any given night."

Carla Meyer recalls being in *An Italian Straw Hat*. "It was hysterically funny. My big scenes were with Stephen Nathan, and I had no idea when I stepped on the stage whether he was going to be doing Groucho Marx or John Lennon or Bela Lugosi. It could have been anybody. He had a wonderful ear for it." Nathan's growing talent and experience with improvisation would have a significant impact on the New York version of *Godspell*.

Another very characteristically 1960s aspect of the summer was the communal living with the entire company. Tebelak had his own room behind the stage and others found spaces around the theater building. Hamburger comments, "John-Michael was taking a step down from being the so called 'director' and was living with his cast members in a somewhat communal way. He had such a talented bunch that lived together, knew each other, and could click and understand what the next move was."

Meyer adds, "You could talk with him and laugh with him about anything, and he was very much a part of the group and the leader of the group, which is a difficult row to hoe."

As effective as Tebelak was part of the time, he was also still young (eighteen), unsure of himself as a fledgling director, and indulgent in recreational drugs (often Robitussen™ cough syrup, the popular "high" of the day). Although some of the shows might have been more effective with a more mature director, it was a season for learning.

As the summer's end approached, the group decided to re-stage *MacBird!* so they could go out with a hit. It worked to win audiences a second time.

> *"I think in many ways John-Michael was an old soul in a young body. He was younger than most of us, not significantly but a year or two. I remember one conversation that we had. We were driving home from a meal at Big Boy or something and talked about directing and producing...I just felt a certain capricious wisdom: he'd be astonishingly insightful, and then, at other times, I'd be thinking 'Huh? What are you talking about?'"*
>
> —Carla Meyer

The Turning Point: 1968

MacBird! was so successful as Limited in Company's first show that Tebelak decided to bring it back at the end of the season. Pictured here: Laurie Faso (Nina's brother) and Bill Phillips in the remounted version.

"The production of 'MacBird!' was probably the closest in essence and creativity and collective group effort to 'Godspell.' It was a very untraditional rendering of the piece, it was highly stylized in many ways, and it was really John-Michael at his collective best. Everybody's contribution or view of the piece was crucial to how the piece ultimately came about. I've always felt that 'MacBird!' and 'Godspell' were close cousins."

–Stephen Nathan

The Godspell Experience

ABOVE: Members of Limited in Company perform a scene from *Marat/Sade* from behind a chain link fence.

"'Limited in Company' seems to be a strange name but it was dead on for John-Michael. He wasn't trying to be anything else than he could be. What he did with limited resources was kind of miraculous."
— Jay Hamburger

The Turning Point: 1968

Several *Marat/Sade* cast members perform in clown makeup.

"John-Michael was a little bit of a Mad Hatter. He was in many ways impossible. And yet at heart extremely lovable and kind...."
— Carla Meyer

Stephen Nathan and Carla Meyer improvise in *An Italian Straw Hat*.

Back in Pittsburgh at CMU

In the fall of 1968, Leon Katz invited an experimental group, The Living Theatre, to conduct their workshop at Skibo Student Center. The Living Theatre was the antithesis of everything expected in dramatic performance. When they came to Carnegie, students were exposed to the extremes of experimentation and confrontational radicalism.

"We all went crazy when The Living Theatre was there," says Nina Faso. "They were absolutely the wildest group of people we had ever seen. They were guerilla theater—all very dramatic people who just went overboard with everything." Peggy Gordon is convinced that they had a particularly strong influence on Tebelak. "The Living Theatre set John-Michael on fire. Many of us were stunned by the wildness and poignancy of The Living Theatre and his entire working process changed after that experience." The presentation contributed to his vision for communicating to the audience through body language and audience interaction.

According to Bill Phillips, "There were a growing number of us wanting to do something current. Experimental theater was everywhere for those who wanted to find it and it certainly fit with the times." Phillips notes that another likely influence for Tebelak was the Open Theater, a New York City-based company that embraced improvisation and social transformation. The Open Theater developed *Viet Rock*, a rock musical that Phillips directed at CMU in the fall of 1968. *Viet Rock* added fodder to Tebelak's interest in new musicals with pop scores.

Chapter 5
The College *Godspell*

By the spring of 1970, twenty-year-old John-Michael Tebelak was ready to complete his B.F.A. degree, having directed and/or worked backstage on nearly a dozen plays in addition to his summer work. According to Nina Faso, "The faculty said to John-Michael, 'If you do your master's thesis within a year, we'll give you your master's degree. If you were to transfer, you could never get it in a year.' And so he was desperate to come up with something for his master's thesis."

For most graduate students, it meant selecting an established play, preferably from a previous century, researching the style and period of the play, directing it, and writing a thesis about it. Tebelak considered revamping a Greek drama or something from Greek mythology and trying to get approval. "The Greek myths seemed to have no relation to my casts or audiences," he commented later. Abandoning that notion, he next considered something from Judeo-Christian sources.

Spiritual Inclinations

Tebelak's affection for religious material had started many years earlier, so it made sense to research spiritual source material for his thesis. In fact, his sister believes his passion for drama may have initially been inspired by experiences with religious pageantry.

While their mother led a more intellectual than faith-based life, their father's parents were from Czechoslovakia and were involved with the Russian Orthodox religion. The older Tebelaks had immigrated to America (in order to distance themselves from the Russian Revolution) and brought with them their religious traditions. Trudy recalls the other-worldly appeal of their grandparents' Russian Orthodox Church building. "It was cool and dark; there was chanting and incense, and everything was red and gold. The chanters were up behind you singing. Frankincense would overwhelm you."

Similar pageantry intrigued the children at the Episcopal Cathedral in Cleveland, where they sometimes attended services after the family relocated from Akron to a Cleveland suburb. An interest in staged group experiences emerged naturally from these moments in impressionable years. Trudy also recalls, "When we came home from church, John-Michael would redo the church service. It was cute. He would take a cloth to make an altar, and burn candles, and do the communion—all the dramatic parts." If not for the somberness of the religious approach and the general confession, which he disliked, John-Michael might have pursued a career as an Episcopal minister.

> *"John-Michael was truly religious. But he was also of the 1960s. So the two things were there in an odd combination."*
>
> –Leon Katz

As a teenager, he'd been looking for spiritual meaning beyond the boundaries of religion. Nina Faso remembers: "Spirituality was something that he discovered. His own life was a quest for some kind of peace. He was a troubled guy. He had a lot more fun than most of us, but it was hard to manage a personality like his. He was brilliant, but his mind was always all over the place. He was someone who had trouble sleeping because he had thoughts all the time." That restlessness was about to stir up an innovative concoction of a musical.

Dramatic Adaptation

While searching for material for his thesis project, Tebelak read through several miracle plays and passion plays, but felt them to be "very heavy." Then, one afternoon, he read the four Gospels of the New Testament in one sitting. "Afterward, I became pretty excited because I found what I wanted to portray on stage... Joy!"

Tebelak resolved to attend a church service, and it was there that a spiritual experience, or rather lack thereof, completed the inspiration for the new musical. On a snowy Easter morning in 1970, Tebelak arrived at the Anglican Cathedral in Pittsburgh wearing his standard overalls and scraggly Afro haircut. The people sitting near him were complaining about the snowfall upsetting their plans.

He explained later to *Dramatics Magazine*, "An old priest came out and mumbled into a microphone, and people mumbled things back, and then everyone got up and left. Instead of 'healing' the burden, or resurrecting the Christ, it seems those people had pushed Him back into the tomb. They had refused to let Him come out that day."

As Tebelak left the service, a policeman who had been sitting a few pews in front of him wanted to frisk him for drugs. "Apparently he had thought I was ducking into the church to escape the snowstorm. At that moment—I think because of the absurd situation—it angered me so much that I went home and realized what I wanted to do with the Gospels: I wanted to make it the simple, joyful message that I felt the first time I read them and re-create the sense of community, which I did not share when I went to that service."

At some point over the next months, Tebelak read Harvard professor Harvey Cox's book *The Feast of Fools: A Theological Essay on Festivity and Fantasy* (Harvard University Press, 1969), or at least the chapter entitled "Christ as Harlequin." Tebelak's notion of working playfully with the Biblical material was bolstered by this book. Cox suggests that while in previous generations, Jesus has been viewed as a teacher, judge, or healer, today these images have lost their power. What can most touch "our jaded modern consciousness" is the clown character—a promoter of joy.

For Tebelak, associating Biblical material with clowns didn't mean he was making fun of religion. Rather, he wanted his project to be an antidote to lifeless and boring spiritual experiences; clownlike performances were a means to an end.

He also needed a play that could fulfill his degree requirements. Cox's treatise seemed justification enough for Tebelak to associate clowning with the Bible in a stage show, and he used *The Feast of Fools* when he defended his thesis choice to his faculty advisor.

He decided to name the play *The Godspell*, using the archaic English spelling for gospel, which means good news.

Next he needed to draft a script. At that time, Tebelak shared a house off campus with five or six renters, most of whom were attending medical school. One of them recalls: "I had the pleasure of watching the sometimes bizarre creation of *Godspell*, at least to walk down the hall by his room or wander in and ask him what he was doing… He spent a lot of time in his room, sitting on his bed tripping or stoned, watching soap operas and game shows on a little thirteen-inch TV and cutting out verses from the Bible to put on his storyboards. (He said he watched the TV shows to 'gauge the sensibilities' of the general public.)"

By early summer 1970, he had collected many of the conceptual and literary ingredients he would need for his future musical: Biblical parables and a vague storyline (that started with the Baptism and ended with the Crucifixion), clowns, and cast members who would improvise and leap up to act out a scene.

He also had memories of scenic designs that would enhance his upcoming project. In addition to a fenced-in arena used in *Marat/Sade*, Bill Phillips recalls showing him a TV show about a religion-inspired production mounted by a Boston repertory theater company in an abandoned building. It included parables of Jesus as well. "I think that helped to focus ideas that he already had," perhaps contributing to his notion of doing something Biblical in an empty enclosure.

This unusual combination of ingredients wouldn't work as a creative stew without a group of cooperative chefs who could blend clown behavior with Biblical expressions. But he would deal with that in the fall.

Meanwhile, Tebelak was directing a show at the Berea Summer Theater when an actor friend, Howard Sponseller, stopped by for a visit. Sponseller had been in *MacBird!* and would eventually perform over 2,000 times in *Godspell*. During a break they sat together in Tebelak's car discussing his master's thesis project.

"I'll just take popular songs and intersperse them into the show as we did with *MacBird!*" Tebelak said about his work-in-progress.

"There must be someone at Carnegie who could write some music for the show," Sponseller replied. Tebelak would pursue that suggestion when he returned to school.

From Idea to Page

In order to transform his ideas for *The Godspell* into a script, Tebelak had to overcome his lifelong difficulty with writing. He gathered his notes and turned to his mother, who could type what he read out or spoke to her. "He had this vision in his head," recalls Trudy Tebelak Williams. "Our mom was the perfect person to dictate it to. I loved her characterization of him lying on the sofa with *Godspell* springing forth. And then he'd sleep on it and then the next day he would say, 'I want to change this' or 'I want to change that.'"

He apparently hoped his future cast would spontaneously concoct theatrically fascinating material, because the script was basically a collection of parables, sayings, and hymn lyrics with no humor lines or staging plans.

Although the show would later be subtitled *A Musical Based on the Gospel According to St. Matthew*, Tebelak actually used quite a few parables from Luke and a couple of quotations from John. But since he did rely heavily on the Sermon on the Mount, which is present in Matthew, the subtitle could be justified.

For the show's opening he collected writings about God and human existence from various philosophers, such as Socrates, Thomas Aquinas, Martin Luther, Frederic Nietzsche, and others. He turned some of their paragraphs into long monologues for what later became known as the "Prologue." (Among the chosen philosophers was R. Buckminster Fuller, a popular futurist of the day of whom he was a great admirer.)

In his early approach to *The Godspell*, the playwright attributed Jesus' comments to Clown 1. He decided to combine the historical John the Baptist and Judas into one character, Clown 10. Other comments would be spoken by Clowns 2–9. He wanted most of the decisions about who says what to be made during rehearsals.

When he returned to Carnegie, he brought his script draft to his faculty advisor, Larry Carra. Although Carra respected Tebelak, he had rules and reasons for guiding his students toward traditional work in regional theaters. Carra read what Tebelak had pieced together for *The Godspell* and rejected it.

Deflated, Tebelak approached Professor Katz, who had been supportive in the past. Katz recalls, "He turned to me when Larry Carra turned down the idea for *Godspell*. At the time it had that twenty-minute introduction [with philosophers' speeches] and Carra did not think it had theatrical viability apparently. So John-Michael showed me the outline of what he had and I thought it was wonderful and I said, 'By all means go ahead.'"

It is likely that the whole matter went before Earle Gister, who resolved it by allowing the show to move forward due to Katz's support for it. Bill Phillips remembers, "For directing students, Carra always had the final word and therefore without Katz's strong support, *The Godspell* would never have been produced at Carnegie, or perhaps ever, because John-Michael needed the time, people, and support to make it happen."

From Page to Stage

In the autumn of 1970, Tebelak's conception started moving from a quote-filled short script and a smattering of songs to the next level of realization.

As a graduate-level directing major working on a project, he could select a modest number of actors from the casting pool comprised of undergraduate drama students even if they hadn't auditioned for the show.

Robin Lamont and Sonia Manzano had started their junior year that fall. One day after class they went to check the board, hoping to see their names in leading roles in one of the larger school productions. Lamont recounts, "We looked and didn't see our names on the main stage production. Then we see a notice: 'John-Michael Tebelak.' We didn't really know him; we just knew he was a strange-looking guy with a huge Afro, who was very tall, walked around wearing overalls, and was a real hippie. The notice said it was 'The Gospel According to

St. Matthew.' All he had listed was Clown 1, 2, 3, etc., through 10 with names after each one. I looked down and I was Clown 4. And Sonia's name was there as another clown. We looked at each other and went 'ahwgggh no!' We had envisioned a bizarre show and we were sort of appalled. The first rehearsal confirmed our feelings."

It would be several weeks before Tebelak was able to translate his ideas in a way that student cast members would understand. At the first meeting in October, when the director tried communicating his intentions for reverent comedy to his recruits, they resisted. He once revealed, "I held a rehearsal with the cast, reading the Bible, saying this is a funny show, and by the end, eight of the ten performers were crying, trying to quit. They thought I had finally flipped!"

Andy Rohrer, who played Jesus, says it took the cast several weeks of rehearsal meetings before they grasped Tebelak's approach. "The clown concept, though it was on paper, didn't penetrate the rehearsal process until late. John-Michael was an idea guy, living in his intellect. You'd listen to him and just think, 'What is he talking about?' You couldn't relate it to any practical reality."

Lamont concurs. "*The Godspell* was just the Gospels. There was no stage direction about who says this and how you react to it. It was just the Gospels, and the ten of us, and John-Michael saying, 'Okay, let's go, let's do this.' We had no idea what he was talking about and no idea where to start. It wasn't part of our theatrical training." She felt "concerned that we were getting involved in some sort of theatrical chaos."

What turned the corner for the group was a physical representation of the "clown" idea that had previously been abstract. One night Tebelak brought in grease pencils to a rehearsal. He said to the cast, "All right, tonight everybody's going to paint everybody else." They started drawing crazy pictures on each other's faces as their mood shifted from worried to light and playful. When they realized he expected them to wear clown faces for the show, they suddenly understood the theatrical context for performing Bible parables. The room exploded with creativity, and the earliest *Godspell* sprang to life.

"Everybody would take the stage and act out a story," recalls Sonia Manzano about clown behavior. "We eventually called it 'Mickey Mousing' the parables, like if you said, 'A sower sowed a seed,' you might mime someone sowing or even sewing for that matter!"

The staging for the show rolled out rather spontaneously. CMU cast member Mary Mazziotti says, "I remember the rehearsal process as being very loosey-goosey. That was sort of the style." The students pondered what a scene was about and then would mill around until they discovered how to perform it. Rohrer explains, "Pretty much everybody relied on their innate theatrical sense to kind of find where to be in this thing."

The group experimented with reverse engineering scenes based on Bible phrases. Knowing how Jesus completed a parable, actors invented a charade or game or other goofy behavior to give him a reason to teach that lesson. As the acting students clowned around, Tebelak either approved or nixed their approach for use in the show.

The show wasn't all fun and games, as Tebelak included Jesus' betrayal, the Last Supper, and the Crucifixion in the mix. Somehow the clowns needed to pull off these moments as well.

Music elevated and brought some consistency of tone for the whole piece. Following up on Sponseller's suggestion, Tebelak asked one of his medical student roommates, Duane Bolick, to write some rock music to go with lyrics from hymns or psalms he'd selected, and form a band with their other roommates who would make up arrangements for an electric organ, electric guitar, and a drum set. Tebelak worked with the group to cobble together songs.

The next step was to teach songs to the cast. Andy Rohrer remembers, "There was no written music. If Duane had it on his piano or organ, we never saw it. I couldn't read music. He just sang it for us and we picked it up from that." With a few exceptions, most of them were ensemble songs, to be sung by all the performers throughout the piece.

The costume budget for the show was $150, which meant it would be a "pulled" show. The designer would go into the Carnegie drama department's large collection of clothing and gather (pull) costumes that could be altered or pieces of costumes that could be sewn together into new ones.

Undergraduate student Susan Tsu had excelled in her design-related classes, and it was decided that Tebelak's ten-character show could be her first costume design assignment. She knew of Tebelak, although he was a graduate student and she a "lowly sophomore" as she describes herself. "I much admired him. He had a wonderful imagination. And was tall and striking, with dark hair to his shoulders."

She remembers that at their brief initial meeting, he said he wanted some combination of "hippies and clowns"—no more specifics than that. She recalls that she and Tebelak together came up with the idea of a Superman shirt for Jesus. She headed for the vintage clothing collection in the College of Fine Arts building to find pieces for costumes for a cast of ten. Tsu sewed most of the new costumes herself, with last-minute help from her advisor for the final three pairs of pants. After seeing David Haskell as Judas in rehearsal, she responded to his personality and performance. "He was like the Ringmaster of the circus,"

Tsu recalls, so she gave him a circus-suited tailcoat, and added things to it like stripes and military epaulets.

Sonia Manzano remembers that the dress rehearsals and performances in costume helped her discover her inner comic. "We were improvising while wearing funny clown outfits complete with oversized shoes and red rubber noses, so it was hard not to find the humor in things. Also, someone would put comical props in our pockets (kazoos, rubber chickens, etc.). So in the middle of a monologue you'd reach into your pocket, pull out a funny party favor and feel compelled to incorporate it into the scene."

In December, the student actors pushed to finish something that resembled a musical. In Andy Rohrer's recollection, the spirit was more 'anything goes' because of the pressure on Tebelak to complete his master's degree. "He had to get it up and get it interesting, so anything he liked went in. I remember Bob Ari bringing in a rubber chicken filled with talcum powder so when you squeezed it, it blew. Yeah, perfect. On we went. There were no debates—Is this in poor taste? Is this right, is this wrong? —No. Shove more junk into this thing. Whatever makes us laugh, get it out there. It was like that.... There was no unifying plan; there was no theatrical conceit. It was just like, 'How are we going to survive this production?'"

First Performances

The Studio Theatre, a small cinderblock building at Carnegie Mellon University, just outside the College of Fine Arts building, had no frills. It didn't even have running water, so bathroom access required walking to an adjacent building. But the theater space with seats for about fifty people was ideal for small student productions. It was there that Tebelak scheduled four performances of *The Godspell* in mid December 1970.

On opening night, audiences savored a theatrical feast: actors with grease-painted clown faces performing parable vignettes with a sprinkling of rock songs. There was a potpourri of charades, comic dancing, send-ups of movie stars, kazoos and guitar performances, and a three-piece band accompaniment. There was wine to sip at intermission, and sorrowful moments at the Crucifixion. At the finale, onlookers watched Jesus in his Superman T-shirt and striped pants being carried out the front door. Then the room exploded with wild cheers.

Sonia Manzano comments, "It wasn't until the audience was there and we did the show for them that I felt the impact of it. I was so touched by it; the whole idea of making people laugh before you make them cry made a big impression on me. I remember bursting into tears at the end of the show with Robin Lamont, because we were overwhelmed by the whole thing. The audience was crying too; it was great theater."

Word of mouth spread and crowds grew every night. "It was a tremendous hit," recalls Robin Lamont. "By the fourth performance, there were kids from the technical department and the sciences trying to get into this little theater, so it was standing room only." The response was so positive that she felt they might have something worthwhile.

By then, Tebelak's advisor had been won over by the musical. Professors Carra and Katz both believed the show should reach a wider audience. One of their associates made an inquiry on Tebelak's behalf with the leading off-off Broadway theater, Café La MaMa.

NOTE: This book includes three "State of the Show" sections for the evolving stages of the new musical, as well as one for the movie adaptation.

The State of the Show at CMU

The Godspell at Carnegie Mellon University was not a pretty, polite show. Although it included uplifting commentary from Jesus and plenty of delightful humor, the presentation was rough.

It began with multiple weighty monologues by famous thinkers that might have held meaning for philosophy majors but were overwhelming for most audiences. After presenting their monologues, the philosophers broke into a raw, free-for-all argument, creating a true sense of incomprehensible babble.

The idea was interesting: *The Godspell* would open with the antithesis of a harmonious community as a contrast for what was later created by Jesus and the disciples—a transformation that could be theatrically compelling. But the presentation was rather wild. Tebelak staged the argument with real trash (that included some garbage). Lamont explains, "As philosophers, we would get more agitated about what we were saying, and then we started to go over to where there were bags of trash on the stage. We'd rip open the bags and throw things at each other. And all the philosophers were getting in each other's way. Then someone would throw an empty can up on the stage and scream 'F--k you!' Then we heard the shofar [ram's horn]. The philosophers would stop arguing and John the Baptist would baptize everybody."

Perhaps Tebelak was remembering the nudity of the musical *Hair* and The Living Theatre when he planned the scene with the Baptism of Jesus. "John-Michael wanted me to begin the show nude," says Andy Rohrer about preparing to play Jesus. "It was the tail end of the sixties and there had been lots of nude performances and appearances at school, so it was not that outrageous an idea, but... I was just not willing to appear nude in a show about Christ that I thought was going to be bad. So I said, 'John-Michael, I have some blue boxer shorts, I'll wear those.' So I brought them in and he said, 'Okay, that's great.' And everybody agreed it was kind of a funny look. So that was my costume contribution."

Overall, "The show had a much harder edge to it than it had later," says cast member Bob Ari (known then as Bob Miller). He remembers there was a marijuana joint passed at the Passover seder. "Tebelak was using *The Godspell* to buck the system." According to Ari, a real-life situation provided a model for comic radical behavior for Tebelak. In 1969, activist Abbie Hoffman made headlines during a trial related to anti-war protests held the previous year. Ari explains, "When you look at the trials of the Chicago Seven, the way Abbie Hoffman behaved with the judge was very clownish—he'd dress up in costume and come to court. So John-Michael felt that the way to buck the authorities was to make fun of them. That's what a lot of *Godspell* was about at the beginning: challenging authority in a clownish way."

Tebelak also had something special in mind with the backdrop for the performance space. "He came to first rehearsal with the idea of the fence going to the edge of the stage," says Ari. "He wanted the audience and the stage to be one. That was what he called the liberated zone." Tebelak was adapting an idea from college sit-ins. Ari explains, "Dupont was very involved with Carnegie at the time, developing Napalm. When we had demonstrations on campus we would liberate the science department; we would break in and occupy it. Police would have to drag us out. So when you had a sit-in, you had a section that was called the liberated zone where you did the sit-in." *Godspell*'s revolutionary cast would have their liberated zone as well.

The college production was designed to play up the dramatic power of the Crucifixion. Behind the fence the audience could see a red light like that of a police car. Sonia Manzano remembers, "The combination of the red police car light and Jesus' first lyric, 'Oh God, I'm busted,' gave the feeling that we had been caught by the authorities while doing something wrong, so it was very theatrical that way."

At the end of the original production, Rohrer as Jesus was carried out by the actors. "It was very dangerous," Rohrer recalls.

"That was typical of John-Michael. It was out of control… Part of the intention was that they took me down like a piece of meat. They didn't take me down with respect. They took me down like children would take a body down. So they had me under each arm, under each leg while they were singing 'Prepare Ye.' It was more like a body carried out of the battlefield in Vietnam. It had a very different imagery to it. It worked for that production because the production was so out of control. But it was very troubling for the actor. So I was fighting for my life. It was like being in a low-budget movie in a bad stunt." (For later productions, the actors lifted Jesus carefully.)

The Songs

Student audiences enjoyed the first score, with music by Duane Bolick, although they may have found it odd to hear hymn lyrics set to rock music. The pieces were mostly group numbers accompanied by heavy drum, electric guitar, organ, and bass. The program listed "Prepare Ye the Way of the Lord," "Save the People," "Day by Day," "Bless the Lord," "All Good Gifts," "Turn Back, O Man," "On the Willows"—many of the same titles that would appear in the final recorded score. In addition, the list included "Sermon on the Mount" and "Oh God, I'm Busted." The show ended by reprising "Prepare Ye the Way of the Lord." (Most of the lyrics remained the same in later versions of *Godspell*.)

The Next Step

For *Godspell* to reach a large and more diverse audience with less risk of offending them, not to mention keeping the cast from getting arrested for drug use, the edgiest elements would need to be smoothed out.

"It was very heartfelt and unsophisticated musically and otherwise. People were over the moon about it. People were screaming and applauding and shrieking, and the place was jammed for every performance. I have to say I was a real Doubting Thomas. I thought, 'What the f--k is this?' We're just sort of lolling around the stage. It was not my thing. I really like things in a row, but people just went insane."

—Mary Mazziotti

The College Godspell

ABOVE: Andy Rohrer and the student cast of *The Godspell* on their stage in the Studio Theatre.

LEFT: Lawrence Carra ran the graduate directing program at CMU. He studied directing under Alexander Dean and co-authored the *Fundamentals of Play Directing* textbook with him. According to Bill Phillips, Carra had difficulty appreciating the experimental approach to directing that Tebelak took. But he liked *Godspell* after seeing the performance at CMU. (Photo courtesy of Great Lakes Theater)

The Godspell Experience

Ta Da! The CMU cast of *The Godspell*. From left to right: Martha Jacobs, Sonia Manzano, Randy Danson, Robin Lamont, James Stevens, Mary Mazziotti, Andy Rohrer, Stan King, David Haskell, Bob Ari.

FROM LEFT: Nina Faso (Photo by Roy Blakely), Susan Tsu, and Leon Katz later in life.

CHAPTER 6

Experiments in New York City

Over the holiday break from school in December 1970, Tebelak traveled to New York City to meet with Ellen Stewart, known as "the first lady of the American avant-garde theater." A decade earlier, after hearing stories from her playwright foster brother who couldn't get his work staged, Stewart had established Café La MaMa as an off-off Broadway performance space combined with a café. Her little enterprise changed many times due to requirements of health authorities, but eventually settled on East 4th Street in the Village, where it remains today (called "La MaMa," without the "Café") as New York's leading experimental theater.

Stewart was receptive to *The Godspell*. "She thought it sounded interesting," Tebelak once explained, "but unfortunately she wasn't then able to do anything for about a year. Two days later she called and asked, 'How soon can you be here?' I very quickly said, 'Six weeks,' and she said, 'Fine!' She had had a cancellation." That meant the show needed to be ready by late February 1971.

One advantage of playing at La MaMa would be that their shows tended to be experimental, edgy, and different in some way or another, so their clientele would expect what *The Godspell* delivered. Tebelak felt confident that he could essentially re-create the show with friends that he'd recruit.

Casting from a Manhattan Loft Apartment

By January, Tebelak had settled into a loft apartment on Forsyth Street belonging to his painter friend, Richard Hannum. The apartment in a Lower East Side tenement building would serve as an initial rehearsal room until the Café La MaMa rehearsal room became available weeks later. It also served as a crash pad for many actor friends who would sleep on the floor when they first arrived on the scene.

Right away, Tebelak contacted Nina Faso because he knew he couldn't run the show without someone like her to help focus on details. "As soon as John-Michael decided to do this show in New York," Faso recalls, "he called me in San Francisco and said, 'You've got to come and do this with me.' I was working in San Francisco at The Committee (an improvisational theater group), and I wasn't making any money. I said, 'I can't come, I haven't the money.' He said, 'Yes you have! I already talked to your mom and she's going to give you the money.' He had called my mother and said, 'Look, I need her. She'll be with her college friends. It will be all right.' So I arrived in Manhattan at Forsyth Street with one suitcase."

It was a phone call from Tebelak that also inspired 10 of his peers to drop their other plans and join him in festive musical making. It was an invitation that would not only launch their careers, but immortalize their names in the future script. Their real first names—"Robin," "Peggy," "Gilmer," "Herb," and so on—became the character names used by future generations of performers.

Among those he called first were members of his 1968 summer stock cast, including Stephen Nathan to play Jesus. Nathan was a CMU graduate, 6' 1" tall, slender, with wavy dark hair. He was newly married and living in Pittsburgh, where he and his wife were about to open a specialty foods store (postponing his show business career). He recalls, "We had rented the space, we had gotten a huge sign, and everything was perfect. We were going to open the business in about six weeks. Then John-Michael called me and said, 'I'm doing *The Godspell* at La

MaMa, do you want to come and do it?' I said, 'Well, is there any money? I have money invested in this business that I'm doing and I'm going to open in a little bit.' He said, 'No, there's not a penny.' I said, 'Okay, I'll be right there.' I knew the piece. I loved John-Michael. It sounded great. It was a spiritual fit as well as a creative fit. I thought, what the hell, I'll just go to New York."

> *"I was dying to do 'Godspell.' I thought it was fabulous and I wanted to be a part of it. John-Michael said we were going to reconceive things and it was going to grow. And it just seemed like the perfect melding of everything that we all wanted to do with the collective consciousness of the time."*
> **–Stephen Nathan**

Jeffrey Mylett and Gilmer McCormick were secure in Tebelak's memory from the summer of 1968 and from CMU. McCormick was in New York, working her way into television roles when she got the call and came down for rehearsals in Richard's loft. Mylett had left college early to live in the Indian ashram of Meher Baba, a popular guru of the day, but he had moved to New York by the fall of 1970. He lived in Greenwich Village behind a store that sold tie-dyed merchandise and was exploring all the arts, including poetry and photography. He and his friends were accustomed to attending shows off-off Broadway, so when Tebelak called about a show at Café La MaMa, he was eager to join in.

Tebelak remembered Herb Braha's performances at Carnegie. (His stage name is listed variously as Herb Simon or Herb Braha.) Braha explains, "I did a lot of comedies at Carnegie and some offbeat things in the Studio Theatre which John-Michael saw and really liked." Braha was living in New

York and had just been offered his first paid acting job in Boston when Tebelak phoned him. "I was really in a quandary," Braha recalls. "The director in Boston said, 'You'd be crazy going to do this showcase in New York.'" But when he went down to Forsyth Street to meet with John-Michael privately, he decided in favor of *The Godspell*.

Peggy Gordon, a New York City native, had studied music, acting, and dance from an early age. After a couple of years at Carnegie, she dropped out to work at the American Conservatory Theatre in San Francisco, which she found more fruitful than finishing her B.F.A. degree. In January 1971, she came home to New York for a few weeks to visit her family. When John-Michael discovered that Gordon was in the city, he called and begged her to join the company in rehearsal for the off-off Broadway production in the East Village, saying, "Please, won't you just come down?! Please?!" She replied that she'd help with the music, but when she arrived to see all her friends and heard that Tebelak would allow her to create her own character, she signed on for the cast. "It was just irresistible."

Tebelak invited juniors Robin Lamont, Sonia Manzano, and David Haskell from the cast of *The Godspell* at CMU, and they officially petitioned department chairman Earle Gister for time off. Although Tebelak had wanted other students from the CMU production, Gister told seniors they wouldn't be accepted back in the academic program if they left. Mary Mazziotti says, "I remember feeling very upset about it because this business is so hard, why would you say to students who have a chance for a New York show that they can't go?" But she and the majority of the others who were in the Carnegie cast either couldn't leave school or preferred to finish their degrees.

To fill out the cast, Tebelak recruited his 1968 summer stock cast member and CMU graduate, "Tina" (Prudence) Holmes, as well as Jimmy Canada, a fellow cast member in a student production of Shakespeare's *As You Like It*.

Meanwhile, Nina Faso started working on assorted production details. As with everything else, there was essentially no budget. Tebelak was able to retrieve a few things from school. He stated later, "My professor in directing had given me a hundred dollars to get a truck so I could move all of my things to New York with our sets and costumes." Faso recalls having a meager $200 to cover all additional production costs.

There was a slight glitch with the costumes. When the show closed at CMU, no one informed costume designer Susan Tsu about the possibility that *The Godspell* garb might be needed again. "After we did the production in the Studio Theatre, we 'struck' everything," she recalls. "Every patch was taken off, every single piece that had fit together was taken apart and made back into its neutral self again and put away." So with a new cast and new production dates, every piece and patch had to be assembled anew or redesigned. Tsu gathered some of the former costume pieces and packed her bags for Manhattan to finish the job. She knew nothing about finding the final costume materials in the big city, but she would figure it out quickly enough.

Rehearsals for La MaMa – Reshaping the Show

Rehearsals began January 18th in Tebelak's shared loft, where he commandeered his apartment mate's painting studio. It was a large enough space that when they started playing theater games and improvising parables, the whole ensemble could move boldly about without hitting the walls or each other.

On the first night, the actors sat on a rug on the floor facing their director, listening to him talk about his intentions. "I'll never forget sitting there listening to him," says Gordon. "He was like a master storyteller."

Her recollection is that he spoke of his disappointing experience at the Easter service: "He couldn't find any relevance to his life based on church dogma. He wanted to strip all that away. He said, 'Let's find out who this Jesus might have been.'" His plan was to re-approach the Biblical parables and texts with the innocence of a child, and to play with the material as if it was a school recess. The rehearsal process wouldn't focus on integrating the funniest pop cultural references the group could find, but would be about discovering the meaning of the stories through play, through improvisation. The best moments would become the musical.

> *"John-Michael wanted the humor to serve the innocence and never to sacrifice it, because that would enable people to open up and have an extraordinary experience."*
>
> —Peggy Gordon

True to his style of directing, John-Michael did not make a record of the final improvised script from Carnegie, but rather wanted to let the new cast create their own version. "When we got a script, it was just the Bible," recalls Gilmer McCormick about the handout with Bible quotations and hymn lyrics. At first the seven members of the company who had not been in the college production were unsure how to proceed. But David Haskell, Robin Lamont, and Sonia Manzano were able to help others catch on to the spirit of the piece based on their experience with the show the previous fall.

For their New York City venture, some actors found temporary day jobs to cover their living expenses, so the group fit rehearsals into their unscheduled hours. Peggy Gordon recalls,

"We would hook up in the early evening and rehearse, and go to a bar for hours, and then get up the next morning for work. We were kids—who needed sleep?" They were soon filling the rehearsal space with parable improvisations.

To help the group prepare for their improvisations with Bible passages, Tebelak started the cast doing theater games and other rehearsal exercises, drawing inspiration from Grotowski and other drama gurus. "Grotowski was about trust," says Herb Braha, who believed this phase of the process was essential. "It was about being sensitive to what was going on around you on stage, having the trust in the other performer, and the courage to go where that performer would go." Some of the Grotowski-inspired exercises spilled over into the show. For example, the ending scene in which Jesus is holding onto the fence and then falls into the upheld arms of the cast came from a trust exercise.

Another rehearsal tradition to help the company bond was a "show-and-tell" session. Every night for about twenty minutes, cast members would bring in outside material to share that might expand the idea pool. That was how a new song came into the show. Peggy Gordon remembered "Marigold's Song," which had been sitting in her guitar case since she was a college student. She played it for her cast mate Gilmer McCormick, who suggested that they bring it in for show-and-tell. When Tebelak heard the piece he said, "I know exactly where that should go. Peggy, you change places with Tina and sing this after the stone throwing." McCormick would sing the haunting harmony that she developed for the piece, and Gordon renamed the song, "By My Side."

Jeffrey Mylett brought in one of his songs, and Tebelak fit that into the show as well (for the La MaMa production only). For other musical numbers, Robin Lamont was able to teach the previously developed songs with music by Duane Bolick.

The actors in this new musical not only originated their roles, but they invented their own characters. Tebelak asked them to consider what their personal experience would be if they met Jesus. He'd say, "If this kind of person came into your life for a period of a day, this kind of perfect soul, what kind of person would you become?" With that guidance they were to derive their character. McCormick told the director, "I would become like a small child. I'm a real daddy's girl, and I kind of want him to pick me up and carry me away at the end of the show." So her approach to clowning was girlish.

> *"We fashioned ourselves after the seven dwarves [from the movie 'Snow White and the Seven Dwarfs']—the shy one, the bold one, the showy one. My concept of my character was that she was the shy one."*
>
> **—Peggy Gordon**

Peggy Gordon remembers, "Everyone found a slice of themselves at the first rehearsal that they wanted to comedically amplify." They were inventing from their own memories and personalities. For example, Brooklyn Heights native Robin Lamont had spent summers in rural Connecticut in her youth, where she rode horses or worked outdoors. "I was not into any of the girl things," she comments. Her persona for *The Godspell* was a playful tomboy.

Sonia Manzano had developed a comic sexy persona for the college production, and re-created it during the La MaMa rehearsals. "Sonia was clearly Puerto Rican and very sexy," recalls Herb Braha about the petite woman. He decided his character would respond to her appeal, and he started carrying her across the rehearsal room as a comic bit. It ended up helping illustrate one of Jesus' cautionary sayings.

Gordon knew she would be singing "By My Side," which includes a line about daring to walk with Jesus. By becoming a shy character, she gave credence to the idea of daring herself to go with him. Peggy explains, "…after my character survives the attempts to stone her, Jesus says lovingly that he doesn't condemn her. 'You may go. Do not sin again.' She, in that moment, knows that she wants to go with him, wherever he goes—but does she have the courage? The lyrics seemed suited to telling the story."

After a week or two, the group moved to Café La MaMa's spacious official rehearsal room on Great Jones Street, a few blocks from the theater. There the playful yet earnest rehearsals continued as the actors developed the show with Tebelak.

Stephen Nathan recalled a Three Stooges comedy routine that they borrowed from vaudeville, and that served as inspiration for one of the show's moments. In the routine, whenever one of the Stooges said "Niagara Falls," another would say, "Slowly I turned, step by step, inch by inch…" and attack the person saying the trigger phrase. For *The Godspell*, at one point David Haskel (John/Judas) reacted to something Nathan (Jesus) said with "Jesus Chr…." Nathan led the others with "Slowly I turned, step by step…" and pretended they were about to attack Haskell.

Many of the other lines in *The Godspell* emerged from the actors' spontaneous response to each other and the material, such as the "Lamp of the Body" segment. "Steve Nathan led us aggressively all over the rehearsal space at Great Jones Street," recalls Peggy Gordon. "Whatever he did, we did. When he crawled, we did; when he jumped up, so did we. He did this for what felt like twenty minutes, gradually increasing the speed so that we would increase our responsiveness to follow whatever and wherever he took us. When we were practically in a fever pitch of responsiveness, he said the line [from Matthew 6:22], 'The lamp of the body is the eye.' We'd been in such a responsive frenzy that we just automatically echoed what he said. It was so powerful. We organically echoed every single line: 'The lamp, lamp, lamp of the body, body, body, is the eye, eye, eye....' John-Michael loved it and had us keep it."

At one rehearsal the actors had been improvising with the Beatitudes. They had been jumping around or somersaulting when suddenly David Haskell spoke his next line to Stephen Nathan in a pained tone of voice. It was a Beatitudes line about being blessed even while being reviled by men. The other actors were startled by the tone, and they froze in whatever position they were in. Mylett had just somersaulted away from Nathan and stopped with his feet in the air. Nathan decided to break the chilled mood and reintroduce joy. "That's when I picked up Jeffrey's feet and went, 'Did I ever tell you I used to read feet?'" The interplay served the show and would make it into the script.

Another of Jeffrey's lines arose from a rehearsal moment. He was saying a line quickly and started flubbing the words. Rather than stopping and correcting, he made it into a line about speaking in tongues, as Gordon recalls. "That's what we would do with our improvisations—we went with the moment to see if it led somewhere interesting."

> *"It was a big collaborative effort with lots and lots of improvisation.... John-Michael was really the driving force behind all this and I was fulfilling his vision."*
>
> — **Stephen Nathan**

Dozens of similar moments were created in that way, although they were not all accepted. "Shaping it was primarily a job of trimming things back, with the help of John-Michael's perspective on it," says Nathan.

The wildly creative group process seemed to yield good results. Faso remembers how they refined the material: "We broke into groups and worked on specific pieces, and never gave too much thought to the aggregate effect.... We did endless versions of endless parables until we felt we had a decent and funny show..."

As there had been at Carnegie, there was some discomfort with the unusual process of clowning with normally serious content. McCormick was hesitant about her *Godspell* work for religious reasons. "I was a minister's daughter. There were six generations of Anglican bishops in my family. And when we started poring over this Bible stuff, I said to John-Michael, 'I'm so offended, I feel like lightning is going to strike.' Yet in the course of rehearsals I found what a reverence he had for whom he called God. He wanted to take Jesus down off the cross and exemplify the joy of the Gospels, the life. Many religions are so concentrated on the death aspect. [Wanting to emphasize Jesus' life] was one of his major motivations for writing."

Setting the Scene

For the dress rehearsal, the group was finally able to move to Café La MaMa with the full set. As with the Carnegie production, Tebelak's set employed two sawhorses and three unfinished wood planks, which meant the actors made all the scene changes. During the show, in addition to performing on the stage floor, the actors could vary their playing elevation by using the boards and sawhorses to form a platform on which they could stand or sit. The drawback was the planks were heavy and potentially dangerous. The group practiced carefully maneuvering them.

Nina Faso remembers how essential the planks and sawhorses were for *The Godspell*'s creative presentation. "You could build whatever you wanted out of them. It was like giving a kid some building blocks. We could have used any modular thing, but planks and sawhorses was it, and they worked like gangbusters. To my mind they are the most brilliant thing, because of Jesus being a carpenter."

For costumes, during the opening scene, the actors wore signs written in block letters displayed on the front of their gray sweatshirts so the audience would know they were hearing from Socrates, St. Thomas Aquinas, Martin Luther, Leonardo da Vinci, Edward Gibbon, Friedrick Nietzsche, Jean-Paul Sartre, and R. Buckminster Fuller. For the rest of the show, the colorful Susan Tsu clown costumes added whimsy to the visual display.

Would It Work? The Opening and Beyond

Several of the cast members had doubts about appearing in the show in public. For Herb Braha, who had enjoyed the process of building a play from the ground up, the La MaMa show seemed too "off the wall." But Jeffrey Mylett, who had worked with Tebelak in 1968 and trusted him, offered reassuring words. "He said to me, 'Herb, this is the greatest thing of all times. You're not going to believe it.' And I just couldn't see it. All through rehearsals I was saying, 'Jeffrey, this thing is a mess. We don't know what we're doing.' And he said, 'Just relax. It's going to be fine. You're not going to believe what happens on opening night.'" Mylett was right and Braha became convinced of the show's value once they had played to an audience.

Peggy Gordon started as a doubter as well. "I thought the show was a mess. And when we did the first dress rehearsal at La MaMa in front of an audience and they all stood up at the end and were applauding, I was stunned." She concluded that their innocent playfulness had a power she hadn't understood before.

By the time *The Godspell* opened at Café La MaMa, word of the inventive show had reached the Carnegie Mellon crowd, including fellow student Colette Bablon, who was spending time in New York and came to visit her friends in the show. "The first time I saw *Godspell* was just before it opened at a dress rehearsal and I thought, 'Okay, this is a hit!'"

Bablon was part of the network of people who kept track of each other. "We all knew where everybody was," she recalls. "That's one thing about being in a class like this. You were either in New York, you were on tour, or you were in California." In that network was her classmate, Charlie Haid, who had aspirations as a producer. She called him to say about their classmates, "They're doing a show and you've got to come see this."

Haid also loved it. He, in turn, invited the producing team of Joseph Beruh and Edgar Lansbury to see it before it closed at Café La MaMa, asserting that if they liked it, he wanted to be an associate producer.

By that point the producers had heard about the Café La MaMa production from Larry Carra, who had phoned his friend Joe Beruh about it. Between Haid's and Carra's prompts, they were not going to miss it.

Once they saw the show, they agreed it could be great. They knew that the Cherry Lane Theatre had an upcoming opening in the schedule. Perhaps *The Godspell* could run there if the young dramatists could give it a quick turnaround.

The State of the Show at La MaMa

Although *The Godspell* was suited to an experimental theater venue like Café La MaMa, it would not likely have worked elsewhere without changes. Even with the refinements that had been made since the CMU production, the show still seemed long on speech and short on song.

It opened, as before, with a series of philosopher monologues, during which time actors tore off their gray sweatshirts and blue jeans, stripping down to not much at all (Manzano taking off more than the others), and dressed themselves in their clown outfits, pieces of which they pulled from the bags of trash around the floor. Faso remembers that because the trash on stage was real, it was actually helpful to have a baptism during which actors were wiped down with water because they could clean off what they'd been handling.

The show proceeded from the baptism scene, through the assorted parable enactments and related material, and on to the Crucifixion. By this point in its development, *Godspell*'s structure was essentially established in terms of the order of parables, expressions, and songs, though it was running long.

The set was similar to the previous production. Sonia Manzano remembers it being stark and she liked it that way. "At Café La MaMa there was barbed wire on the top of the fence, like a concentration camp—that was the image that came to mind for me," Manzano states. "And there were these bare bulbs hanging down, and the brick in the back. I always thought concentration camp." (She believed the look was worth keeping. "I was very disappointed that they took away the barbed wire when we went more legit.")

For this second production, Susan Tsu had a chance to closely design costume pieces for specific actor/character personalities. She adjusted them again for the Cherry Lane Theatre, based on further experiences with the group. For example, she remembers, "Peggy Gordon was soulful and more of a hippie. Robin Lamont had a kind of spunk." Gilmer McCormick recalls that when her character responded to Jesus' presence as if she were a little girl, that informed Tsu's choices. "She knew I needed a dress, and she knew I wanted a Baby Huey hat." The costumes essentially remained the same from Café La MaMa through the early days at Cherry Lane.

The Songs

The songs at La MaMa were still the energetic rock music pieces that had been heard at CMU, with the addition of "By My Side" and Mylett's piece. Tebelak had recruited the Quinn brothers to perform as the band, as they had for *MacBird!* years earlier. Their parents had relocated to Westchester County, just north of New York City. When Duane Bolick declined to come, Tebelak invited the brothers to form the band: 18-year-old keyboardist Richard Quinn, 16-year-old guitar player Doug Quinn, and 14-year-old drummer Marty Quinn. Peggy Gordon explains that while the young men were talented, the arrangements they used "didn't do the songs justice," as they were so similar it made the songs hard to distinguish.

Audience Response and the Next Step

Tina Holmes remembers the reception to the show being positive. At intermission when the cast handed out wine and wafers, some of the audience members embraced the actors and told them what a profound spiritual experience the show was for them. *The Godspell* was still too wild for the general public, but at least the nature of each clown character was coming into focus. The whole piece needed conscious reshaping; that's what the evolution of a musical is all about.

The entrance to La MaMa.

The cast performs at Café La MaMa. Pictured: Robin Lamont, Tina Holmes, Jeffrey Mylett, Peggy Gordon, Herb Braha, Jimmy Canada. Not pictured: Gilmer McCormick, Sonia Manzano, David Haskell.

Chapter 7
Enter Lansbury, Beruh, and Schwartz

Essential to the future of the show were producers who could present it to a broader audience. Fortunately, Edgar Lansbury and Joe Beruh were seeking something like *The Godspell*. They were regularly booking shows at the Cherry Lane Theatre in Greenwich Village and had a certain amount of control over what went into it. They also had created the Promenade Theatre, an Off-Broadway venue on the Upper West Side with a 299-seat hall designed by Lansbury. So they were in the habit of looking for material and talent for both theater spaces.

Lansbury and Beruh were not high-stakes gamblers in the producing business primarily for financial rewards, but were genuinely motivated by a love of the theater. To take a small show and try to make a success of it was more their style. They kept abreast of social trends and had a feel for ways the American theater could reflect that. "Joe Beruh and I had been actually looking for something that had its roots in religious and philosophical beliefs," says Lansbury about the early 1970s. "We looked at a number of possibilities and then heard about *The Godspell*. We just felt the time was ripe for that kind of thing."

Edgar Lansbury, born in London in 1930, came to America as a child. His older sister, Angela, was a star of stage and screen. Edgar built up his own show business credits, working as an artist and scenic designer for stage, television, and movies before becoming a producer. He enjoyed a major success when he produced a Tony-winning Broadway play, *The Subject Was Roses*, in the mid 1960s. Tall, elegant, and cultured, Lansbury's refinement contrasted with that of Joe Beruh, who was general manager for *The Subject Was Roses*.

Joseph Beruh (1924 to 1989) was a Pittsburgh native and a graduate of Carnegie Mellon University's drama school. Beruh's demeanor would readily shift between cheerful and stern for business purposes. Lansbury recalls, "He was an amusing fellow. He had a fund of Jewish jokes and a whole background of that kind of theater." He had trained under the infamous producer David Merrick, and had a tough approach to the theater business.

> *"Joe was much shorter than Edgar, very round, and had a little pot belly. So together they looked like Laurel and Hardy."*
>
> —Nina Faso

When Lansbury and Beruh saw *The Godspell* at Café La MaMa, they found themselves moved by the show and believed that it might work well at the Cherry Lane Theatre. They decided to produce it without altering the basic approach, but wanted a new score. "The storytelling was wonderful but a lot of the music wasn't," Lansbury states.

Enter Stephen Schwartz

It was raining on Sunday, March 7, 1971, the day Stephen Schwartz was supposed to see *The Godspell* for the first time. His friend and college classmate, Charlie Haid, had called him the previous day about coming to see it, but Schwartz and his wife were staying at his parents' home on Long Island, about an hour's drive or train ride to the theater, and he considered not making the effort.

Since his days at Carnegie, as well as during his summer breaks, Schwartz had been expanding his experience with professional theater. In summer stock at the New London Barn Playhouse in New Hampshire, he'd performed multiple tasks, such as musical direction, musical staging, and/or directing for shows like *How to Succeed in Business Without Really Trying*, *Oliver!*, and *Camelot*. Occasionally, he appeared on stage, such as when he was in the chorus for *Kiss Me, Kate*.

It was in that summer stock program that he met his future wife, Carole Piasecki (stage name Carole Prandis), whom he married in June of 1969. He also met dancer and singer Joanne Jonas, whom he would soon recruit for the cast of *Godspell*.

Schwartz settled in New York City where he picked up some music directing work, and got a job as an A & R (Artists and Repertoire) representative for RCA records, helping them find new acts for their label.

He and Carole lived in a first floor apartment at 155 West 81st Street, a relatively quiet section of Manhattan's Upper West Side. At a furniture store around the corner, Stephen bought a heavy, used upright piano for $100 and had it hauled into the apartment's living room. He was pleased that "it turned out to be such a good piano." This was the instrument on which he would write much of the music for *Godspell* and *Pippin*.

By his twenty-third birthday on the 6th of March, 1971, he was feeling discouraged about his prospects for fulfilling his dream. Although he had been accepted by talent agent Shirley Bernstein, the musical *Pippin*, for which he'd been revising the score since college, had yet to be produced. A few months earlier, Lansbury and Beruh had heard Schwartz play his original songs from *Pippin* and they liked the young man's style. So when *Godspell* came to their attention, they thought Schwartz might be able to make it into a commercially viable musical.

Schwartz's mother and wife prodded him to follow up on Charlie Haid's phone call and go into the city to explore the opportunity. Once at Café La MaMa, he discovered that he liked the piece.

"My first impression of the show was that it was messy but inspired."
–Stephen Schwartz

On Monday, March 8th, Schwartz walked into the producers' office in the Theatre District, feeling a little more optimistic about his future. When asked if he could write a new score for *Godspell*, he felt ready.

"Sure, I'd be happy to," he told them without hesitation.

"Great. We go into rehearsals April 11th."

And that was that. About the absurd deadline Schwartz later remarked, "I was so young and stupid, I had no idea that you couldn't do this. I didn't say to them, 'But that's impossible.' I just said, 'Uh, okay.'"

In later years, Schwartz shrugged off his entry into *Godspell* rather than claiming he deserved it. "If I put myself in their position, that's not what I would have done. It's not the smart thing to do—to go to somebody completely unknown and inexperienced." Lansbury, however, is quite sure Schwartz was the first they called upon. He remembers being in Shirley Bernstein's office, hearing Schwartz play and sing. "We thought of him immediately for *Godspell* because we were so impressed with his *Pippin*. He played the score of *Pippin* as far as he'd taken it at that point. And we were enormously impressed with the talent—with this young guy who seems to be fluent in all kinds of ideas and styles. And serendipitously, he'd been to Carnegie and knew all these people. So it was just a short hop and a skip to put the whole thing into action and get the rights and go into rehearsal and start Stephen to work writing some more songs."

Lansbury also had high regard for Tebelak when he saw the show, and he believed the two young men could be a team. "I just saw a wonderful idea and a lot of talent in the person of

John-Michael Tebelak, who had conceived of the idea and developed it thus far within the context of the theater department at Carnegie. And it was exactly what we were looking for. It had to do with faith and religion and philosophy. It was very theatrical, very unconventional, and used story theater techniques, which of course had been used Off Broadway prior to that, but John-Michael took it a step further and used them to illustrate the Gospels in a most imaginative, humorous, and wonderful way. All of that was terrific. We just thought the music could be better. That was our reason for calling on Stephen."

A New Start with New People

With an opening scheduled for May 17, 1971, at the historic 180-seat Cherry Lane Theatre, preparations began in earnest for the revised musical. Somewhere in the transition, *"The Godspell"* became *"Godspell,"* probably because it was simpler.

The young dramatists were now aligned with experienced producers twice their age who provided guidance, hired publicists, set up the management, and raised funds. After Café La MaMa, the actors had about five weeks to regroup personally before rehearsals began at the Cherry Lane Theatre, but there was much work to be done on other aspects of the new commercial production.

Tebelak had agreed with the producers that *Godspell* needed a new score. "I wanted something a little more eclectic than pure rock," he once said in an interview. Eclectic was not a tall order for Stephen Schwartz, who was naturally diverse in his musical tastes and had broad composing talents.

Director Tebelak also wanted to replace two cast members whom he and others felt weren't coming across vocally: James Canada and Prudence Holmes. As Schwartz reports, "We made two cast changes, one male and one female, in order to get a slightly stronger singing ensemble."

Lamar Alford had been noticed performing in another production at La MaMa, and was approached to join the *Godspell* cast. He was a classically trained baritone with a powerful voice and an imposing build. It didn't hurt that he was an African-American and would add some diversity to the group in addition to Hispanic cast member, Sonia Manzano. Schwartz loved Alford's voice and was really pleased to have him on board.

Schwartz wanted to recruit an actress who could belt songs in a musical theater style. He sought out Joanne Jonas, whom he remembered from summer stock. As a skilled singer, actor, and dancer, the agile young woman would easily integrate into the *Godspell* cast. He composed the vocally demanding song "Bless the Lord" with Jonas' vocal talents and range in mind.

Jonas recalls a conversation with Schwartz in which he invited her to help out with a unique musical he was working on. "He said he was writing a Laura Nyro-esque song for me, so how could they refuse?! It would be Off-Broadway and would I like to sing it for the producers so they get an idea of the music?"

When she came in to meet with him, she learned "Bless the Lord" on the spot, and then debuted the song an hour later. The producers loved both the song and Jonas, so she was selected as the final cast member.

Schwartz enlisted his friend Stephen Reinhardt as music director and keyboard player for the show. While working at RCA, Schwartz had auditioned Reinhardt, a singer-songwriter at the time, for a recording contract. They were about the same age, and Schwartz noticed that they played piano in a similar way, partly because they had often played pieces by the same pop and Broadway songwriters.

As interesting as the offer for *Godspell* was, Reinhardt hesitated. "I've never been a musical director for anything in my life," he emphasized.

"I know you can do it," Schwartz affirmed. It was a vote of confidence that he would give many aspiring musicians in the coming years.

A Face and Subtitle for *Godspell*

Among Lansbury's projects was planning the show's visual imagery for promotions. He contacted artist David Byrd, who was famous for his psychedelic poster art. Lansbury explains, "He had done a poster for a Hal Prince show, *Follies*, and I admired that tremendously. I told him what I felt *Godspell*'s logo needed: it should just be the head of Jesus in a very stylistic way. And that's what he did. And we put it on T-shirts, we put it on programs, we put it on everything. That logo was very successful."

Lansbury was an experienced scenic designer, but Tebelak had developed a set that seemed to suit the show (planks, sawhorses, and fence), so that would stay. Lansbury worked out details for a platform for the band above the acting space, still visible to the audience.

Another thing on Lansbury's To Do list was hiring a publicist who could promote this unusual musical in the most tasteful and helpful manner. He remembers when the husband-and-wife team Edwin and Michael Gifford came to his office looking to expand their work as publicists ("Michael" here is a female name). He especially noticed Ms. Gifford's flair. "I remember she came in with this great big hat, and I was very impressed with her." He felt that the role of the publicist needed a lot of imagination. "We went with the Giffords, which was a very good choice because they really got a handle on the show. She had connections among the clergy as well, which was helpful."

The producers also believed the show needed a tagline. They wanted a few words to define the show a little better for potential audiences who might not otherwise grasp what something called *Godspell* would be, and so they added, "*A Musical Based on the Gospel According to St. Matthew.*" Even though Tebelak never claimed the show was based on that particular Gospel, much of the material did come from St. Matthew, so the subtitle stayed.

Peggy Gordon notes that the Gospel according to Mark was written first, followed by Matthew, and that Tebelak especially loved this second one. She says, in comparison to Mark, which is bleaker, "With Matthew, suddenly we have the resurrection, we have hope, we have joy." And that suited Tebelak's purpose.

CHAPTER 8
An Off-Broadway Collaboration

At the center of *Godspell*'s next phase of development was a pair of young men in their early twenties who were now under contract as the official authors of the new musical. As a team they were a study in contrasts. The older of the two, by a year and a half, was the assertive, trim Stephen Schwartz, 5' 8", usually wearing a brightly colored shirt and sporting a haircut that made him look a bit like one of the Beach Boys. The more laid back and pensive one was John-Michael Tebelak, habitually dressed in oversized blue denim overalls over a casual shirt. His long bushy hair accentuated his height of 6' 1". Whatever their physical and personality differences, they worked together smoothly and symbiotically, as Schwartz recalls.

> *"John-Michael was somewhat shy, but he could also be gregarious and occasionally even grand. Like any genius, he had his own particular and peculiar way of looking at things. He was quite a large man physically and so he could be somewhat overwhelming, but his basic soul was very gentle."*
> —**Stephen Schwartz**

Right after the show closed at Café La MaMa, the two started meeting at Stephen and Carole Schwartz's 81st Street apartment. Tebelak provided a mimeographed script that included psalms, hymns, sayings, and parables. Schwartz recalls about the script: "It was basically just passages from the Bible edited together. And then, out of that, this amazing theatrical piece got created."

Later in his career, Stephen Schwartz might spend a few weeks on one song, and several years to complete a musical. Using his imagination, he'd step into a character and try to feel what that character might feel in a particular situation in order to write emotionally appropriate music and lyrics. He'd consider the whole emotional arc of the characters and what the song needed to convey.

For *Godspell*, Schwartz recalls, "It was only five weeks between the time I saw the show at La MaMa and the time the show went into rehearsal, when there had to be a score. So there was really no time to think about anything except trying to get it done, and responding to the lyrics, finding the places that I wanted to musicalize, and, obviously, consulting with John-Michael about all these decisions—playing the stuff for John-Michael and getting feedback from him, and so on. It was very, very tight."

Schwartz decided to keep "By My Side," a song he'd heard at Café La MaMa. In his meetings with John-Michael he said, "I could try to write a new song for this spot, and maybe I would write a song as good as this, but why bother if we have this wonderful song?" All the other music needed to come from him.

Neither Schwartz nor his casually Jewish parents saw a problem with him working on *Godspell*. He rather hoped that being unschooled in Christian tenets would prove an advantage in terms of a novel perception. "I don't come from a Christian upbringing and therefore I really didn't know the New Testament," he once explained. "I was reading some of these parables for the first time, and the hymns that I set with new music for the show are from the Episcopal Hymnal. I basically was responding to the material fresh."

It helped that he could write music and new lyrics after witnessing a version of the show in action. "I had seen the show itself at La MaMa, so I already knew what the tone was, the theatrical journey, and the specific characters the cast members had created. None of it had to be imagined from scratch."

Schwartz and Tebelak evaluated the "event" of each song, so that the actors wouldn't just be stopping the story to sing. In most instances, songs suggested characters' moments of revelation or conversion or commitment. "They are pledging their loyalty, their belief, their faith to become a member of this community that's being formed," Schwartz explains. Accordingly, he wrote specific songs for a featured cast member to lead.

For example, he decided that Robin Lamont, instead of singing "Turn Back, O Man," as she had sung in the previous two versions of the show, instead would sing "Day by Day." The Robin clown became the first character to sign on to a community that explored the parables as lessons. Her character's breakthrough occurs after she listens to a parable about a man who doesn't forgive his brother's debts and is condemned. Jesus then explains the parable's meaning in terms of the importance of forgiveness, inspiring the Robin clown's epiphany and motivating her to sing from her heart.

Joanne Jonas remembers that Tebelak and Schwartz based the song spot for "Bless the Lord" on a moment during the rehearsal when she personally experienced a revelation. "One day, while we were rehearsing the 'rich man' parable, I had a revelation about the power of love that was coming through Jesus. A light bulb went off inside me, the actress, and I said, 'Oh, I get it!' out loud. John-Michael and Stephen said, 'Right there—that's when you should sing 'Bless the Lord.'"

Schwartz also reviewed the spoken material to consider whether any might work better as song, especially the show's opening scene with the monologues. "It was reeaally long! That thing went on forever." He began paging through the philosophers' quotations in the script and extracting the kernel of what each said. He then generated a multi-part fugue-like piece that became an exciting opening ("Prologue"). "I kind of shaped it so it had a build as a musical number, instead of just being an amorphous thing where everybody came out and made speeches and then threw things at one another."

He also decided to write an original duet he'd call "All for the Best" for Jesus and Judas, and to musicalize the lengthy speech in Act II about lawyers and Pharisees, turning it into the song, "Alas for You."

He did a little editing on the "Finale." The lyrics at the time included "Oh God, I'm busted." Schwartz thought the "busted" line was over the top and trivialized the Crucifixion. "I just said to John-Michael, 'You can't. That's a really bad idea.' And he got it right away."

See Part III of this book for more details about the songs.

Music director Reinhardt was one of the first people (after Tebelak) to hear all the new *Godspell* songs. He remembers, "They were really wonderful, very clever and very heartfelt."

He needed to quickly learn the pieces in order to play piano for rehearsals and performances. In those days, Schwartz trusted his memory for retaining everything he composed, so except for some hand written lead sheets, there was no printed score. Reinhardt brought along a small cassette recorder as he listened to Schwartz play the pieces in his apartment, and then went home to practice with the recordings and lead sheets. "I wouldn't play it note for note; I would basically interpolate what he was doing and get it as close as possible to how he played it."

First Presentation of the New Score

Once Tebelak and the producers heard and approved the music, it was time for an in-house debut. The cast assembled at the apartment of one of the producers on Manhattan's Upper West Side. Stephen Schwartz, Steve Reinhardt, Joanne Jonas, and Lamar Alford performed the songs.

Until that moment, the show had been freewheeling and eccentrically nontraditional. The actors had memorized the previous versions of songs and were not prepared for hearing polished musical theater tunes. Schwartz accompanied at the piano, with Joanne debuting "Day by Day" and belting "Bless the Lord;" Lamar sang "All Good Gifts" and Schwartz and Reinhardt performed the other pieces.

When they finished, the room settled into a fidgety silence. There was no warm applause or supportive praise. Peggy Gordon recalls, "We were stunned when we first heard this music. It was not only different, but there was so much more of it. We were protective of the old and a little reserved toward the new." Without saying anything, two cast members pulled out their guitars and others joined them in singing the familiar old songs.

> *"We were all very anti-showbiz at the time, and Stephen wanted to turn 'Godspell' into a musical comedy. He managed to do it successfully, but it took a little while to get into the spirit of what he wrote."*
>
> —Nina Faso

Edgar Lansbury believed Schwartz was on the right track, even if the cast "balked a little bit" when asked to let go of their previous songs. "Actors are like that. They become very possessive of the way things are done."

Although they were not initially swept away by Schwartz's work, it wasn't long before the cast appreciated the more theatrically ideal music. Stephen Nathan had already been convinced of the new score's merits. "John-Michael had me over to his loft and said, 'I want you to listen to the score and tell me what you think.' I remember listening and going, 'Oh my God, these songs are phenomenal.' It was exactly what the show needed. ...Godspell could so easily have turned into a bunch of self-indulgent young people acting for themselves. The beauty of the score for me was that it became a performance piece. It became accessible to a wide audience [and] commercial in the best sense of the word. It elevated, for lack of a better word, the vibe of the cast. Our vibe was a bit different. The parables also became a bit more accessible."

Rehearsing at the Cherry Lane Theatre

The theater on Commerce Street where *Godspell* finished its birthing process was in Greenwich Village, where a walk down Bleeker, Commerce, or other side streets can evoke the mood of a European village. There are no skyscrapers; trees grow along the sidewalks, and in summer some of the apartment dwellers fill window boxes with fresh flowers. In years past, legendary writers and musicians frequented the cafés and clubs in the area. The Cherry Lane Theatre had contributed to the Village culture by presenting the works of pioneering playwrights like Albee, Beckett, Ionesco, and others. *Godspell* would soon add to the legacy of innovation in its own warm-hearted way.

In mid April 1971, an ambitious troupe of young actors and their also-young leaders entered the Cherry Lane Theatre through the front door under the theater's red awning (since there was no stage door or even any backstage space). The building had started as a brewery in 1836 before becoming a warehouse, box factory, and then a theater. The overall tone of the seating area and brick wall that formed the stage backdrop was a muted red. There was only one aisle between the seats, down the center, a little space for a rehearsal piano in front of the first row of seats, and a small wood stage where they could work.

Unlike their part-time labors for La MaMa, the actors had now been hired for a commercial Off-Broadway run, so they could revamp *Godspell* all day. The band, once hired, rehearsed in the same space at night.

One of the immediate goals for Tebelak and the actors was to integrate the two new cast members, as well as return to the spirit of the show after their break. The foundation for this next incarnation of the musical was primarily in the memories of the eight actors who would be continuing. (A 32-page typed script found amongst Tebelak's papers appears to be one developed early at La MaMa, but it was never completed. The sayings and teachings of "First clown"—a.k.a. Jesus—were all marked, and clowns two through ten had some of the Bible quotations from parables assigned to them.)

According to Peggy Gordon, most of the structure remained the same, although many of the spoken bits changed during rehearsals when actors further divided up the material and added their own playfulness. "We started from scratch, from the vantage point of letting Joanne and Lamar create their characters," remembers Gordon. "Once this was achieved, we began the necessary reshaping of the show through judicious cutting, and continued that process all through previews."

It didn't take long for Joanne to find her clown. She took cues from her experiences as a dancer: "I fashioned myself as a marionette. Being double-jointed and very flexible, I would contort into some wild shapes kind of like a marionette pup-

The Godspell Experience

pet could do." As she flexed physically, her vocal performance also morphed into different impressions to suit the moment. She remembers: "Ed Wynn, Mae West, high funny voices, low voices—many different voices."

Gordon especially remembers one of Jonas' voices. "Joanne does the best Ed Wynn impression in the entire world. Think of Ed Wynn in the *Mary Poppins* movie during that wonderful song where he's laughing and flying up in the chair—that was Joanne's character."

Lamar's clown character evolved gradually during rehearsals.

Towards a Stable, Artistically Structured Show

In April and May, the actors finalized their formerly improvised parts and practiced performances together. Stephen Schwartz brought the new songs to the cast, and together they shaped the musical with input from Tebelak, who usually sat in the theater seats and watched most of the rehearsals.

Music director Reinhardt remembers the first day that the cast rehearsed the "Prologue" song. Schwartz brought index cards with the music solos written out for each cast member. He'd play a part on the piano for one actor and then send him or her outside to the quiet Greenwich Village street to rehearse the song a cappella with Stephen Reinhardt.

Fortunately, by then the actors were sold on Schwartz's new tunes. "It was heaven," says Gordon, "pure, blissful, joyful, exuberant heaven to learn these songs; to learn our individual harmony parts and then sing them in the context of the show."

Not only were they learning songs, but they were practicing a variety of other talents. Gordon recalls, "Stephen Nathan played the ukulele; Jeffrey played the concertina, recorder and guitar; Gilmer and I played guitar; and David played the shofar as his particular rite. Edgar Lansbury said to us, 'You are the most unbelievably multi-talented group of people I have ever seen. You are dancers, you are singers, some of you are acrobats, and some of you play instruments. We want you guys to do everything you do in this show.'"

Comedic Movement and Casual Dance

While much of the play's blocking was collaborative, the overall theme for the actors' movements on stage came from Tebelak. Gordon remembers, "It was a fascinating challenge to create what John-Michael wanted…. goofy rather than slick and polished! His mantra was 'keep it childlike.'"

Jeffrey Mylett instigated a lot of the physical movement for the scenes, says Robin Lamont. "He had the most energy of anybody in the show. It was really hard to keep up with him. He'd say, 'Let's just jump up and land on our knees here.' Sure Jeffrey."

No official choreographer was ever assigned to *Godspell* at the Cherry Lane Theatre. Tebelak had little experience with staging musical numbers and yielded to Schwartz and the cast. As director, Tebelak would say things like, "I don't know how to make it feel like this, but here's the way I want it to feel," and his cohorts took it from there.

For "Bless the Lord" and other songs, Schwartz sent groups of two or three off to different parts of the rehearsal space or the dressing rooms, saying, "See what you can come up with for this verse." The whole group process delighted the actors and helped them bond with each other emotionally.

"Everybody really pitched in with everything they had."

—Stephen Reinhardt

When specific dance moves were needed, trained dancers Joanne Jonas and Stephen Reinhardt recommended steps. For the "All for the Best" duet, Reinhardt worked out a soft-shoe dance with Stephen Nathan that would be entertaining and doable while singing.

Carole Schwartz was watching a rehearsal one day and had the idea for a particular cake walk strut they could perform during "Turn Back, O Man." That worked because it was simple enough that it could almost have been invented on the spot.

Gordon recalls Tebelak's interest in "comedic choreography that even adolescent children could dance." Gordon also says that it was Sonia Manzano's idea to have the backup dancers for "All for the Best" do a faux tap dance. "Sonia talked about what children look like when they're learning to tap but haven't mastered the steps yet. It was a very funny illustration and perfect clown behavior!"

Let Songs Be Heard with a Band

With opening night quickly approaching, Schwartz set out to find musicians who could handle the new material and agree to work almost every night in an Off-Broadway show. The Quinn brothers were not available at that time. Schwartz asked several other musicians who declined because they didn't think the show would fly.

Joanne Jonas remembered a band from high school on Long Island, and Schwartz telephoned the drummer, Rick Shutter (then called "Ricky"). Shutter was 19 years old at the time, and living with his parents in the suburbs, but already a professional performer. He was part of a rock band called the Young Executives that played regular gigs and backed up acts like Chuck Berry, Bo Diddley, and the Shirelles.

The composer took a train out to Shutter's house to audition him. With Schwartz at the family piano, Shutter set up his drums and played along for a few songs. Schwartz said, "I think you're perfect for the show, but I want to try 'Alas for You.' This song is trouble. It's got a lot of time changes."

Shutter decided to play by ear rather than read lead sheets. He recalls, "I started drawing on Elton John's style of music, Procol Harem's B.J. Wilson, and Ringo Starr of the Beatles. I started to play, drawing from that musically, and Steve loved it."

"That's what I'm looking for," Schwartz affirmed.

Next, Shutter telephoned his and Jonas's guitar player friend, Jesse Cutler, who lived down the block, insisting that he come over right away with his guitar. Cutler was also 19 and had also been a professional musician throughout his teen years, performing as part of the Young Executives with Shutter.

Whatever Cutler played pleased Schwartz. The two recruits were then invited to a backers meeting the following week. Soon they and Richard La Bonte (a bass player who was also a friend of Joanne Jonas) joined Stephen Reinhardt as the official band for the show and the original cast recording.

Pay Caesar What is Caesar's

It was up to Edgar Lansbury, Joseph Beruh, and their "silent partner," Stuart Duncan, to raise the capital to bring this musical to the public. Duncan, a Princeton, New Jersey-based businessman, had joined Lansbury and Beruh the previous January to produce *Waiting for Godot* and *Long Day's Journey Into Night*, and he had previously co-produced several others with Lansbury. Duncan was "silent" with respect to not being involved in day-to-day artistic decision-making. Rather, he focused on raising funds for the show while maintaining his position as vice-president of Lea and Perrins, a company that made Worcestershire and other sauces.

The producers held several gatherings to find investors for the show. One of the important backers auditions was held at Stuart Duncan's home in Princeton. "We had invited a lot of investors," Lansbury recalls. "The whole company and John-Michael and Stephen went out there and did the whole show. The people all loved it, and in very short order we had raised what we needed."

The producing team felt that they could launch *Godspell* as a low-budget piece. Lansbury explains that their plan was to capitalize the show at $40,000, although, according to several sources, they raised only about half of that before the opening. It would all work out if they could pay the actors about $50 a week and they didn't have to pay too much for marketing. As with all new stage musicals, it was a gamble with a high potential for failure. But it could also succeed.

See "The Godspell Commune Company" chapter in Part IV for more details about financing and payment.

Cherry Lane Theatre in Greenwich Village.

CHAPTER 9

Mishaps, Miracles, and a Completed New Musical

Godspell was headed for many unpredictable moments. Company members expected the usual oddities of live performances, like forgotten lines, mishaps with props, odd responses from audiences, and perhaps some magical or serendipitous experiences as well.

They hadn't counted on rats. As with other old theaters in the city, rats had infested the Cherry Lane Theatre where they were spending all their days finishing the show. The actors compensated with humor. "We called ourselves 'The Rat Family,'" Gordon recalls, "because the rats were humongous. So we were 'Peggy Gordrat,' 'Jeffrey Myrat,' and so on."

For Lamar Alford, a rat actually assisted his integration into the show. He was new to the group and not quite sure about the clowning process or when to commit to the Jesus character's teaching. Gordon recollects, "We were improvising on stage during the first week, and we were having a conversation about revelation. Suddenly, Lamar ran straight down the stage toward John-Michael, who was at the back of the theater, yelling 'Rat! Rat!' John-Michael said, 'That's it, you've got it!' And Lamar said 'No, there's a rat the size of a Buick next to your foot.' John-Michael jumped up and ran to the stage, shrieking. We laughed hysterically and Lamar suddenly felt like he understood how large the moment of revelation would be for his goofy, dumb clown."

At that point the staging and organization of props was happening on the fly as the show evolved. On one occasion, a miscommunication added to the show. While the cast was rehearsing "We Beseech Thee," Stephen Schwartz asked Nina Faso to find some batons and colored banners or posters to use with the staging. He wanted the song's often-repeated lyric, "hear us," to be displayed visually, assuming she understood that the words could all be on one banner. Faso returned with small banners displaying two letters each (HE AR US). When the cast began using the letter groups, they would often hold them up in the wrong order, which Schwartz thought was funny and it became a standard part of the antics.

The Miracle of Magic, Lights, and Creativity

Although Tebelak did not include the Bible's miraculous healing stories in *Godspell*, he and the other show creators were interested in stage magic, such as the appearance of something new coming out of nowhere in a seemingly miraculous way.

Stephen Nathan had been a fan of magic for many years, and brought in props from his own collection to make the show more magically entertaining while illustrating points. For example, he made flowers appear magically from nowhere when he spoke of lilies of the field. While delivering a line about not letting the right hand know what the left hand is doing, he transformed a scarf from one color to another with the sweep of his hands.

During "All for the Best," Nathan, acting as Jesus, conjured up a cane to use for his performance. After demonstrating he had nothing up his sleeve, he held out his hand and presto! A long black cane appeared out of thin air. He also gave an "appearing cane" to David Haskell to use. Haskell, in the role of John/Judas, acted as if he couldn't muster the same conjuring power. Finally, Nathan touched his hand, and suddenly Haskell held a long black cane as well. Then they both proceeded to dance with them. "I just did everything I could," Nathan comments about adding special props to the show.

Tebelak wanted to make theatrical magic with lights. He had always been fascinated by lighting effects. Conceptually, he liked simplicity and a kind of "theater of poverty" effect with minimal production values. He hung inexpensive lights in three rows over the stage. These were cone-shaped light bulbs known to theater crews as "PARs," or parabolic aluminum reflector lights. When an actor jumped up to begin a parable, he or she could pull the cord in order to be lit. This eliminated the need for more costly spotlights that would require extra personnel.

Tebelak also liked dramatic or inventive visual effects. He asked cast members to swing flashlights around the theater as they scurried up and down the center aisle singing "Day by Day." He used a strobe light to create a silent movie type of effect during the final segment of "All for the Best." And he arranged for stark red lighting during the Betrayal and Crucifixion.

As the show neared completion, the creative group even adapted the plain silver chain link fence backdrop to suit *Godspell*'s needs. Faso, as stage manager, operated from behind it and hung props from it that actors would grab as needed. She remembers, "When Stephen Schwartz saw the show, he loved that, and so he kept giving me more stuff to put on the fence. The musical instruments like the vibraslap and the other rhythm instruments—all of that was on the fence." The fence also substituted for a wooden cross at the end of the show. Stephen Nathan would lean against the fence while others tied red ribbons to his outstretched hands, and untied him when they were ready to carry him away.

Who's In Charge Here?

As with any creative work, the more *Godspell* developed, the more it took on a life of its own. Musical theater is a collaborative art form anyway, and with *Godspell* it was inevitable that many chefs would add flavors to Tebelak's original broth. Who could say what the best flavor would be? Who should be in charge of deciding?

Lansbury and Beruh worked from their office in the Midtown Theater District and mostly left the young artists alone down in the Village, although they did expect some editorial control over the material. However, the twenty-something actors refused interference from an older generation. Stephen Nathan comments, "We were new to the whole thing and we didn't know what the hell we were doing. I remember we told the producers to leave. They wanted to see a run-through and we said no. We said, 'You saw one the other day and you just had these notes, and we don't want to listen to them.' And they said, 'We are going to go through the run-through!' And then we said, 'Well then we're not going to do the show. We'll just leave!'" So Lansbury and Beruh backed off temporarily.

Regarding who was in charge for the completion of the show, it was never really specified how much was Tebelak's responsibility and how much was Schwartz's. In Schwartz's mind, he was preparing *Godspell* for a commercial run with the new score, so it was natural for him to take over much of the rehearsal time. While Tebelak preferred to focus on ideas, Schwartz handled the more nitty-gritty rehearsal details well, such as song practice and blocking.

This last part of the process of creating a musical was mostly Schwartz's territory anyway. Nina Faso, who had seen several of Schwartz's college musicals, explains, "Stephen had been writing musicals and studying musical theater for so long that he knew things that we didn't know, like how to get applause on a number."

> *"When we met with Stephen Schwartz, he was completely confident. Like a shooting star, he knew where he was going to take us."*
>
> —Herb Braha

Schwartz would always run new material past Tebelak, and he respected him for the creative work he'd already accomplished. "John-Michael and I talked a lot about what went where, who was singing what, and what was the feeling of the song—what it was about," Schwartz recalls. "He had clear ideas; like for 'Day by Day,' he knew that he wanted everybody to be doing everyday activity. He was very clear about things like that." Schwartz focused on staging the new songs with help from others. From his point of view, he was taking charge of the rehearsals for practical reasons.

Faso, who had been directed by Tebelak as a student, explains, "John-Michael never liked that part of directing—he never liked the endless jumping up there with the actors. He liked to sit in the house and say, 'Use your talent. You're the actor; you decide how to do it.' Stephen was much more hands on than John-Michael." So it seemed to work out well that the dynamic composer finished off the process, while the quieter "director" added his two cents from the back of the hall.

A few people who were personally closer to Tebelak watched another story unfold. Since moving to New York, their friend had been slipping in and out of personal crisis. Alcohol played a large part. Tebelak had always been a lover of food and drink. He'd learned to cook in his youth and he often partied with the family, so kicking back with a food-related celebration was a meaningful part of his life. But by his early twenties, alcohol had become an addiction—one that on occasion undermined his creative functioning. "That was the time before the recovery movement [was popular], and drugs and alcohol just flowed," recalls his sister, Trudy. During his early months in New York City, he would occasionally collapse and have to be transported to a hospital.

Besides the addictive quality of alcohol itself, there were likely a number of factors that set him drinking. Nina Faso and Edgar Lansbury noticed he had relationship issues, often quarrelling with his apartment mate, artist Richard Hannum, with whom he had settled into a romantic partnership. (They remained a couple for many years despite their differences.)

Bill Phillips believes Tebelak experienced inner turmoil on account of *Godspell*: "Stephen Schwartz was such a force, and rather than battle him for directorship of the show to run rehearsals, John-Michael chose to withdraw and go to drink." Nina Faso noticed Tebelak's emotional and drinking issues around that time, sensing a tension relative to Schwartz's running of rehearsals. "That's when John-Michael started putting vodka in his cokes," she recalls.

It probably didn't help that Tebelak and Schwartz had opposite sensibilities when it came to shows. Schwartz comments, "When I was at Carnegie and shortly thereafter, I was not someone who was studying Peter Brook and being influenced by the Living Theatre. I was on a trajectory toward trying to write Broadway musicals. And so I wanted to learn what works in them and what doesn't and why." He wanted to make the show more audience-accessible, as if it were a mainstream musical, even though the score featured his new amalgam of pop-folk-rock styles. Tebelak loved experimental approaches and directing them was no doubt part of his self image. "John-Michael longed to direct avant-garde theater, as I did," says Bill Phillips.

The goal was not always to please an audience but to challenge the audience. Although he had wanted new music, and didn't mind that people would make money on a commercial show, he apparently wasn't expecting it to change tone quite so much from the shaggy, evocative piece that played at CMU to a perkier, polished musical.

Whatever drove Tebelak to drink, it impaired him then and continued to be a problem, on-and-off, throughout his abbreviated life. Peggy Gordon watched the drama from her own perspective. "We smoked a lot of marijuana when we were rehearsing at La MaMa, but after that there was nothing. What stunned all of us is that John-Michael was so immoderate in his use of drugs and alcohol that he became paralyzed. He literally became paralyzed and Stephen Schwartz had to take over. If Steve hadn't taken over, we never would have opened."

Faso also played an essential role in preparing the musical for its debut. Gilmer McCormick recalls, "Nina often did a lot of re-communicating for John-Michael. She just had a way, and was very calming. She never raised her voice. She was kind of a mama of everything else. She was always able to smooth things out and help us understand what she needed to get the result that he wanted."

Robin Lamont concludes that ultimately having two lead creators in Tebelak and Schwartz was ideal. "My recollection is that John-Michael was sort of an ethereal person, and *Godspell* happened out of his incredible imagination. It was Stephen Schwartz who made it commercial. So it might have lost something from John-Michael in the translation because Stephen was there to say, 'Hey, we need an uptempo number in the second act.' And John-Michael was going—'That's too commercial. That doesn't fit my vision.' But it was the two of them that created this piece. Probably neither one of them could have done it alone."

Last-Minute Preparations

One of the late-in-the-game twists came when Joe Beruh worried about attracting crowds and wanted to change the female cast members' appearance. "You can't tell the boys from the girls," Peggy Gordon recalls him wailing. She and others were horrified that he wanted Sonia to dress in a bikini with a cape. "Joe and I had a screaming fight in the Limelight Café where we would all go to drink after rehearsals."

Costume designer Susan Tsu was as stunned as anyone. "I was a kid, still in school, and I said, 'But this is about clowns and Jesus, and it's not about sex!' Beruh said, 'Well, we need you to do something!' I made a fringed bra for Sonia on top of a dress, so that was my concession to make it sexier for her."

Schwartz and Tebelak also stood up for the work they were doing. "When the producers decided to change the costumes and have the girls look sexier, there was a little revolt from the cast," Schwartz recalls. "John-Michael and I went to Edgar and Joe and said, 'We have things we're trying to do, so you've just got to leave us alone and let us do the show. Then, if you come back and you don't think it's working or you're not happy, say something, but we've got to finish what we think we want to do first.' And they did! I never forgot that. That they had the faith to leave us alone."

One of the other problems was the show's excessive length. "Steve Schwartz joked Act II is three hours long and it should only be forty-five minutes," says Gordon. She explains that during their improvisations they'd come up with some long bits they wanted to include; for example, a twenty-minute-long depiction of the Parable of the Talents. "We loved the Parable of the Talents but we had to cut it."

What else could be sacrificed? Any song with a verse that wasn't essential; any parable that seemed too similar to others. One of Schwartz's favorite verses from "By My Side" had to go.

During the final week of preparations, Schwartz also realized the musical wouldn't be complete without one more song. He quickly wrote "Learn Your Lessons Well" for Gilmer McCormick to sing. It would break up a section that seemed too thick with parables and give Gilmer her own song.

Before the show opened in previews, Stephen Reinhardt came down from the band platform and said to Schwartz, "I'd really like to see what's going on down here because I don't have any idea what this show is about; all I can do is hear it. He said 'Oh my God, of course.' So he played a run-through while I watched. I was just on the floor, pounding the floor laughing. I had never seen anything this funny. I said, 'This is wonderful.' That was the first time I got the feeling that we were involved with something very special. I laughed through the whole first act and then I saw the second act as it gradually transformed into a completely different kind of tone. And by the time that run-through was over I was in tears. I realized, I don't know what's going to happen to this thing, but it's a momentous show."

Previews and Opening Night

Godspell's run at the Cherry Lane Theatre started with three previews. Tebelak had enough to worry about without thinking of his academic program that he'd left behind. But the professors at Carnegie Mellon hadn't forgotten about him. "I had not returned to school, obviously, from the time I had left at Christmas," he said later in an interview, "and I was a little afraid of what the school would think about my—in a sense—running away…. Opening night, the department sent me a telegram that said, 'No matter what the critics say, you've passed with us,' and then announced that I would graduate."

On Sunday night, May 16, 1971, critics started attending the show. More came the following night for the official opening, and then dashed off to prepare their assessments of the new musical. Later that evening the first notices would appear.

The opening night party was to be at Sardi's restaurant on 44th Street, where theater casts and companies traditionally gathered to await praises, pans, or mixed reviews.

After the final curtain call, the entire company headed uptown. Susan Tsu remembers the restaurant scene: "It was a real eye-opener about the commercial world. There were people sitting there at tables tabulating and making charts. They were there to give an estimate of how well the show was doing right then. The reviews were going to come out that night. We had worked hard birthing a baby, so recognizing that there was a whole other world involved with this was interesting."

Schwartz joined his fellow *Godspell*ers at the party, but he was worried because he didn't believe it had been their best performance. "I was quite trepidatious," Schwartz recalls, "as one would expect from my first major show in New York." His heart sank when he heard that the review from *The New York Times* wasn't positive, but later headed upstairs to catch the television reviews. "The doors of the elevator open. There are three televisions: Channel Two comes on, and Channel Four comes on, and Channel Seven comes on, and they're unqualified raves. And then we start to find out that everything but the Times is a rave."

Schwartz and his colleagues had reason to celebrate that night. The show was not only finished at last, but it had worked its magic and touched an audience.

State of the Show at the Cherry Lane Theatre

By the time *Godspell* opened in its final incarnation, it had coalesced into a poignant musical that could consistently be shown anywhere. This was the version that was made available for licensing a few years later.

Among the many refinements since the Café La MaMa production was the addition of Stephen Schwartz's varied music and new lyrics. Group numbers had mostly been replaced by songs that were led by one of Jesus' followers. Schwartz comments, "Everybody had a number that began with him or her that became his or her signature tune."

From the spoken part of the libretto, Schwartz trimmed two lengthy prose sections to create the "Prologue" and "Alas for You." Tebelak and company decided to drop several Biblical parables and expressions, including:

- the Parable of the Workers in a Vineyard
- the Parable of the Talents
- the story of Jesus interpreting a rule of Moses about childless widows

Audiences watched actors playfully enact some of the key parables and stories told by Jesus (with songs interspersed):

- The Persistent Widow (Luke 18:1-8)
- The Tax Collector and the Pharisee (Luke 18:10-14)
- The Unforgiving Servant (Matthew 18:21-35)
- The Good Samaritan (Luke 10:25-37)
- The Rich Fool (Luke 12:16-20)
- The Prodigal Son (Luke 15:11-32)

The Godspell Experience

- The story of the Rich Man and Lazarus (Luke 16:19-31)
- The Sower and the Good Seed (Matthew 13:1-23)
- The story of a woman protected from a stoning (John 8:3-11)
- The Sheep and the Goats (Matthew 25:31-46)

From the four canonical Gospels, with nearly 90 chapters between them, Tebelak selected the majority of his non-parable text from the popular Sermon on the Mount found in Matthew chapters 5 through 7. This included the Beatitudes as well as familiar comments of Jesus, like: not nursing anger, reconciling with your brother, turning the other cheek, loving your enemies, praying in secret, and setting your mind on God (seek first His Kingdom and all the rest will follow).

Mishaps, Miracles, and a Completed New Musical

LEFT: In this publicity photo, Stephen Nathan (as Jesus) and David Haskell (John/Judas) form a cross while the cast looks on. From left: Sonia Manzano, Jeffrey Mylett, Robin Lamont, Lamar Alford, Nathan and Haskell, Peggy Gordon, Gilmer McCormick, Herb Braha, and Joanne Jonas. (Photo by Martha Swope/©The New York Public Library). ABOVE: The original cast performs in *Godspell* at the Cherry Lane Theatre. From left: Stephen Nathan, Sonia Manzano, Peggy Gordon and Herb Braha, Robin Lamont, Jeffrey Mylett, Lamar Alford, Gilmer McCormick, David Haskell, with Joanne Jonas on the floor. (Photo by Martha Swope/©The New York Public Library)

For his set design, Tebelak drew from a theatrical tradition of using large wooden planks for a temporary stage. Spanish playwright Lope de Vega (1562-1635) once made a remark about what he needed to create a play. He famously said, "Four trestles [sawhorses], four boards, two actors, a passion." The use of planks and sawhorses remained a staple of *Godspell* productions for many years.

Gary Gunas, assistant company manager for Lansbury and Beruh's producing office, sometimes substituted in the petite Cherry Lane Theatre box office shown here, or in the one at the Promenade Theatre once the show relocated in August 1971.

Whoever worked in *Godspell*'s box office would inform cast members when famous people were attending the show. The actors remember performing in front of Paul Newman, Joanne Woodward, Lily Tomlin, Leonard Bernstein, producer David Merrick, Lee Strasberg, Mayor Lindsay, Jackie Kennedy, and others. Herb Braha recalls that when Ed Sullivan saw *Godspell*, he came backstage afterward and said, "It was a really wonderful show."

Mishaps, Miracles, and a Completed New Musical

ABOVE: The original Cherry Lane Theatre cast enacts the Prodigal Son parable. (Photo by Kenn Duncan/©The New York Public Library). BELOW: John-Michael Tebelak (middle) chats with band members Jesse Cutler (left) and Ricky Shutter (right) on the set at the Cherry Lane Theatre.

The Godspell Experience

ABOVE: The original Cherry Lane cast of *Godspell* gathers around John-Michael Tebelak: Front row from left: Peggy Gordon, Jeffrey Mylett, Herb Braha. Second row, from left: Sonia Manzano, Robin Lamont, John-Michael Tebelak, David Haskell. Top row, from left: Lamar Alford, Joanne Jonas, Stephen Nathan, and Gilmer McCormick. BELOW: The original cast performs a parable. Front: Joanne Jonas and Stephen Nathan. Front row, from left: Robin Lamont, Lamar Alford, David Haskell. On the platform, from left: Jeffrey Mylett, Peggy Gordon, Gilmer McCormick. Top row: Sonia Manzano, Herb Braha. (Both photos are by Martha Swope/©The New York Public Library)

Chapter 10
Long Live *Godspell*

It seemed likely that the show would run for a while, although no one could really judge how long. One of the first challenges that the new company faced was that they hadn't trained understudies, so when Gilmer McCormick tore her foot on the fence opening night, they weren't prepared. She had finished the show, but didn't realize how badly she'd been cut under the bandages that Charlie Haid had wrapped around the wound. When her father took her to the hospital after the Sardi's party, she was given twenty-two stitches. They told her if she had waited half an hour longer they would have had to do a skin graft. She would be out of the show for a week. Peggy Gordon injured her knee in an early performance and also had to be out for a week. The only possible person who could step in was Nina Faso.

That meant the director would need to be stage manager for a week. Faso had previously worked with Tebelak in college when they had stage managed each other's shows. She knew that staying calm and organized was not his strength. "Let me just tell you, he's a terrible stage manager! So when John-Michael had to 'call the show' he was a nervous wreck. He had to call the lighting cues, call the music cues, call the acting cues, and make sure all the props were there beforehand. Usually, the stage manager is backstage, but in *Godspell* the stage manager is visible behind the fence because that's where I always used to call the show from. And he had no idea how to call the show. I mean none. So while trying to get through the performance, I kept dancing over to the fence and saying, 'John-Michael—

don't forget….' this and that." They survived the week but then quickly started casting understudies.

Another urgent duty in the producers' office was the completion of an official, typed script that actually represented everything spoken and sung on stage. The group knew the show by heart, so Faso had only written out a few stage managing notes. She remembers Lansbury and Beruh beginning to panic about copyright. "There was no script and you can't copyright something that isn't on paper," Faso says. "And the characters had to have names—they had just been clowns one through ten."

Dean Pitchford, an actor and an English major at Yale University, came in as a typist. He later played Jesus for several years and went on to become an Academy Award-winning lyricist for the song "Fame" (from the film by the same name) and multi-award nominated writer for other films and shows (including the popular musical *Footloose*). But in 1971, the urgent need was for his typing skills. Pitchford spent four or five days hovering over a typewriter in a small office at 1650 Broadway while Faso put her feet up on a desk and dictated the entire musical from memory, including stage directions.

For character names they used the actors' names, including "Stephen" for Stephen Nathan and "David" for David Haskell. (In later years, the script was amended for these two to be "Jesus" and "John/Judas," but the other characters maintained the first names of the original actors.)

Although Faso and Pitchford recorded the humorous expressions of the original group, that didn't mean that the comic moments stayed static. Robin Lamont recalls that as the show continued its run, the cast was eager to find new takes on the material. "We'd come in and say, 'Oh I have a good idea! Did you see *The Dick Cavett Show* last night' or whatever, and we would want to change stuff up. We tried to keep it fresh for ourselves by changing some of the bits as it went along."

Getting the Word Out

With positive reviews, the marketing team's efforts, and word-of-mouth publicity, *Godspell* started finding its audience. Still, the actors were spooked by a closing notice posted backstage a few weeks into the run until Beruh explained it. "He said, 'Calm down, this is what we do,'" recalls Faso. Budget-watching producers release themselves from the obligation to pay ongoing salaries if poor ticket sales require a show to shutter suddenly. But Lansbury and Beruh had paid for a publicity team and were planning to give *Godspell* a chance.

Peggy Gordon remembers how hard *Godspell*'s publicists, the Giffords, worked to inspire a broader interest. They realized that new spirituality was popular, including the so-called Jesus movement. "All of these news outlets were doing stories, so Ed did cold calls. He said, 'We've got a show, it's about this, and you can use it as a lead-in.' That's what *The Today Show* did and *The Midday Show*." The cast members did a lot of press interviews and presentations.

Soon, theatergoers were pouring into the theater every night to sample this new experience that was *Godspell*, and everyone felt more confident about its longevity. Edgar Lansbury attended the show regularly to watch the phenomenon he helped create. "It was wonderful because everyone was so moved by it, and entertained by it. So it was always a lovely experience."

> *"'Godspell' was like a fire lit in a cold neighborhood and people came and warmed themselves by it."*
> —**Gilmer McCormick**

Whatever was happening at the Cherry Lane Theatre, it seemed to satisfy both audiences and actors. Performances were getting standing ovations almost every night, and the cast members were enjoying themselves more than for other shows. "When I did *Godspell*," recalls Sonia Manzano, "I'd feel so good that I really felt like my feet weren't touching the ground, I was so elated—it was the most exhilarating, euphoric feeling." Others reported similar experiences. As the lyrics for "We Beseech Thee" suggest, being able to "come sing about love" was its own kind of blessing.

Cast Album

Bell Records arranged to record an Original Cast Album in the summer of 1971. Because Schwartz had worked as a producer at RCA, he planned to record the songs the way pop albums were recorded. Schwartz explains that they tracked the music, first recording instruments with no vocals, then adding lead vocals, and then backup vocals. He also doubled the backup vocal tracks, which is something he liked to do to enhance the power and richness of the sound.

It was a tough session for the cast because they had just finished a five-performance weekend and they were weary. In addition, they were asked to complete the recording in one day. If there were pitch problems or a performance sounded tired, there wasn't much time to fix things.

Peggy Gordon recalls the challenge. "We literally did all the vocals on Monday, our day off. I remember glancing at the clock on the wall of the recording studio when it was time to record 'By My Side.' I think it was something like 1:20 a.m. Tuesday morning. That's why I refer to it as my somnambulistic vocal!"

The album was released in July and sold moderately well, at least enough to help the show gather an audience (and later sold so well it earned gold record status).

Clowning Off Broadway and Beyond

When the producers determined that *Godspell* would be popular outside of New York City, they started arranging additional concurrent productions. The first would be in Los Angeles that November, followed by Boston in December, and then other cities.

Actors flocked to auditions when calls went out for understudies, replacements, and additional productions. Among the first to get cast was Jeanne Lange, who ended up marrying David Haskell by the end of the first year of performances. Also on board were Lynne Thigpen and Katie Hanley, who later landed roles in the *Godspell* movie. Actor Dean Pitchford, whom Nina Faso knew well from the script typing sessions, was cast as the Jeffrey clown (to replace Jeffrey Mylett, who was about to start rehearsals for the Los Angeles production) and as a Jesus understudy.

Meanwhile, by late summer 1971, *Godspell* had outgrown the cozy Cherry Lane Theatre in Greenwich Village, and Lansbury and Beruh decided to swap their shows—they moved *Long Day's Journey Into Night*, running in their Promenade Theatre, to the Cherry Lane Theatre and shifted *Godspell* uptown. The redbrick wall behind the fence had worked so well at Cherry Lane that they installed a similar brick wall at the Promenade.

Pitchford remembers the unusual move that began after the Sunday afternoon matinee. "They immediately struck the sets, working through the night and all through the day Monday. Sometime Monday afternoon, trucks carrying the two shows passed each other on the street. They got to the new theaters and began to set everything up, working all the way through the night and into Tuesday. Tuesday night we went to the Promenade Theatre, we had a sound check, and we did a show!"

In the new venue, *Godspell* became a New York theater staple. The show opened August 10, 1971 at the Promenade and would ultimately run for 2,123 performances before transferring to Broadway.

Beginning in early September, actors started shifting around to different productions. Stephen Nathan left to take a role in the movie *1776*. Andy Rohrer, who played Jesus at CMU but stayed on campus to finish his degree, stepped into the Jesus role for the New York production and later in Los Angeles.

Nina Faso and Stephen Schwartz co-directed *Godspell* in L.A. at the Mark Taper Forum with original cast members Lamar Alford, Herb Braha, Peggy Gordon, David Haskell, Robin Lamont, and Jeffrey Mylett reprising their roles. The company welcomed recruits Rebecca Baum, Lynne Thigpen, and Jeanne Lange, in addition to Andy Rohrer. *Godspell* opened there in November to mixed reviews.

Jeanne Lange noted that *Godspell* was part of the Mark Taper Forum subscription series. "This particular audience didn't know what to make of it," said Lange. "A couple of the reviews were wonderful and a couple of them were saying, 'What is this?'" She sensed that there was an adjustment period. "It was like somebody seeing Cirque du Soleil for the first time. It was so unique. *Hair* had been around, and *Jesus Christ Superstar*, and *Grease* was just starting, but *Godspell* was one of the first rock musicals." Still, *Godspell* continued playing for much longer than expected in Los Angeles, well past the scheduled slot for the subscription series.

Shortly after it opened in L.A., *Godspell* became a huge hit in Boston and other cities. The administrative work to support it swelled. To help deal with the intense levels of expansion, Beruh and Lansbury brought in a new general manager, Marvin Krauss. Their offices also expanded beyond the small space where they had started, on the fifth floor of a high-rise building at 1650 Broadway. They added rooms down the hall to house more administrators and accountants.

At one point, as many as seven resident companies of *Godspell* operated simultaneously in North America, plus a tour. Once the New York City and Los Angeles were established, Nina Faso directed the show in Boston, Washington, D.C., San Francisco, and the first national tour. Howard Sponseller directed productions in Chicago and Toronto. "We really had to hustle in order to get enough casts together," Lansbury recalls.

Multiplying the Casts of 10

The *Godspell* approach to casting had a special wrinkle to it. Not only did the actors need a singing audition, but also a parable audition. They were given three parables and they had to choose one. Then they had to enact the parable, improvising a way to make it come to life. "That's very challenging for some actors," comments Stephen Schwartz who helped cast the productions. "There were many talented actors who didn't come in because they were terrified of the parable audition. They just thought, 'If you give me lines, I'll do that, but I can't just come in and do an improv.'" Only those who excelled at the process would be asked to the call back. During this new session, the group of actors would create a parable performance together so that the director could see which actors seemed to fit as a team.

Among the other strategies the show's leaders used to deliver the full *Godspell* experience to new audiences was to cast at least one actor in every new company who had experience in the New York City company. "There was a *Godspell* zeitgeist—a

Godspell ethos," explains Dean Pitchford. "It was very important that those of us who knew the show close to the source carried the message out." He remembers Stephen Schwartz making an analogy to sourdough bread that is helped to grow with a starter from a previous batch of dough. The practice seemed to work because all the productions met with success.

Assistant company manager Gary Gunas recalls what it was like handling so many American productions, with casting, payroll, and other operations being run from the New York City office. When flu season hit, there was trouble. "We had four Jesuses down with the flu," Gunas recalls. "I'd be on the phone calling people who'd been in the show in the previous two years, saying, 'Could I get you to Chicago for the weekend? We can get your costume together—we have your file here, so unless you've gained weight, could you go straight to the airport? I'll pay you back when you get home on Monday.' So there were lots of crises like that. We had one guy who had understudied it without ever having gone on. We sent him out and he was fine, but we got lucky."

One day, Gunas called Dean Pitchford to set up another unusual temporary replacement. "What are you doing for the next three days?" Gunas asked Pitchford, who by then had played both Jeffrey and Jesus in the New York City production. "If I sent a car for you right now, could you go to Boston?" The show was opening there but the actor for Jesus got sick suddenly and the understudy wasn't yet familiar enough with the Jesus role. Pitchford agreed to the urgent plea. He recalls, "A car pulled up in front of my New York apartment and I was whisked off to LaGuardia and flown up to Boston where, by this time, it was early evening. Somebody at the theater had some clout with the police department and I was met by a car and was then escorted by screaming police sirens to the Wilbur

Theatre." The curtain was delayed for about 15 minutes, and so the audience was informed about the new Jesus coming in from New York City. Pitchford rushed into his makeup while being briefed by the stage manager, and then went over a few points with the unfamiliar cast. "I walked on the stage at the Wilbur Theatre that night, having been in my New York apartment four or five hours before. We did the show with no hitches and got a screaming standing ovation."

Over the years of greatest expansion, the *Godspell* company employed hundreds of actors, especially recruiting those with multiple and flexible talents. Actor Bob Garrett played seven of the 10 roles at various times during his professional *Godspell* career, including belting "Bless the Lord" in the original key (Am/A) when the actor playing Joanne was out of the show due to an injury. Tebelak's friend from his Ohio theater days, Howard Sponseller, served as an actor, assistant stage manager, and director over a six-year period. Wardrobe supervisor Reet Pell worked for many years keeping all the actors in costume.

Starting Fresh Each Time

In each region the show was performed, the players tweaked lines during the rehearsal period to make the show more relevant to themselves and audiences. "We 'localize' it for each particular city—each part of the country," Tebelak once explained. The actors came up with references to locations, major personalities, or local history. Jerry Sroka played the Herb clown in Boston, where the show ran for two and a half years. He recalls, "Filene's had a big department store in Boston. I remember crossing downstage during some money lines as if I was Groucho Marx, saying, 'I'm on my way to Filene's basement, you wanna come with me?' We localized everything that we could." Audiences loved it.

The groups made additional changes based on rehearsal experiences. Rather than assume that the script was fixed, they explored the Bible material anew and used theater games to help the actors bond emotionally. As his friend Bill Phillips explains, "John-Michael was trying to be Grotowski, the famous director. He was trying to develop the show from scratch, from the raw, from the ground up. It was all about building relationships… and it's trying to get at that inner-core connection. They're not just up there reciting lines and going through blocking. That's the last thing he wanted to do."

Although Tebelak guided the ideals of the show, it was often Nina Faso and Stephen Reinhardt who put them into practice as they traveled to different cities to lead new casts. Faso would begin with parables, working with the groups on improvisational skills; Reinhardt taught the songs and later guided the dance sessions. Faso was intent on helping the actors create a feeling of family as they worked together day by day.

Whenever directors guided actors in *Godspell*, they were concerned with how effectively the show communicated to an audience. Faso notes, "We felt really strongly that we wanted to be able to develop an acting style that could be understood by anyone. We always told the actors, with this kind of acting you have to make the story clear to everyone in the audience. Imagine you have an audience of children, and half of them are deaf, half of them are blind. You tell the story using every part of your body and psyche." This encouraged the group to focus on physical movements to express the story, as well as to try out interesting voices and sounds for anyone who was listening but couldn't see.

Rex Knowles, who was among the cast members for the first American tour company, had also worked closely with Paul Sills and the improvisational approach to theater. Knowles remembers that for *Godspell*, "We became an improv group. When we started working on the parables, we said, 'Hey, let's try this, do this theater game, or try that game.' As I recall, the first three days for eight hours a day it was all improvisation." That didn't mean abandoning *Godspell*'s structure as the rehearsal proceeded. It was more about asking themselves (in Knowles' words), "How do we put our own unique contribution onto this form that works?"

Katie Hanley appreciated the "privilege of being able to do our own improvisations," and learning that clowning was about joy coming from within.

"The more we worked together and the more the spirit of the show rubbed off on us, the better we all got. The show just made us happier to be ourselves. So ourselves equaled our clowns. What a wonderful experience to be part of that show!"

—Katie Hanley

Global *Godspell* and Stock and Amateur Productions

Godspell productions sprang up around the globe in the early 1970s, all supervised in some way by the home office in New York City. (See Chapter 33 for more stories.)

One day, Nan Pearlman, an acquaintance of Lansbury and Beruh, approached them and suggested that they could start their own licensing business for *Godspell* for stock and amateur production rights. Pearlman knew the ropes, as she had been working in music publishing and the play licensing business for some years. With the financial help of Stuart Duncan, they first formed Music Maximus, an umbrella company for music publishing. Then they arranged with Schwartz and Tebelak's representatives to start Theatre Maximus, also operating in an office at 1650 Broadway, to license *Godspell* performance rights around the world. Pearlman has run the company ever since.

After Tebelak passed away, Music Theatre International (MTI) made arrangements to be a second licensing agency for *Godspell*, although only within the United States. MTI also developed *Godspell Jr.* for the Broadway Jr. program.

One reason *Godspell* quickly became a mainstay of amateur theater groups is that it is one of the few musicals that can be molded creatively by actors and directors, which means the group can experience more of the joys of creative expression. This was all part of Tebelak's plan for the show.

Other significant incentives in the musical licensing business include lower costs, flexible cast size, and unspecified age of actors. For *Godspell* the set requirements are minimal and the show can be played by as few as 10 people. Larger groups often cast the traditional 10 roles and then add additional ensemble members who share lines or just sing, dance, and witness the parable enactments. Clown characters are no specific age.

To make *Godspell* work requires an understanding of the clown concept, subtext, and everything else that the early *Godspell* groups understood about the show, as will be described in Part II.

Licensing *Godspell*

Godspell must be licensed before it is performed. For the contact information, please see the Bibliography page at the back of this book.

LEFT: Nan Pearlman helped to found the original licensing company, Theatre Maximus.

Long Live Godspell

ABOVE: The marquis for *Godspell* at the Promenade Theatre. BELOW: The New York cast of *Godspell* enjoys the company of actress Helen Hayes. Front and second rows, from left: Joanne Jonas, Mark Planner, Randee Heller, Elizabeth Lathram, Michael Forella, Helen Hayes, Dean Pitchford, Katie Hanley, Sonia Manzano. On top: Howard Sponseller.

The Godspell Experience

In early July 1971, the *Godspell* cast and company gathered at NBC Studios for the filming of a segment that aired on *The Today Show* on July 8th. Here they celebrate their success. Standing left to right: Reet Pell, Steve Nathan, (unknown), Lamar Alford, Harvey Cox, Stephen Schwartz with John-Michael Tebelak behind him, Peggy Gordon, Herb Braha, Joanne Jonas, Jesse Cutler, Rich La Bonte, Andy Rohrer, Peter Kean; seated left to right: Joe Beruh, Robin Lamont (by the cake), Nina Faso, Jeff Mylett.

Backstage Christmas Eve 1971. Seated: Katie Hanley. Behind her, from left: Elizabeth Lathram, Sonia Manzano, and Joanne Jonas. Manzano's sweatshirt is the type actors wore for the "Prologue."

Long Live Godspell

ABOVE: Nina Faso, Edgar Lansbury, Carole Schwartz, and Stephen attend the opening of *Godspell* in London, November 1971. BELOW: Stephen Schwartz (right) performs a song for the wedding of Gilmer McCormick (left) and Stephen Reinhardt (behind), February 1972.

The Godspell Experience

A publicity shot for the Washington, D.C. company of *Godspell* at Ford's Theatre.

> *"I explained to a Jewish fan who said she thought the show was preaching Christianity: that wasn't our purpose at all... Our purpose was to celebrate the essential message of the unconditional love taught by this one clown, to love thy neighbor as thyself. As Steve Nathan always said, 'Our hope is that we could make the world just a little bit better.'"*
>
> —Peggy Gordon

PART II
Understanding *Godspell*: Concepts and Colorful Details

One of the Australian casts of *Godspell* performs "We Beseech Thee."

Understanding *Godspell*: An Introduction

What is *Godspell*, really? Is it a revue, a musical, a mystery play, a celebration, sketch comedy, Spirituality 101? From the moment Tebelak brought the idea of clowning with parables to his first college cast to the present, people have wondered how to regard this unusual amalgam.

Not only do they ask what it is, but they wonder why and who? Why are the actors clowning around with "serious" material? Who are the characters and who is Jesus here? What insights might audiences of different faiths derive from it? Part II of *The Godspell Experience* fathoms the layers of meaning intended by the show's creators and provides answers to frequently asked questions.

Godspell's playfulness leaves the impression that anyone can easily put a production together. Several hundred school, church, amateur theater groups, and professional theater companies stage the show each year around the world, but not all succeed in making it work artistically. The show is actually multi-layered and is as challenging to bring to the stage as any other musical.

What can go wrong with *Godspell*? For one thing, it can be thrown off by an overly showy clown. "The important thing to remember is *Godspell* as the show is the star," Herb Braha reminds us. He cautions against performances that draw attention to themselves and away from the whole.

Sometimes the director and actors can make it too saccharine. Peter Filichia, theater critic and author of *Let's Put on a Musical* and other books comments, "A production can often suffer from 'the cutes' when the cast gives the audience too much peace, brotherhood and smiling." The show has an emotional range that is not always honored, and a need for honesty as well as delight. It can be less fulfilling for audiences if it's too jokey, too political, set in too strange an environment, not understood by the cast, or not felt authentically.

Inexperienced *Godspell* actors and directors may assume the show is suited to mugging and horsing around with no purpose, but there is a purpose to keep in mind.

According to Stephen Schwartz, at its core the show is about community—about having a group of people bond emotionally and feel transformed by the experience. Schwartz's notes for directors are included in the script to help ensure they understand key points like this.

In Schwartz's words, "a group of disparate people slowly become a community built around one charismatic individual (Jesus), who then leaves them and they have to carry on as a community without him." He then warns, "If this basic dramatic arc is not achieved, *Godspell* does not exist; no matter how amusing and tuneful individual moments may be, the production has failed."

So it is important that performing groups understand the show to make their production more satisfying.

The first question to answer is: Who are the characters?

The Godspell Experience

Andy Rohrer makes a flower bouquet magically appear during the Beatitudes in the New York production of *Godspell* at the Promenade Theatre. Front row, from left: Judy Kahan, Andy Rohrer, Bob Garrett, Jeanne Lange, Elizabeth Lathram, Herb Braha. On the table: Bill Thomas, Linda Sherwood, Marley Sims, Bart Braverman (Photo by Sam Freed)

Chapter 11
Why Send in the Clown Characters?

For John-Michael Tebelak, the memory of a dour Easter service in a formal Anglican church motivated him in the opposite direction. He resolved to make brightly dressed, joy-inspiring clown characters the centerpiece of *Godspell*.

But what did "clown" mean to him, to cast members, and to Schwartz? They didn't just have a dictionary definition in mind. Yes, *Godspell* clowns would be comic performers who wear outlandish costumes and entertain by acting out common situations in an exaggerated or ridiculous fashion. But there were nuances of meaning for the original group that enriched their experience.

Clowns as Shakespeare's Truth-telling Fools

For Stephen Nathan, the dramatic tradition of the "fool" character came to mind when he performed as Jesus in the early New York productions. "A clown and a fool are the same," he explains. "It was my job to be the fool—the classic Shakespearean fool who is the only one who tells the truth; the only one who has no fear of authority and no bond with social convention. It's being anti-social in an odd way. My job was to destroy convention in the same way King Lear's fool was the only one who could tell Lear the truth. He is the only one safe in any kingdom because he has been given permission by the king (or in the case of *Godspell*, God) to tell the truth.

"For Jesus," Nathan continues, "there was an ultimate price to pay, which was the story, but his job in *Godspell* wasn't to be sweet; it wasn't to preach. It was to wake up the cast. It was to show them what was really there."

When Robin Lamont heard "clown" in the first meetings about *Godspell* at Carnegie Mellon, she also thought of Shakespeare's clowns, who she felt were "more comic and robust in nature" than circus clowns.

Clowns as Revolutionaries

Bob Ari, who performed in the college production, remembers Tebelak discussing clowns as social teachers advocating radical change. "We were clowns teaching the parables, but also we were revolutionaries," Ari comments.

Tebelak no doubt realized it was revolutionary for Jesus, in his own day, to reverse earlier teachings, such as one from Leviticus 24:19-20 (and elsewhere) about retaliating in kind for a wrong. *Godspell* includes a scene derived from Matthew 5:38-39, when Jesus transforms the advice from "an eye for an eye" into "turn the other cheek."

In the song "Alas For You," based on Matthew 23:13-37, Jesus rejects the status quo of his spiritual society. He labels the Pharisees and interpreters of the law as hypocrites and blind fools.

So *Godspell*'s creators didn't view clowns as passive jokers, but as individuals standing apart from others, actively promoting transformation or truth revelation.

Clowns as Joyful Rescuers

For Tebelak, it was the clown who could rescue humanity from its greatest problems. Tebelak is quoted in one of the *Godspell* souvenir books as saying, "I wanted to show Christ as a happy man, as a joyous soul. As someone not brooding on how he was going to die, but preaching joy. In the theater the supreme entertainers are clowns. If a trapeze artist falls, a clown is the one to divert the audience's attention to save the show. In a sense, Christ came along to save the show."

David Haskell said something similar to an interviewer in 1973: "Clowns can ease tense situations. Take rodeos. If someone is hurt, out come the clowns. They make everyone feel better. Jesus was like that. He taught what was wrong with the world. He also tried to make people feel better."

Godspell even includes a literal depiction of a rescue in the Good Samaritan parable. The clown version of a Samaritan rescues a needy stranger who might otherwise have died on the roadside.

Clowns as Comics

For Schwartz, the laughter-generating role of *Godspell's* clowns seemed obvious. "That was clearly what we were doing—something that was funny." A clown's role has to do with humor.

Sonia Manzano modeled her clowning on laughter-inducing performances she saw on television. She loved physical comedy and remembers that it was Jewel Walker, her Carnegie instructor in movement, who introduced her to the magic of Charlie Chaplin. "That summer after my freshman year, I came home and PBS was having a Charlie Chaplin retrospective. I sat in my living room and watched every single thing that he ever did. I read his story and I was obsessed with it, and all I could think of was Charlie Chaplin and trying to imitate those gags."

She valued the universal communication that physical comedy provided. "It was the kind of humor that everyone understood, meaning my mother laughed at the same things I laughed at or a Hungarian would laugh at. You slip on a banana peel and it's a constant humor. It's not topical according to what just happened in the society that's watching it. And I was flabbergasted about this." Her interest in physical comedy supported her performances in *Godspell*.

Actor George Salazar, a fan of comics like the Three Stooges and Jim Carrey, used a lot of physical comedy for his performance in the 2011 Broadway revival of *Godspell*. For example, during the Prodigal Son parable, when Salazar played the angry son who was jealous of the father's treatment of his wayward brother, he performed a kind of interpretive dance rant that put the audience into hysterics every night. "My character was so angry that he couldn't express himself in words so he had to do it in dance. It was just such goofiness."

Salazar says that being a clown required stepping out of his own comfort zone. "I wasn't afraid to poke fun at myself. That's crucial for a clown. You've got to be able to first, know the show really well, and then second, to put yourself on display in a fun way where the audience can laugh with you."

In Tebelak's day, he often recommended to new cast members that they read *The Feast of Fools* book to learn about the relevance of clowning to spirit, and the idea of Jesus leading through clowning behavior. "I thought that the clown concept was pure genius," says Dean Pitchford, while recalling the days of being trained for his *Godspell* role. He had been raised Catholic, and for him, listening to Tebelak and reading *The Feast of Fools* was a revelation. "With *Godspell* I thought of Jesus as the greatest prankster of them all, of the most infectious fun meister. What a wonderful way to think of Jesus, because religion had always showed him as a very serious man with a very serious mission who gets terribly persecuted and murdered. And *Godspell* opened my eyes. This is funny. All my life I've been worshipping a tragic story. What about giving people another version of that story?!"

Clowns as Childlike and Playful People

Young people naturally clown around before they add layers of social inhibition to their psyches. For Tebelak's troupes, releasing their inner child or inner clown was part of the job.

Peggy Gordon explains how the cast developed their particular clown characters: "We sort of retroed our personas back to what we would be like as children.... Since innocence is the objective, what would it be like to have someone who is, for example, a mischievous adult like Jeffrey? What would be the innocent version of that? What would be the innocent version of someone who is chronically fearful and shy? What would each one of these adults have been like when they were innocent?"

> *"It's not surprising that John-Michael chose for the actors in 'Godspell' to do the clown version of themselves. He sort of did that himself in his own life."*
>
> —Stephen Schwartz

When Clowns Take On Other Roles

Godspell actors behave as talking clowns, but on the surface, they may have other roles, depending on the setting the director uses for the show. Some groups have imagined their actors to be homeless people on park benches or in homeless shelters. In one case, a homeless shelter was in New York City's East Village and John/Judas ran a local soup kitchen. Some have tried playgrounds with a swing set and monkey bars, the circus, a diner, various work environments, and at least one group tried a beach with Jesus as the lifeguard. Colorado's Candelight Dinner Theatre staged it as if their group was part of Habitat for Humanity, building a new home for a family in need. They held a fundraiser for the charitable organization during the run of the show.

With each setting, the clowns are transformed into characters that suit the environment. Stephen Schwartz comments, "What I think is important, as I say in the Note to the Director in the script, is that these eight strangers are looking for answers to their lives and become increasingly hostile to each other's ideas and points of view, until John/Judas arrives and announces the coming of someone who will show them another way ('Prepare Ye')."

Sonia Manzano (right) uses physical comedy to enhance a scene in *Godspell*. Stephen Nathan as Jesus and Robin Lamont respond to her clown moment. (Photo by Kenn Duncan/©The New York Public Library)

CHAPTER 12

What Holds *Godspell* Together?

"It is easy for the show to appear formless, or worse—for the ten performers to degenerate into ten stand-up comics vying with one another for laughs and attention," Stephen Schwartz remarks. "This is the diametric opposite of what *Godspell* is all about."

But if the script text is basically a couple of dozen separate stories from the Bible threaded between songs, what are performers of local productions expected to do? How are audiences, trained by popular entertainment media to love a well-plotted story, to enjoy a show without a compelling central storyline? An answer can be found by discerning several threaded stories on both textual and subtextual levels.

Text: The Jesus-as-Teacher Story

On the most basic level, the show holds together through Jesus' expanding role as a wise guide. It begins with the baptism scene that ritually launches his position as a teacher. After a middle section of assorted parable teachings, it runs through the Last Supper and Crucifixion.

During the bulk of the musical, the Jesus clown teaches his followers through his expressions, through coaxing, and through his own example. For instance, he encourages the clowns to act out a parable about an unforgiving servant, and then gives the moral of the story, which is about forgiveness. Another example is when he coaxes the brothers in the Prodigal Son story to reconcile with each other.

Joanne Jonas recalls appreciating this during the rehearsal process when she joined the cast. "The flow of *Godspell* is that the Jesus clown inspired us to listen and try to understand some very profound concepts about love, care, integrity, humility, sacrifice, and so on." The cast, working with Tebelak and using the Bible quotations he provided, found a way to structure this into a show.

Tebelak specifically wanted the people attending *Godspell* to witness the teacher-student relationship that was blossoming on stage. That's why many moments involve clowns facing their leader, Jesus, who has his back or side to the audience. Peggy Gordon explains, "John-Michael wanted for Jesus to be looking at us as his audience, so that we are facing him, doing whatever we are doing and then we look to him." Examples include:

- After singing three verses of "Save the People," Jesus dons his costume while the cast sings the choral section of the song. Jesus stands facing the cast with his back to the audience, conducting the final refrains of the song.
- At the beginning of "Day by Day," Robin sings to Jesus while they face each other. "The whole point is the intimacy between the two of them," says Gordon about Tebelak's plan for the moment. "He's teaching her."
- During the Good Samaritan parable, performed by the disciples as a little puppet show, Jesus watches so that he can see they are learning something.
- By the scene with "All Good Gifts," the group is ready to send love and gratitude back to their teacher. Says Gordon, "It was important from John-Michael's perspective to have us looking at Jesus so he would see how much we loved him."
- Lastly, for "By My Side," Gordon specifically remembers

Tebelak's direction to her: when she sang to Jesus, they were to face each other. "He wanted the audience to see me looking at him" as she sang "...Where are you going? Can you take me with you?"

Schwartz, Tebelak, and other directors were always very careful to cast a charismatic head clown to help fulfill the Jesus-as-teacher story. If audiences watched a Jesus who wasn't a natural leader, the *Godspell* experience wouldn't be as meaningful. Schwartz comments, "Jesus is the driving force in the show; therefore, he needs to have the most energy, the most humor, and the most willpower of all the characters. He starts the games, he teaches the lessons, and he motivates the action."

All About Subtext: Personal and Community Evolution

Primarily, Tebelak believed the show held together by way of a deeper structure, or "subtext." Producer Edgar Lansbury recalls that Tebelak looked beneath the surface of things. "I remember that he was always thinking in terms of subtext.... His whole attitude was geared to that—to the inner meaning of what was going on. In directing the show I think he expressed that."

Subtext in *Godspell* can be understood in several ways that are not mutually exclusive. One perspective focuses on the inner growth of each character, and the other on an awareness of a coherent community.

The Personal Evolution Subtextual Story

Following the experimental version of *Godspell* at college, the show's creators refined the character arcs and thereby enhanced the overall story. Stephen Nathan remembers about the first New York productions, "It was very important to John-

Michael, and to us, that this not be a collection of parables—a sketch—but that the show have a clear narrative where people started at point A and ended at point B." Each character's journey followed its own arc, contributing a spirit of growth to the total drama. The outer actions of spending time with a wise teacher resulted in inner transformation over time. Their personal growth wasn't something the characters spoke about specifically, but it was demonstrated through their interactions, their growing ease, and their change of spirit.

For Gilmer McCormick, the way to understand *Godspell* was in terms of how the characters evolve as they "try on" Jesus' lessons. "Stephen Nathan as Jesus spent a lot of time with us in rehearsals, taking us through that journey as disciples," McCormick explains. "He would give us a lesson and we would act it out to be sure that we understood what it was, what the consequences were, and what the point was. We'd always look at him and say, 'Is that right?' He would go, 'That's right' or 'No, no, no, no, that's not right. This is what's right.' So with each little vignette, the clowns grew a little bit more."

For the casts working with Tebelak, discovering their character's inner emotional arc was an essential part of learning to clown within *Godspell*. One example is the arc of the "Peggy" clown. Although it took her a while to figure out what it would be, Peggy Gordon made sense of her clown's story by way of the song she would sing in Act II. "Everybody found something right away for a clown except me," she recalls. "And so we're improvising wildly all over the place and John-Michael said, 'Peggy I'm not seeing—what's happening with you?'" She didn't know. Finally, when Tebelak accepted "By My Side" into the show and she knew she'd be singing about daring to walk with Jesus with a pebble in her shoe, that's when she realized that her clown would suffer from an "amplified comedic form of shyness." She could overcome it in time, but to begin with, she held back. "I made a point of not stepping out very much. I made a point of being part of the body of the group. And the places that I chose to step out and take the lead… it was because I could work on the element of shyness." She eventually narrates the Parable of the Good Seed with Jesus' encouragement, finally daring to step out more, and then sings "By My Side."

Tebelak not only wanted audiences to witness the setup of a teacher-student relationship, he also wanted them to note the results: the Jesus clown's spiritual classroom supported the other clowns' personal development.

Halfway through the show, the growth process shifts. In Act I the followers are in a safe learning environment where they could, in Nathan's words, "uncover all the goodness in ourselves." Act II is about solidifying the spiritual growth through application. Nathan continues, "In Act II we're in the real world [asking ourselves] 'How do we take what we learned about ourselves and bring it to the world?' That's what changed people who saw the show, I think."

The Community-Building Subtextual Story

After Tebelak passed away in 1985, Stephen Schwartz became a spokesperson for the essential artistic story of *Godspell*. He focused especially on one aspect of character growth: the way they connect to each other. In interviews and in his Author's Note to the Director in the licensed version of the script, Schwartz explains, "Above all, the first act of *Godspell* must be about the formation of a community. Eight separate individuals led and guided by Jesus (and helped by his assistant, John the Baptist/Judas) gradually come to form a communal unit."

"The way we set 'Godspell' up is we would each fall in love with this character, Jesus, and with each other, so we would go through this extraordinary emotional journey."

—Peggy Gordon

As part of the process, each of the actors on stage has an "aha!" moment during which he or she effectively signs in to the community with Jesus. Most of the clowns had songs in Act I, and it was during their scene with their song that they really connected. (Robin: "Day by Day," Gilmer: "Learn Your Lessons Well," Joanne: "Bless the Lord," David: "All for the Best," Lamar: "All Good Gifts," Herb: "Light of the World")

The remaining three clowns who had songs in Act II found their moments during Act I scenes, according to Peggy Gordon. Her Peggy clown realization moment was when Jesus made a bouquet of flowers appear from nowhere (using a magic prop) and tossed it to her during Beatitudes.

The Sonia clown's was after "All for the Best," when Sonia Manzano got carried away by the exhilaration of the number and continued singing and dancing. Jesus gently encouraged her to get with the group and move forward.

Jeffrey's "aha!" experience can be linked to his recorder break performance in "All Good Gifts." Schwartz recalls, "They were all singing to the Jesus character and Jeffrey was in front with the recorder, and just the way he looked up at him, you could feel it."

This meant that by the end of Act I, all nine clowns were unified in their understanding of the group purpose and the significance of their leader, the first clown. The process of creating this sharing community, evolving as it does over time, provides an overarching theme for *Godspell* that unifies the disparate elements.

Ken Davenport, the lead producer for the 2011 revival of *Godspell* on Broadway, once commented on the value of this community-building arc for audiences today. He began one of his email memos to *Godspell* investors by reflecting on an article he'd read on CNN.com about the "era of increasingly shrill and unyielding partisanship" that America seemed to have reached. Davenport wrote: "This 'era' is exactly why I decided to bring *Godspell* back to Broadway. Because yes, *Godspell* is super fun, yes, it has a spectacular score, and yes, it's filled with joy, but there's also something underneath it all that's worth talking about. When I first met Stephen Schwartz and Danny Goldstein well over a year ago, they described *Godspell* as the story of a group of people who, at the beginning of the show, can't communicate, as if they are speaking different languages. (For those of you who know the show well, that's the 'Babel' sequence.) And then, through the course of the show and thanks to the leadership of one individual, they learn how to talk to one another and how to get along . . . regardless of religion, race, or political party affiliation. And by learning what is really important, they learn how to live each day by day together in harmony (literally!)."

A Loving Tribe

Schwartz notes that community-creating is not just an act that's put on for an audience, but it also emerges through the process of preparing the show. Thus, in addition to the story of clowns growing closer to Jesus and each other, the acting troupe members are working cooperatively together, so that they are, in a sense, walking the talk.

Edgar Lansbury understood that this was part of the original plan. "That's what John-Michael did when he brought them all together. They would have exercises in which they got together and practiced this sense of family." Tebelak once told an interviewer, "It's very important for the performers to feel close to one another. After all, the play is about people coming together to create a new way of living."

Joanne Jonas remembers the Cherry Lane cast learning how to work in harmony. "Our personalities could get in the way from time to time in terms of clashing egos, and so on. But Jesus, as portrayed by Stephen Nathan, was trying to get us to see ourselves as one. He constantly brought the oneness theme to the nine of us—Love thy neighbor as thyself. We were learning these principles in real time as we were creating the show."

Stephen Schwartz explains that a unifying dynamic is part of any production. "To create the show each time, *Godspell* requires a community made of the cast, the director, and usually the musical director. And since that's what *Godspell* is about, essentially, the experience of doing the show recapitulates the content of the show."

This is relatively unusual for a musical, although there are other examples, such as *Hair*. "It's about this tribe," Schwartz suggests, "and the process of doing the show and the way it's performed is part of that." He also cites *A Chorus Line*—the musical that depicts the audition process for a Broadway ensemble—as a related example. "The way the medium of theater is used has a lot to do with what the show is about."

While *Godspell* is not literally about its own rehearsal process, it is (in part) about the loving spirit that can be shared. This has important implications for thespians working on productions of this show. If the group does not work together well during rehearsal, the artistic experience for performers and audiences will not be fulfilled. One amateur group reported hiring a professional to play the role of Jesus, but the professional never bonded with the group and the result was a show that was less emotionally satisfying than it could have been.

Many groups report that the experience of putting together *Godspell* is so engaging that not only is the performance enhanced by their mutual love, but the actors become lifelong friends. Community spirit emerges, in part, from spending time with improvisation that requires letting go of resistance, says Paul Kreppel, one of the long-time *Godspell* actors in the early 1970s. He suggests, "The 'Prologue' comes from the place of justification where the thoughts are so ingrained in these people's minds. [After that] each of the characters surrenders at some moment to whatever is being taught. They let down all resistance. I think that's part of the process of acting. When it came time to do the show, you didn't really need to think about it. You just needed to listen and be in the moment; to fall in love with those other nine people on stage. It was a fascinating journey and we loved to do it."

Breaking the Fourth Wall and Community Building

Godspell's connection to the audience is integral to the show itself, and involves what is described in theater terms as "breaking the fourth wall." Shows that don't break the fourth wall are self-contained ones like *My Fair Lady*—a show that runs along independent of the audience, as the actors don't interact with the theatergoers at all. Most shows function in this way; they have "walls" on the two sides and back of the performance space plus a fourth wall being the imaginary line across the front of a stage between the performers and the audience.

Following the notion that *Godspell* is about community, this show essentially requires breaking that fourth wall to be effective. When *Godspell*'s actors are spilling up and down the aisle at various times, engaging the audience in hand-clapping during "Day by Day" and carrying Jesus on their shoulders down the aisle at the end of the show, they are involving the audience in their community.

Schwartz notes, "The actors are definitely aware of the interaction between them and the audience. I don't think the show works as well when there is more of a fourth wall." Lansbury concurs. "The actors all come from the house and they leave through the house. In the meantime, we have an intermission where the audience comes up on the stage, meets the actors, and has a glass of wine. This all makes the audience part of the experience. I think you always want to do that in a theatrical presentation. You always want to make them feel part of it, but it's not always possible because of the fourth wall syndrome. But in this case, the actors came in and out of the audience space."

With the aid of an interactive intermission, *Godspell* has a consistent tone that helps hold the show together. There is a whole that is more than the sum of its parts: disparate pieces seem part of a coherent, unified musical because of an atmosphere of openness and love that gets created.

> *"There's something hard to describe about the 'Godspell' experience. When the show is performed correctly, the audience becomes part of the show and thus part of the community that is being formed at every performance. When that happens, it can be transformative for the audience."*
> —**Stephen Schwartz**

CHAPTER 13

The John/Judas Relationship Arc with Jesus

The relationship between the John the Baptist/Judas character and Jesus in *Godspell* deserves special attention because of its importance to the show's creators and to an understanding of how the pieces of the show fit together.

John/Judas is the only character with essentially the opposite arc of the other clowns. Rather than being an individual who gradually grasps Jesus' greatness and commits to the loving community he is creating, John/Judas connects emotionally to Jesus immediately at the Baptism, then questions Jesus' teaching mid show, and ends up isolated.

In the original production, when David Haskell originated the role, he blew the shofar at the beginning, danced with Jesus/Stephen Nathan in "All for the Best," and betrayed Jesus at the end by blowing a shrill police whistle.

Haskell helped set the tone of the character. His wife, Jeanne Lange, notes that he was the calm one on stage who didn't flit about. "Everything needs a straight man," says Lange. "You have to have somebody to be grounded around all this." In terms of his relationship to Jesus, he was, in Lange's terms, "the negative to the positive. He was the down to the up."

John/Judas' lines tend to change the point of view being expressed. For instance, when Jesus teaches about turning the other cheek, John/Judas is incredulous and begins to say, "Oh, Jeeeeesus Chr..." before he is stopped by Gilmer. Judas is the first to realize that Jesus' life could be in peril and while everybody else shares cheery Beatitude lines, Judas, in a heartbroken wail, foreshadows things to come.

Acting the Part

Tebelak and Schwartz considered it vital that John/Judas be played by one actor. That way the audience is able to observe him interacting with Jesus in varying ways over time, from the innocent moments of the baptism through the betrayal.

From an acting standpoint, Haskell differentiated the two aspects of his role. He started in John mode for "Prepare Ye." By the end of "Save the People" he essentially stepped into Judas mode, which is how he remained for the rest of the show. This is according to Peggy Gordon, who explains: "As John the Baptist he is deferential and grateful; as Judas he is plucky, far more assertive and finally, heartbroken, because he's betraying one whom he's grown to love."

Friend or Foe?

Don Scardino, who directed one of the New York City revivals, remembers Tebelak's view of Judas' nature in *Godspell* as being inspired by a book, which he recommended to those around him. Scardino explains, "John-Michael had read Kazantzakis' book, *The Last Temptation of Christ*. The book says Judas is his ally, his closest friend. It's almost as if Jesus is saying that the others are my children in a way. 'They are my disciples, so they cannot betray me. You are the only one who can do this because you love me the most. And if you love me the most, you will help me complete what I must do.' Judas, being human, is confused and feels betrayed himself, but runs off to do it because he has to do it."

Schwartz suggests, along the lines of Kazantzakis' book and film adaptation, that Judas is expecting something different from Jesus than what Jesus actually offers. "Judas wants Jesus to be more of a revolutionary—to sweep out the old order and the fat cats, by violent means if necessary. When he begins to see that Jesus' philosophy is 'turn the other cheek,' he grows disillusioned, and it is this that leads to the betrayal."

The Kiss and Betrayal

In *Godspell*, Judas doesn't betray Jesus with a kiss, but rather Jesus kisses him. It still works as the infamous betrayal moment when Jesus is identified, but it means that even under pressure, Jesus doesn't change his philosophy—he even forgives Judas.

In the original production, when Stephen Nathan as Jesus kissed David Haskell on the cheek, David would flinch as if it had burned him. Schwartz comments, "Judas is so conflicted about what he has done that to be forgiven is more painful than if he was chastised for it. It would be easier for him if Jesus was angry or brutal to him, but that's not the philosophy that Jesus espouses through the entire show. The fact that he once again forgives is very painful to Judas. I liked that there was a physical manifestation of that. I found it very moving."

Some actors in the role of John/Judas use a "glass box" mime routine. Wallace Smith played the role in the 2011 Broadway revival and approached the scene in this way. With gestures he showed that he was surrounded on three sides by invisible flat surfaces. Finally, he reached out a hand in Jesus' direction, but found no wall and fell through. Smith explains about the character's experience: "The only place he can go is through that space and he falls at Jesus' feet. Jesus comes down and gives him a kiss and tells him, 'Do what you have to do,' and then he goes to do it because he realizes he can't get out of the situation. Jesus is calling him to do it."

All in all, the John/Judas role adds valued dramatic tension to the musical. The show's creators developed the role with a varied emotional throughline that contributes to the story as a whole.

The Godspell Experience

ABOVE: Barrett Foa (as Jesus) and Will Erat (John/Judas) dance together in the *Godspell* revival Off-Broadway 2000. (Photo ©CarolRosegg) BELOW: Andy Rohrer (Jesus) and Dan Hamilton (Judas) are shown in the betrayal moment in Act II during a performance at the Promenade Theatre. (Photo by Sam Freed)

Chapter 14
Symbol Wars
or Is Clown Makeup a Message?

When *Godspell's* clowns apply or remove makeup in front of the audience as part of the staging, they are defining the show's dramatic arc in a visual way. For directors today, the use of this traditional visible symbol or any other symbol is an important artistic choice.

Godspell actors in the early productions always used greasepaint to fulfill a dramatic purpose. Stephen Schwartz explains what adding makeup means symbolically. "When Jesus applies clown makeup to their faces after 'Save the People,' he is having them take on an external physical manifestation that they are his disciples, temporarily separating them from the rest of society." Removing it is also meaningful. He continues, "When Jesus removes their makeup, just prior to the Last Supper, he is saying that they have assimilated this teaching into themselves and no longer need the outward trappings that brand them as disciples. And when Jesus is taken from them at the end, the rest of the company remains fused as a community, ready and able to carry forth the lessons they have learned."

Later productions have interpreted the clown characters' step into Jesus' world in other ways. Jesus might give out an item of clothing or jewelry that performers don as they join the group. Examples include things like colored bandanas, glow-in-the-dark bracelets, or brightly colored T-shirts worn over darker clothes. Then near the end of the show, these items are removed.

Whichever symbol is used, *Godspell's* actors need to understand that they are dramatizing a community building process.

Over time they are likely to find that these small actions become heartfelt expressions of their relationship with their stage friend, Jesus.

Is one approach better than another? Is it possible to have a deeper experience with *Godspell*? Here are some thoughts from people interviewed for this book.

In Favor of Alternative Symbols

The argument for not using the makeup routine is primarily to adapt to a particular production's design concept. Danny Goldstein, director of the 2011 revival, had several reasons for not using clown makeup for the production at Broadway's Circle in the Square Theatre. He didn't think *Godspell*'s characters needed a clown appearance because their comedy was of a different sort. "I think of Buster Keaton as a clown, and today, Martin Short is his own sort of clown. They each create heightened versions of themselves, which I would refer to as clowning without makeup."

He also wanted the revival to show a fresh face. "From our standpoint, it felt like if we were going to do clown makeup, then we may as well do a museum copy of the original production, which I didn't want to do."

In searching for a symbol, what came to mind was a kind of vaudeville act scenario for which actors might wear red carnations on their lapels. The audience in this theater-in-the-round setting could readily see the bright silk flowers as the actors faced them.

Several years earlier, director Heather Hutchison, who had already staged the show numerous times using makeup, wanted to try something new for a community theater production. For her setting, she conceived of an old vaudeville theater being used temporarily as a storm shelter. At the appropriate moment during the show when the clowns would have applied the makeup, she had Jesus pull distinct personal props from a trunk for the players to use or wear, including a feather boa, a slide whistle, a ventriloquist's dummy puppet, a showman's hat and cane, a Charlie Chaplin-esque oversize tuxedo, and other items. Later, during "On the Willows," they returned the items to the trunk with the attitude that they had formed new identities based on what they had learned from Jesus, and the outer trappings were no longer needed.

In Favor of Makeup

Tebelak and company associated makeup with *Godspell*'s clowning and believed that using it contributed extra meaning to their experience.

Most of the actors came up with their own designs—a zig zag, or dot, or something else inventive. The Jesus clown makeup developed by Stephen Nathan was consistent for all the early *Godspell* companies. He came up with a red dot on the nose and a red heart on the forehead. Under his eyes he drew tear-like designs in black that extended to a point to make them "a little bit more the Harlequin clown that John-Michael had talked about," he says. The tears and large heart suggested Jesus' compassionate nature as well as the emotional range of his experience on Earth.

Dean Pitchford relished the whole process when he played Jesus in New York and at the Ford's Theatre in Washington, D.C. Sitting in front of a mirror in his robe and applying Jesus makeup wasn't an ordinary show preparation. Using a stencil for the heart, he dabbed red greasepaint there, and drew the tears with a special brush. He recalls, "I would sit there and I would transform. I felt like I was behind a mask and I could be anybody and do anything." He believes it also helped the group of actors bond emotionally. "It was almost like we all met behind the makeup...like we had secret decoder rings."

Other actors also experienced the way makeup seemed to make over their subjective experience. "I was transformed in that seminal moment when I put makeup on whomever and they put makeup on me," recalls Herb Braha of the original cast. "All of a sudden I could do anything; I was fearless."

When Don Scardino directed the first Off-Broadway revival after performing as Jesus for many years, he used the makeup approach to enhance the storytelling. He suggests that the process was essential to, among other things, communicating the characters' transition from intellectual philosophers to people of a spiritual bent. "Jesus needs to say to them, 'You are not all the way there yet. If you're going to follow me, this other transformation has to be done.' So he holds up a mirror, he starts applying their makeup, and then they put makeup on each other, and so the community begins."

Removing the Makeup

In Tebelak's conception of the show, the makeup isn't removed at the end of the show, but rather just before the Last Supper. The moment initiates the next phase of the show. Scardino says it signaled "a time to have no illusions—to be naked in the world again and accept what's about to happen."

Stephen Nathan comments along similar lines and adds another perspective on clown characters in *Godspell*: "The removal of the makeup was such a crucial and important part of the piece because it was that moment when superficial personality—those traits we believe give us our identity—dissolves and all that remained was our humanity. We put our personality on, like an affectation, and we then take it off. Our nature is something else.... What is revealed to the audience is that mere personality is not our true nature. The love we feel is that truth."

"Removing the greasepaint symbolizes a new phase. It's Peter Pan leaving Neverland; a time to assume a new responsibility of carrying the message forward."

— Robin Lamont

Peggy Gordon had a special fondness for the gesture of removing the makeup. Whatever the philosophy of it, the actual experience for the actors was sublimely meaningful. "At the end, we'd take the makeup off each other, slowly, lovingly, seeing each other and ourselves unmasked...as we began to say our goodbyes to this special clown."

She insists that no other artistic device (and she has seen many) has the same emotional power. In other words, wearing a piece of jewelry or item of clothing and then removing it isn't the same. The act of "...removing each other's makeup, looking in the mirror, seeing ourselves, touching each other's faces as we'd see the other, truly seeing! Nothing equals the sheer emotional intimacy of that transaction. I still get chills when I watch that moment in *Godspell* productions."

Directors are still able to use another symbol, but for the record, Stephen Schwartz agrees with the original cast on this point: "I understand that directors want to do it another way, and that's valid. It doesn't cripple the show or uncut the message, but if you ask me what I feel is the most artistically successful choice, I think the makeup is the best, at least as I've seen it so far."

The Godspell Experience

ABOVE: Dean Pitchford played Jesus in the Washington, D.C. company of *Godspell* at Ford's Theatre. He appears here in full makeup. At his side are Baillie Gerstein (in pigtails) and Berlinda Tolbert. LEFT: Jerry Sroka and Carla Meyer are the makeup-wearing Herb and Peggy clowns in the Boston company of *Godspell*.

CHAPTER 15

Q and A:
Is *Godspell*'s Comic Tone Spiritually Appropriate? (and Other Concerns)

Over the years, hundreds of people have reflected on *Godspell*'s meaning and implications. Reading a few of their observations can stimulate our own search for spiritual truth.

Godspell has collected a range of critics when it comes to spiritual content. Some say it's too religiously specific. For example, it includes quotations from Biblical Gospels used by Christians. Others say it's not religious enough, as it doesn't offer miracle stories or an explicit Resurrection, and therefore doesn't convey that Jesus is divine.

Most audience members enjoy the show as a work of dramatic art—one that doesn't proselytize messages from specific religious denominations. Tebelak, after all, didn't write a church service, but only had a stage musical in mind.

Contrary to accusations from *Godspell*'s detractors, Tebelak was not making a theological statement with his artistic choices. For his purposes, it was sufficient to show Jesus in action as a catalyst for personal transformation and as a model of love and compassion. He was not asserting anything about what he didn't cover, such as miracle or healing stories.

The material that follows covers some of the questions that have been raised about the show's stance. The answers provided by early cast members and others are offered for the sake of enriching the reader's experience of *Godspell*.

Is *Godspell*'s Comedy Spiritually Appropriate?

If you walk into any sanctuary in the world—a church, temple, mosque, or other house of worship—you expect to find a solemn atmosphere. If you buy tickets and attend a production of *Godspell*, you find anything but solemnity, at least in the traditional sense. Jesus jokes, dances, laughs, plays, and sings, as does everyone around him.

From the beginning people have wondered if this jovial behavior is even appropriate. Does *Godspell* mock Christianity? Is it sacrilegious or blasphemous?

For Tebelak, Harvey Cox's book, *The Feast of Fools*, helped him justify his feelings that good cheer is spiritually appropriate. He commented in a published interview, "*The Feast of Fools* says we can not only revere Christ but we can also have fun with Him. Too often we have locked Him into this face of agony that He experienced only within the last few hours of his life, thus wiping out the thirty-three years of his life when He spread happiness around Him."

If anyone needed to discern the show's suitability for the spiritually inclined it was Rex Knowles. At the time that he and his wife, Sherry Landrom, auditioned for the first *Godspell* touring company, Knowles was studying to be a minister. His father and grandfather were ministers, his mother had a master's degree from Hartford Seminary, and one of his mother's distant relatives was William Tyndale, who translated the Bible into English in the 1500s and was martyred for it.

Knowles felt at home with the show. Traveling to perform *Godspell* hundreds of times made clear its universal power. "Touring for a year was an exquisite experience: whether we were in Westport, Connecticut, or Jackson, Mississippi, or New Orleans, the show resonated. That was on an observational level; on a personal level, saying the words every single night and hearing the words, they go deep into the psyche and to the spirit. I was honored to be a part of it, and it's still with me."

According to some contemporary Christian writers, the whole notion that religion should frown on fun and joy is itself based on a misunderstanding of the scripture and Jesus' role. James Martin, SJ, in his book, *Between Heaven and Mirth: Why Joy, Humor, and Laughter are at the Heart of the Spiritual Life*, explains that because humor is culture-bound, many Bible readers have missed the humor in the passages. He notes, as an example of humor, that Jesus' expression about putting a light under a bushel would have been quite funny to those around him.

Christian traditions have tended to remove the natural humor, a tendency that is even carved in marble, in the dour looks on the saints in church statues. But dourness is not required for spirituality. Martin writes, "Why are we naturally drawn to joyful people? One reason, I believe, is that joy is a sign of God's presence, which is naturally attractive to us." Martin fills his book with references to the reasons for mirth, including psalm phrases like "Make a joyful noise to the Lord," which is the spirit that permeates *Godspell*.

Who Is Jesus in *Godspell*?

How is Jesus depicted in *Godspell*? Is he a mortal man of great purity and integrity? Is he the son of God? Is he superhuman?

In practical terms, Jesus is a leader. "He is the best summer camp counselor you could ever have," says Dean Pitchford. "He is the pied piper. The others all followed Jesus," Pitchford continues, as he recalls listening to Tebelak talk about the relationship of the clowns. "John-Michael was very clear that [in the context of the musical] nobody had ideas but Jesus. Jesus set things in motion. He would announce a parable and they would all spring into action. He would put the first dab of makeup on somebody's face and everybody else would go 'Ohhh, that's a good idea.' And we would turn and decorate our assigned cast member."

Godspell's Jesus can also be described as a teacher. He inspires those around him by expressing universal principles. One of the many lessons he offers those around him is the principle known as the Golden Rule—moral wisdom that can be found in the teachings of many different religions. In the musical, Jesus speaks the Golden Rule, an adaptation of Matthew 7:12, in a rhythmic way: "Always treat others as you would have them treat you!" to which the followers affirm, "Yeah, yeah, yeah," just before they sing "Light of the World."

Some directors of *Godspell* have come from a Jesus-can't-have-fun background. Schwartz cautions, "When the show goes wrong it is usually because Jesus is played too reverently, standing off to the sidelines and watching beatifically as the rest of the cast clowns around. The exact opposite is what is needed."

An actor playing Jesus doesn't need to add on an artificial persona, whether comic or beatific. Stephen Reinhardt suggests the character is like an evergreen tree that is left in nature at Christmas time. "Picture a perfectly shaped blue spruce growing in a pristine wilderness. That is the Jesus of *Godspell*—the Jesus not cut down and dragged into our churches and homes to be gaudily festooned with elaborate and bizarre ornaments that completely obliterate the simple beauty of that once noble tree."

As to any debate about whether or not Jesus is divine, as with everything else in *Godspell*, the show's creators wanted to leave it up to the audience, many of whom come to the show with a cherished particular belief.

Q & A

Over the years, Stephen Schwartz has been asked about Jesus' nature. He suggests that *Godspell* works its theatrical magic without assertions as to the spiritual status of its leader. "Each audience member can draw his or her own conclusions; similarly, each actor portraying Jesus in a production of the show can make his (or I suppose her) own decision about it. The content of the show, in contrast to many of the other re-tellings of the Jesus story, focuses on Jesus' teachings, what he actually said, and the power of those teachings to lead to a sense of community in a fractured and fractious world."

> *"The divinity of the character is immaterial to what the show is about. You can believe that or not, but the show is equally valid."*
> —Stephen Schwartz

Who Are the Followers?

In *Godspell*, Jesus is seen teaching a group of people who are sometimes referred to as clowns, followers, disciples, or simply as players. Productions can include any number of people in the ensemble, although the script calls for nine actors in addition to Jesus. Tebelak's choice was partly practical. It would have been hard to manage the original production with more than 10 actors in the Studio Theatre at Carnegie Mellon University. He also may have made a philosophical choice of 10 instead of a group of 12 apostles plus Jesus, as in the Bible. "He didn't want to hit the nail on the head and have twelve," Nina Faso recalls about her friend's decision, "because he didn't want it to be the actual Bible story. He wanted it to be an inference."

In the same light, the other clowns were not meant to stand in for specific Biblical personalities, other than John/Judas. There is no specific Andrew or Peter or anyone else. The Peggy clown is not the woman caught in adultery through the whole play, even though she plays that part in the stoning story. The players step up to take on various roles in the parables as they are called upon to do so. The printed programs for shows either list the script names like "Robin" or "Sonia," or the actors' names because these actors are clown characters who temporarily take on roles and illustrate points.

How do *Godspell* and *Jesus Christ Superstar* Compare?

Both *Godspell* and the Andrew Lloyd Webber/Tim Rice rock opera *Jesus Christ Superstar* emerged as part of the spiritual renaissance and cultural transitions of the 1960s. Yet the two musicals are quite distinct. The latter is a rock opera about Jesus' last week in Jerusalem. It differs significantly from *Godspell* in tone and substance, and is not designed to open up the story for interaction with the audience.

Tebelak focused on creating a fresh experience with the parable teachings. He and his peers believed that spiritual teachings must be lived, not merely described, and the *Godspell* approach brought them closer to the living experience.

Neither show's authors copied the other. Schwartz avoided listening to the album for *Superstar* until after he penned *Godspell*'s score. "I didn't want to be affected either by subconsciously imitating it or consciously striving not to imitate it. I just wanted not to know about it at all."

Tebelak recalls not listening to the album until three days after *Godspell* opened. He also shared the story about Webber and Rice attending *Godspell*. "About two weeks after we had opened, Andrew Lloyd Webber and Tim Rice came down to see our show. They had heard we were playing a pirated version of their show. They came in very tersely, with looks like 'We're not going to enjoy this.' Afterwards, we met with them, and they had enjoyed it a great deal and were happy we were so totally different. It was fun then, to sit and compare notes."

Is *Godspell* Compatible with Judaism?

As *Godspell* was introduced to the world in the early 1970s, religiously inclined Jews and those with a cultural Jewish background had a chance to evaluate their comfort with the show. Four original cast members with Jewish backgrounds acted out parables of Jesus. Actors Stephen Nathan, Peggy Gordon, Joanne Jonas, and Herb Braha had no qualms about what they were doing in this show.

"The actual formation of Christianity as a separate religion and not just as various sects of Judaism didn't occur during Jesus' lifetime," Gordon reminds us.

Historically speaking, since Jesus was a practicing Jew, the gathering with his disciples at the end of his life was a seder, the ritual meal held in commemoration of Passover. Stephen Nathan in the role of Jesus spoke the traditional mealtime prayer in Hebrew. Nathan comments, "I felt it was important to make that a seder rather than the Last Supper. If it's a seder, it's a more shocking moment. If it's the Last Supper and everybody's expecting it, then it's just the Last Supper." The seder prayer reminds audiences of the historical Jesus' life context.

Over the years, a great many non-Christian actors have performed in *Godspell* and enjoyed the experience. Marley Sims was Jewish and she performed in *Godspell* full time for about five years, both at the Promenade and on Broadway. She remembers working with people who were not particularly religious or who were Jewish. "I think what we hooked up to was this was a fun show to do and it had a universal message, sort of like the Ten Commandments. You don't have to believe in God to appreciate the Ten Commandments. I think every one of those parables in *Godspell*, written down on a piece of paper, makes sense. *Godspell* had such a universal appeal."

Is There a Resurrection?

Since no one speaks explicitly about a Resurrection in the show, this question is often raised. It can be answered in many ways. Some people say there actually is a Resurrection depicted physically; others say it wasn't shown because Jesus is not being presented in terms of a particular religion and therefore the show is not positing a Resurrection. As with any material presented on stage, ultimately an interpretation is personal to anyone watching.

Many people have considered the curtain call to be a Resurrection, as Jesus bounces back on stage with all the other actors. *Life Magazine* reviewer Tom Prideaux praises the approach toward the end of his 1972 review of the show: "And when the Christ and his followers leap exuberantly back onto the stage for the curtain call, the audience rejoices in the implied Resurrection. This is brilliant theatrical shorthand."

Others seek a more literal representation. Nina Faso asserts, "The Resurrection is the end of the show — it's 'long live God.' It's when they raise Jesus over their heads and they start singing. It starts there, and that's it." A fan of *Godspell* who once met with Tebelak, asked him about the Resurrection. His comment to her was similar to Faso's. He suggested it is when the music shifts from "Long Live God" and becomes faster when "Prepare Ye the Way of the Lord" is added in. And then the actors lift Jesus over their heads.

Broadway cast member Valerie Williams notes that one of the final scenes included shadowy lighting effects and actors writhing against the fence and shaking it. She felt that this was Tebelak creating a storm mentioned in the Bible. She continues,

"You saw all the suffering in that one particular scene and then [the cast except for Jesus] just dropped to the floor on cue. And we lay there for, I think it was a count of ten, and then we got up very slowly as if rising from the dead. Therefore, 'Long Live God' is the Resurrection."

Stephen Schwartz has provided his perspective in a questions-and-answers forum: "Over the years, there has been comment from some about the lack of an apparent Resurrection in the show. Some choose to view the curtain call, in which Jesus appears, as symbolic of the Resurrection; others point to the moment when the cast raise Jesus above their heads. While either view is valid, both miss the point. *Godspell* is about the formation of a community which carries on Jesus' teachings after he has gone. In other words, it is the effect Jesus has on the others that is the story of the show, not whether or not he himself is resurrected. Therefore, it is very important at the end of the show that it be clear that the others have come through the violence and pain of the Crucifixion sequence and leave with a joyful determination to carry on the ideas and feelings they have learned during the course of the show."

Robin Lamont has her own variation on the theme. One of her favorite memories from *The Godspell* at college was from the final moments of the last showing on a December night. Word of mouth had spread and there was a standing-room-only crowd. "Because the theater was so small and so packed with students, we couldn't get out through the audience. The only way we could get out was through the back doors behind the fence, which is where they used to load the scenery in. At the last minute, John-Michael said, 'You're not going to be able to get out the back. What I want you to do is when you take him off the cross, walk around, we'll open the back bay doors for you which are about ten feet wide, and what I want you to do is take him out and leave.' That night it was snowing. I can imagine what it must have looked like to the audience because people came up to us for days to tell us about this. As we walked Jesus back on our shoulders, and the crew people opened the doors, it was pitch black except for the falling snow. And we walked out and they said, 'You disappeared into the world.'"*

How Far Can Performing Groups Go with Their Changes?

Directors and performers often wonder how far their creativity can wander from the official *Godspell* script. Every play production involves some interpretation for scenery, costumes, staging, and acting, but companies performing *Godspell* are also allowed to personalize some of the non Biblical lines. For example, when Jesus says he can read feet, the Jeffrey clown might reply in a new way, such as with a different brand of shoe than the original Keds or with some other quip. Or in the exchange between Jesus and Judas over turning the other cheek, the actors might find a different way to depict the moment than is described in the script.

Godspell actor Howard Sponseller explains that Tebelak was using a story theater approach: "Whenever we got to do a parable, the idea was look at the words and figure out how to tell the story—are we going to use props, mime, or whatever? That freed us to try something new."

The original cast told the Good Samaritan parable, using a broomstick to represent the road on which the travelers were walking and finger puppets to represent the people in the parable. Sherry Landrom, who performed in the *Godspell* tour and has directed the show in a university setting, comments: "It's effective because the Jesus character is just beginning to draw the group together to say, 'Now we're going to tell these stories so we can learn,' and a puppet show is where kids often start [with dramatics]." Groups are allowed to customize the scene based on their own experiences. For instance, the actors in the 2000 touring production presented the parable as if they were in the reality television show *Cops*, utilizing model cars and a closed-circuit TV camera.

The Prodigal Son parable is the most elaborate one to enact. Actors work together to make numerous choices, such as how to demonstrate the dividing of the estate or where they want to send the wayward son when he travels. Some productions use the original cast's image for dividing the estate: Gilmer (playing a servant) broke a slab of Styrofoam over her knee and gave a piece to each of the two sons. A Chicago-area theater director, Heather Hutchison, who has staged the show twenty times, remembers that one of her groups tore up a real estate listings book for the dividing the estate scene. Another group used a CNN news bulletin approach, with someone reporting on a state being divided. Her groups have imagined the wandering son heading to locations like Rio, or to Hawaii where he is donned with leis. One group included a quick air travel moment with a funny remark by an air flight attendant.

In the early productions, director Tebelak helped the actors find the subtle difference between clowning with a purpose and just performing comic shtick. It was sometimes challenging to understand when antics went too far, but Tebelak witnessed the whole and made choices. Gilmer McCormick comments, "What he was so brilliant at was allowing us that freedom and fun; he kept a very careful eye on the through line and on the message, so that each character [performance] would be appropriate for that scene. If we weren't appropriate, it was gone."

Peggy Gordon also remembers hearing Tebelak discourage political references in particular. "Richard Nixon was president so we had reams of material had John-Michael wanted

Godspell to be topical. John-Michael said the humor 'could not upstage; could not obscure.' There was one irresistible thing that Joanne and I showed John-Michael in rehearsal. He turned to Andy, our Cherry Lane Theatre box office guy and asked, 'Can you tell me what that parable was about?' All Andy could remember was something about Nixon. John-Michael said to us, 'Congratulations, you just subverted *Godspell*'s singular purpose."

Dean Pitchford, who played in *Godspell* for almost two years, comments, "I think that John-Michael was generally allergic to current political commentary because that was constantly changing. This was a piece that could be lifted up and dropped into any decade, and if your references are to the people who are sitting in the White House right now, that's not going to translate. Whereas, if you are making pop culture references to King Kong and the iconography from the movies, that is part of our generally inherited cultural treasure. I think that there's a big difference between those two."

For new productions of *Godspell*, licensing companies allow performing groups to improvise and invent new comedy lines and staging, but it is expected that the groups will use good taste and follow some guidelines. Schwartz explains in his Author's Note to the Director, "While a creative director is free to alter the specifics, it is important to remain true to the subtextual content, motivations, and dramatic structure."

PART III
Godspell's Score: Song by Song

Larry Uttal, President of Bell Records, speaks with Stephen Schwartz at the Grammy Awards dinner party March 15, 1972, after *Godspell* won two Grammys. Schwartz recalls, "This was the night when I said to Larry, 'Listen, if the 5th Dimension is never going to release a single of 'Day by Day,' why don't we release the recording off the cast album?'" The "Day by Day" single quickly rose to the top 40 chart where it remained for nine weeks. The album earned a gold record. (Photo by William "PoPsie" Randolph © 2008, Michael Randolph www.PoPsiePhotos.com PoPsie-photos@att.net)

The Godspell Experience

ABOVE: Jesse Cutler (in back), Stephen Schwartz, and Elliot Scheiner (front) at A & R Recording for the movie soundtrack recording session. BELOW: The album cover for the Broadway revival album. Revival cast member George Salazar in the Sh-K-Boom/ Ghostlight Records studio.

Chapter 16

Notes on the Score, Recordings, and Lyrics

Part III of *The Godspell Experience* explores Schwartz's much-loved pieces, providing stories about their creation, some musical details, and complete lyrics. The comments here are based on interviews with Stephen Schwartz, Peggy Gordon, Jay Hamburger, various music directors, arrangers, band members, and actors. The chapters are organized by song order within the musical, from the "Prologue" through the "Finale." Commentary on the optional song "Beautiful City" is at the end.

Godspell Songs: Overview

"It's been said that a character in a musical doesn't really land until he or she sings, and I think that's true," says Stephen Schwartz. "And if there are important themes or ideas, they need to be sung about too." For *Godspell*, he made sure there were songs for each character, key moment, and central theme.

When composing the score, he changed the basic approach to the songs to reflect what was being communicated. In the show's earlier incarnations, the songs had primarily been group numbers in a rock band style. For the new version, Schwartz wrote most of the songs for one cast member to lead before the others joined in. Within each song, he let the sound build through choral harmony representing the expanding emotional harmony of the group.

Schwartz drew inspiration from his favorite music and intuited his way into an appropriate style. He sometimes brought to mind particular combinations of chords or styles of playing used by songwriters he liked, such as a James Taylor style for "All Good Gifts" or a Laura Nyro style for "Bless the Lord."

"I would describe the score for *Godspell* as pop pastiche," Schwartz once stated. Specific pop styles that he was fond of became, in a manner of speaking, his musical diving boards. "It wasn't that I was trying to imitate or make an homage to any given pop artist, but that they were the jumping-off points. Because I was writing the score so quickly, I would put a lyric in front of me and think, well, how do I jump into the pool this time? What's my diving board? And I would pick something. And I'm sure there were ones I picked where I hit my head on the cement, and went back up to the diving board and tried a different entry point."

As much as the score leaned toward popular music of the day, it retained some of the Broadway spirit that was Schwartz's background. Also, the cast member's voices were not necessarily similar to those on hit records. "You have to consider that it was a Broadway-styled cast that was singing," Elliot Scheiner points out about the *Godspell* movie soundtrack for which he did the engineering work. The soundtrack and all the cast albums featured the vocal talents of actors who primarily performed in the stage musical rather than in popular music concerts or recording studios. "So it was pop in a sense," Scheiner continues, "but it wasn't like James Taylor doing a vocal. It was Broadway kind of stuff. That's what it was meant to be."

Arrangements

After Schwartz composed the music, band members, under his guidance, developed accompaniments that enhanced the piano-based score. Reinhardt recalls, "Steve was there in all the rehearsals and he'd say, 'Okay, this is where the guitar comes in.' He would talk to Jesse (the guitarist) and say, 'I need something like this.' Jesse [Cutler] made up his guitar solo for 'On the Willows' and for the 'Finale.'"

For vocal arrangements, Schwartz encouraged cast members to come up with harmonies as they were working with the pieces. Joanne Jonas remembers being involved, especially as she was the first to learn the score. "Stephen didn't actually go, 'Here's your harmony, and here's yours.' It was [in part] up to the singers. In every other venue that I've ever sung in I always put in harmony because I naturally go to a fifth or a seventh or whatever. So many of the harmonies that you hear throughout were written by us."

Schwartz also remembers harmonies being created in this participatory way. For example, with "Day by Day" he says, "Robin sang the song and we would assign certain people to do the melody with her. Then the stronger singers would come up with harmony, and they just made them up. It gradually came together. I would sit there and edit it together." Robin Lamont's recollection differs. "I have quite specific memories of Stephen teaching us harmonies to 'Day by Day' and Lamar's song ('All Good Gifts'). They're actually complex and nothing we would have come up with ourselves."

Stephen Reinhardt believes that Schwartz came to rehearsal with definite ideas of how he wanted the songs to sound. "His intention was to have it sound like a pop score. The basis of pop harmony is three parts. I can imagine him matching voices with certain parts, getting the right blend, fitting harmonies to what an actor naturally heard, but he was always open to the creative additions that the cast would come up with—like Joanne's descending harmony line in 'Day by Day' and Jeff's beautiful, resolving harmony at the end of 'By My Side' that are some of the most delicate and elusive harmonies in the show. So the process of creating vocal arrangements was a microcosm of how we put the show together."

Ultimately, it seems that the vocal arrangements are the result of all these artists working together in a creative fervor to get the show on its feet.

In the context of the show and the era, ad hoc harmonies fit right in. *Godspell* album collector and director Tom Peters comments, "Seeing the original production of *Godspell*, even though you knew the show couldn't be created on the spot, as an audience member you got that vibe that it was all generated right before your eyes. The arrangements were what I call campfire harmonies that people could pick up if they were sitting around a fire, like if someone would sing a familiar tune from a Peter, Paul, and Mary album or Crosby, Stills, and Nash, and then everyone would lay on a harmony."

The process of creating musical material didn't alter the central credit. Various musicians added harmonic textures, but the notes were always contained within, or suggested by, Schwartz's chords. History will remember the score as the world's introduction to a young American composer whose ability to match a musical's needs with the right song led to his stellar career that included not only *Godspell*, but *Pippin*, *Wicked*, and many others.

Godspell Recordings and Arrangers
See www.TheGodspellExperience.com for album purchasing details.

Godspell albums have been abundant and popular. Each version has its own special features. Many of them came on the market as vinyl records and are no longer in print, such as the London recording, several different Australian recordings, and the original French cast recording.

With half a dozen albums currently available as CDs or digital music files, there's no shortage of ways to enjoy performances of this musical score:

1971 Original Off-Broadway Cast Album: Bell Records released the *Godspell Original Cast Recording* in July 1971, as a vinyl record. Bell was later absorbed into Arista, which reissued the album in 1974. This first album preserves the playful song renditions of the original cast and band. It doesn't include the "Prologue." Schwartz wrote "Beautiful City" later for the movie so the song is absent from this first album.

Godspell **soundtrack:** This album showcases the vocal talents of the movie cast, including Victor Garber, Lynne Thigpen, Katie Hanley, and others. A large band presents a rich accompaniment for each piece. The album doesn't include "Learn Your Lessons Well" or "We Beseech Thee" because the songs were not used in the movie, but the soundtrack does feature the original version of "Beautiful City."

Godspell **(1993 London Studio Cast):** One of the reasons Schwartz went into a studio in London in 1993 was to include the "Prologue" on an album, as well as to provide a record of British singers Darren Day, John Barrowman, Ruthie Henshall, and others.

'*Godspell*' 2000 Off-Broadway Cast Recording: This album includes all the show's songs performed by the York Theatre Off-Broadway revival cast (2000) that starred Barrett Foa as Jesus, Will Erat as Judas, Shoshana Bean, Leslie Kritzer, Chad Kimball, and others. It features updated orchestrations by the show's music director, Dan Schachner.

2001 *Godspell* tour: Beneath the bright yellow cover on this CD is an album that features sprightly orchestrations by

Alex Lacamoire, who drew inspiration from popular music songwriters he admired. For example, the style of the Dave Matthews Band gave Lacamoire ideas for his version of "Beautiful City," while the piano-rock style of Tori Amos inspired "By My Side." DRG label.

40th anniversary album set: This is simply a set that combines the first two albums.

2011 Broadway revival: The most thoroughly reconceived orchestrations and vocal arrangements are featured on *Godspell: The New Broadway Cast Recording.* Michael Holland wrote them and worked with Stephen Schwartz on refinements. The album includes a new section of "Learn Your Lessons Well" that Schwartz wrote for the revival, a unique take on "Turn Back, O Man," and a slow ballad version of "Beautiful City." Two bonus tracks enhance the album: an up-tempo version of "Beautiful City" sung by John Ondrasik and Five For Fighting, and a cabaret-styled version of "Learn Your Lessons Well" performed by Telly Leung, Lindsay Mendez, and Wallace Smith.

Credits

On each recording, the authorship for "By My Side" is noted to be Peggy Gordon (music) and Jay Hamburger (lyrics).

Stephen Schwartz is normally credited as providing "music and new lyrics"—meaning that all of the music is new and the lyrics have mixed origins. More details are provided in the chapters that follow (and on the copyright notices on the Lyrics Permissions page at the back of the book).

Chapter 17
Godspell's "Prologue" and the War of Words

John-Michael Tebelak invented the unusual opening for *Godspell* while first conceiving the show. He nicknamed the scene "Tower of Babble," evoking the Bible story in Genesis 11, verses 1–9. These verses describe a time in Shinar (thought to be the city of Babylon, in present-day Iraq) when people built a heaven-reaching tower called "Babel" and their languages were "confounded." The use of the word "babble" in *Godspell* connects it to the commonly used term for uttering meaningless or confusing words. For the script he collected conflicting comments by numerous philosophers.

Peggy Gordon explains, "John-Michael conceived it as philosophers standing on a world stage, each articulating a belief in God, which then erupted into a literal war of words." Physically, the actors rejected each other. It was "meticulously staged by John-Michael to enact their conflict of ideas. This builds to a crescendo that is interrupted only by the blowing of a shofar. John the Baptist heralds the arrival of one whose belief system is utterly simple—love thy neighbor as thyself."

When Schwartz saw *Godspell* at Café La MaMa, he felt that the lengthy quotations from Socrates, Thomas Aquinas, Martin Luther, and others were not really suited to musical theater in their present form, so he offered to edit them down and musicalize the whole scene. Heading to the piano, he composed a lively tune in a traditional musical theater style, knowing it would contrast with the folk-rock music style he was using for the rest of the show. By varying melodic and rhythmic styles for each singer/philosopher, the composer extended the concept that each had a distinct point of view.

He also arranged the war-of-words section of the song in a complicated, counterpoint style that becomes a cacophony chorus. He'd written a four-part fugue for a musical in college, and for this *Godspell* song he was able to weave eight parts together. He explains, "Once I had the basic chord structure, then it was a matter of making sure that whatever was being sung in each verse or by each philosopher conformed to that chord structure. And also, obviously, I needed to spread the melodies around so that they were on different notes of the chord at different times. That's like working out a musical puzzle. It takes time, but it's not too hard to do. It's fun."

The "Prologue" has always been part of the official libretto for *Godspell*. However, when the composer left the song off the *Godspell Original Cast Recording*, and the *Godspell* movie director left it out of the film, some regional directors in later years felt justified in staging the show without it.

Schwartz's intention for omitting it from the album was to help the album advance on the pop charts. He states, "The 'Prologue' was not recorded because we wanted to make it an album with pop cross-over potential, and I felt starting with the long piano-only and essentially theatrical 'Prologue' would hurt that. I thought we were just much better off starting with 'Prepare Ye,' and it worked; the album became a cross-over hit."

But that didn't mean he wanted it deleted from the licensed version of the show. He believes the musical only makes sense dramaturgically with the "Prologue" included. "Since the show is about the formation of a community, the 'Prologue' is the audience's only chance to see how the disciples-to-be function (or dysfunction, if you will) BEFORE they start to become a community—the obdurate clinging to dogmatic philosophies, the inability to cooperate or admit other points of view, the descent into violence, the loneliness and despair, etc. (If this sounds rather like contemporary America, it's not coincidental.) Without the 'Prologue,' what is their problem to be solved?"

Updates

Over the years, Schwartz has adjusted some of the philosophers. He once commented, "I revisited the philosophers at the opening [because originally] I didn't actually understand what they were. I was just doing what John-Michael did. But after a while I got what this was supposed to be, and I tried to make that a little bit clearer to the audience." The new philosophers he has included are Galileo, Hegel, Jonathan Edwards, L. Ron Hubbard, and Marianne Williamson.

"The God Speech"

Before the "Prologue" begins, *Godspell* opens with what is sometimes called "The God Speech" because it is spoken as if God is orating. Tebelak staged the show to open with actors standing in a circle in the dark, humming at a low pitch, perhaps suggesting the music of the spheres or the "Om" sound of Eastern mysticism. Then Jesus speaks a few opening lines about God's nature being without beginning or end, and related points.

It is likely that Tebelak pieced the monologue together from several medieval mystery plays. In using the lines, perhaps he wanted to signal to the audience that they were about to see a new take on old mystery play pageants, or that the freewheeling style that followed had roots in an earlier dramatic tradition.

When Jesus completes the monologue, the humming stops. At this point the circle breaks, both literally and figuratively—

the moment of quiet unification slips away and the discord of the "Prologue" begins.

Socrates speaks from his trial, saying he shall obey God rather than the men and will continue to teach the youth who come to him. He is the first to sing and is followed by the other philosophers.

LYRICS

"Prologue"

SOCRATES
Wherefore, O men of Athens
I say to you:
Therefore acquit me or not
But whichever you do
I shall never alter my ways
Never adjust my approach to this maze
Never reform 'til the end of my days
Even if I have to die many times

THOMAS AQUINAS
God is apprehended by imagination, intuition, reason, touch, opinion, sense and name

And so on
But on quite the other hand, we find we can't begin to
Understand Him, so to some it seems a shame
To go on
But He is all things in all
And He is nothing in any
He is often found in one thing small
Conversely He is often missed in many

MARTIN LUTHER
God almighty has made our rulers mad
God almighty has turned our people bad
For the German nobility

"Prologue"

With typical agility
Have so applied their skill at egregious laws
That the people are led astray
They feel beholden to obey
It may be just the German way
But God, it gives one pause!

LEONARDO DA VINCI: The rise of man

EDWARD GIBBON: The decline of Rome

BOTH: Was natural

GIBBON: and inevitable…

DA VINCI: Man is so levitable!

GIBBON: Instead of inquiring why Rome was destroyed…

DA VINCI: Instead of admiring man's filling of the void

BOTH: We should rather be surprised

DA VINCI: That God had man so tyrannized…

[SIMULTANEOUS]: DA VINCI: Man will be strong/

GIBBON: That Rome remained so strong

BOTH: So long.

FREDERIC NIETZSCHE
What…
Is noble
Nowadays?

JEAN-PAUL SARTRE
Atheistic existentialism
Which I represent
Is more coherent—I do believe it…

The Godspell Experience

BUCKMINSTER FULLER
Man is a complex of patterns and processes…

SARTRE
There is no such thing as human nature
Not in all or few men
Since there is no God to conceive it…

BUCKMINSTER FULLER
Man is a complex of patterns and processes…
(Voice over music): I live on earth at present, but I don't know what I am.
I know that I am not a "category." I am not a thing, a noun.
I seem to be a verb, an evolutionary process, an integral function of the universe

ALL EIGHT CAST MEMBERS
So high
In my
Lovely I-
V'ry tower of Babel
Babble, babble, babble
Babble, babble, babble, babble
High above the rabble
Rabble, rabble, rabble
Babble, rabble, babble, babble, rabble, babble
Greatest mind of history
Solving life's sweet mystery

GROUP ONE: So listen to me

GROUP TWO: So listen to me

GROUP ONE: Know how life should be

GROUP TWO: Know how life should be

GROUP ONE: Oh,

ALL EIGHT: What does it matter if they don't agree!?

"Prologue"

(They each sing their own philosophies in counterpoint to one another, and then all eight face front.)

Ahh ahh
Ahh ahh
Ahh ahh
Ahh ahh…

REPLACEMENTS FOR, OR ALTERATION TO, ORIGINAL VERSION:

Used instead of Martin Luther:
GALILEO
God endows us with sense and intellect;
God endows us with reason we neglect.
And despite the abolition
By the current Inquisition
Of any intuition
That they don't choose
When it comes to God, I find
I can't believe that He designed
A human being with a mind
He's not supposed to use.

Used instead of da Vinci/Gibbon
DA VINCI: The rise of Man
JONATHAN EDWARDS: The wrath of God
DA VINCI: Is natural
EDWARDS: Is natural
DA VINCI: And explicable
EDWARDS: We are despicable
DA VINCI: If God by inaction has given man the stage
EDWARDS: If man's malefaction sends God into a rage
DA VINCI AND EDWARDS: We can hardly be aghast
DA VINCI: That up we're raised
EDWARDS: That down we're cast
DA VINCI: That we should be sublime
EDWARDS: That God damns us
DA VINCI AND EDWARDS: For all time!

Used in 2011 Revival Script to replace da Vinci/Gibbon
HEGEL: The rise of the state
GIBBON: The decline of Rome
HEGEL AND GIBBON: Was inevitable…
GIBBON: Rome had to fall
HEGEL:
The state above all!
The state is as God
Walking on the earth
GIBBON:
The seeds of Rome's decline
Were present at her birth
BOTH: We should therefore be surprised
HEGEL: That man was ever individualized…
GIBBON: That Rome remained so strong
HEGEL: The state will be strong
BOTH: So long…

Replaces Nietzche
L. RON HUBBARD
Nothing is true unless observed by you

Replaces FULLER
MARIANNE WILLIAMSON
The glory of God we were born to make manifest

CHAPTER 18

"Prepare Ye"
Solving the Problem of a One-Line Lyric

When Stephen Schwartz sat at his piano to write the second number in the show, the entire scope of the piece was a one-line lyric. The phrase that Tebelak wanted the John the Baptist character to sing was "Prepare ye the way of the Lord" from Matthew 3:3 (as well as Malachi 3:1 and Isaiah 40:3). It wasn't part of a hymn or psalm, so there were no other lines to go with it.

Duane Bolick's music for the Carnegie and Café La MaMa productions repeated the same note for the entire phrase "Prepare ye the way of the Lord," except for rising by one whole step on the word "way." The accompaniment had a heavy drumbeat, and the cast added frenzied handclapping.

For the same piece in the Cherry Lane Theatre production, Schwartz wanted to compose something with melodic interest. He had only seen an earlier version of *Godspell* once, at Café La MaMa. "I didn't remember any of the music except I remember that I really liked 'By My Side.' And so there was nothing in my head. I wasn't trying to fix something [that I recalled]. I was trying to solve the problem of—here's the line, 'Prepare ye the way of the Lord' repeated over and over again. What am I going to do about that to make it musically interesting? I wanted to come up with a really memorable tune for that line, which involves some sort of interval skips, etcetera, so that it would really land on the ear and you would remember it. And then it was just a matter of layering vocals on it."

He realized he could expand his melodic options if he let at least one part of the lyric fall on more than one note. "I made it 'Pre-ee-ee rather than 'Pre-pare-ye-the,' and added a lot of melodic jumps."

The song needed to build, over time, into a choral number. Schwartz says, "First of all, it's the statement by John the Baptist, and then the group joins, and as they become more committed and more ecstatic and exhilarated by the experience, then these other vocals come in, so that you get the feeling that they become a choir before your eyes and before your ears." The choral section moves musically into a kind of gospel pop sound that expresses a joyous spirit, anticipating what is to come.

For the transition into this scene, Tebelak specifically wanted David Haskell (as John/Judas) to blow a loud note on the shofar, the traditional ram's horn used as a call to prayer in Jewish holy day ceremonies such as for Rosh Hashanah and Yom Kippur. Suddenly, his note on the horn stops the cacophonous overload and creates a moment of stillness that focuses everyone's attention.

Haskell had to master the shofar, which was not an easy task. "David had a terrible time learning how to do it," remembers music director Stephen Reinhardt. On the cast album, Haskell's blast provides the authentic sound at the beginning of this song.

"Prepare Ye" Context

Schwartz recalls about his collaboration that Tebelak had specific notions for some of the dramatic shifts in the musical. One of those shifts happened between the "Prologue" and "Prepare Ye the Way of the Lord."

Just as *The Wizard of Oz* movie begins with Kansas farm scenes in black and white, so would *Godspell* begin in black and white and suddenly switch into vibrant color, like the color Dorothy discovers as she steps into Oz. Schwartz says, "One thing that John-Michael was very specific about was that he wanted the opening to be the black and white section of the show…. The 'Prologue' is interrupted by the arrival of John the Baptist and then [with 'Prepare Ye'] the whole band comes in and all the colored lights bang on corresponding to the switch in *The Wizard of Oz* movie from black-and-white to Technicolor." Tebelak literally designed the lighting so that all the colored lights would come on during "Prepare Ye," and Schwartz echoed this idea musically.

LYRICS

"Prepare Ye (the Way of the Lord)"

JOHN/JUDAS
  Prepare ye the way of the Lord (4 x)

ALL
  Prepare ye the way of the Lord (4 x)

The Godspell Experience

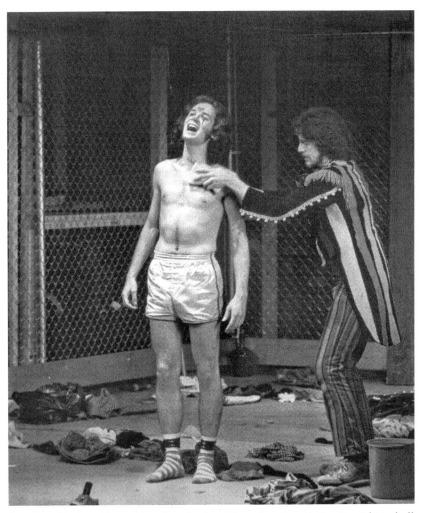

Stephen Nathan (Jesus) begins singing "Save the People" as David Haskell (John/Judas) baptizes him. Cherry Lane Theatre in June 1971. (Photo by Kenn Duncan/©The New York Public Library)

Chapter 19

"Save the People"
Is This What Jesus Wants?

The scene starts with an unusual baptism: Jesus, wearing boxer shorts before dressing in his full costume, approaches the baptizer for the ritual. As can happen in a musical, Jesus breaks into song while he's being sponged with water from John the Baptist's bucket.

At first he sings a rather gentle, folk music-like solo. Baptism over, Jesus grabs a microphone as the piece builds to an assertive choral number with the entire cast.

Schwartz explains that he wrote the music of "Save the People" to follow the Jesus character's emotional arc: "The first verse is just guitar accompanying him and then it grows a little bit, but it's still very acoustic. Then when he starts becoming more of a charismatic figure who is going to draw people to him, the music becomes more electric pop. Suddenly, he picks up the microphone and starts singing into it."

Stephen Nathan remembers the transition to using the microphone in terms of what it communicated to the audience. "To me it was going from that sweet, ethereal, somewhat innocent character to someone who is basically saying, 'Come on now, we've got work to do. Now let's get this show on the road.'"

One reason Stephen Schwartz wrote "Save the People" in folk song style was he knew it would suit actor Stephen Nathan's voice. "I kept the music small enough and contained enough. I knew he had a sweet voice, a folk voice, but a pretty limited range and not much power." Schwartz notes, "It fits the character. Here was this guy who was very simple and unadorned, and the song is unadorned."

"Save the People" is the third song in *Godspell*. In traditional musicals, the second or third musical number is often termed an "I Want" song during which one of the lead characters expresses an unmet desire. This usually sets the main action in motion, as the character seeks to fulfill said desire. When Tebelak selected "Save the People" as Jesus' song here, he probably wasn't thinking about an "I Want" number, but the piece does roughly set up Jesus' wishes as expressed in phrases like, "Man's clouded sun shall brightly rise/and songs be heard instead of sighs/God save the people."

Other performers contribute the refrain "O God save the people," and the piece punctuates its message with a firm rhythm. Paul Shaffer comments from his perspective on the Toronto production, "I thought of 'Save the People' as very theatrical. The cast takes it out to the audience. At one point they plant their feet and look directly out at the audience and sing 'When wilt thou save the people?' and then, bang!, it comes in fast."

Tebelak had selected hymn 496 in the 1940 Episcopal hymnal as a source of lyrics. Lyricist Ebenezer Elliott was a social reformer. His words used in the hymn were first published in 1848 as a song known as "The People's Anthem." His refrain "God save the people!" was a parody of the British national anthem, "God Save the Queen," suggesting that support for ordinary people is the more worthy prayer. Lyric lines like saving "Not thrones and crowns, but men!" seemed to suit Jesus' character in *Godspell*.

What did Jesus want? To protect the ordinary people he had gathered around him; for God to save them from despair and all the problems that come from lack of love. And that sets up the rest of the action of *Godspell*.

LYRICS

"Save the People"

JESUS
When wilt Thou save the people?
O God of mercy, when?
Not kings and lords, but nations
Not thrones and crowns, but men
Flowers of thy heart
O God are they
Let them not pass like weeds away
Their heritage a sunless day
God save the people

Shall crime bring crime forever
Strength aiding still the strong?
Is it Thy will, O Father
That man shall toil for wrong?
No, say Thy mountains
No, say Thy skies
Man's clouded sun shall brightly rise
And songs be heard instead of sighs
God save the people

When wilt Thou save the people
O God of mercy, when?
The people, Lord, the people
Not thrones and crowns, but men
God save the people
For Thine they are
Thy children as Thy angels fair
God save the people from despair
God save the people…

ALL

O, God save the people
God save the people (O, God save the people) (3 x)

When wilt thou save the people
O God of mercy, when?
The people, Lord, the people
Not thrones and crowns, but men
God save the people (save us!)
For Thine they are (for Thine they are)
Thy children as Thy angels fair (O God, save the people)
God save the people (God save the people)
From despair (God save the people)

God save the people (O God, save the people) (3 x)
God save the people
God save the people
God save the people!

Chapter 20

The "Day by Day" Sing-Along

"Day by Day" was *Godspell*'s breakout hit song. Over the years it has not only been presented on the many cast albums, but has been covered by Judy Collins, Andy Williams, the 5th Dimension, Shirley Bassey, Colleen Hewett, and many others.

Stephen Schwartz originally wrote the music with Robin Lamont in mind. The actress had a wholesome appearance and openness—Herb Braha describes her as "The girl-next-door classic." Schwartz and Tebelak appreciated the vocal talent she had displayed while performing at Café La MaMa. "She had this wonderful rich voice," recalls Schwartz. "We both really liked her voice and we wanted to start off with one of the strongest singers in the cast…and it seemed to suit her character. She was the lesson getter of a very early parable where we were going to include 'Day by Day,' so the decision [for Robin] was both contextual and musical."

When Schwartz approached writing music for the six-line stanza of "Day by Day," he believed it should be "deliberately accessible." He wanted an audience to be able to remember it on the first hearing. "The goal was that it be something that by the end of the number the audience could sing along."

Lamont comments, "I took a wonderful musical theater class once where the teacher told us the idea for breaking into song is when words aren't enough anymore. So the song bursts out of feelings that are bigger than words. Stephen created that moment for each one of us. It was a way for each clown to go, 'Oh, I get it.'"

The "Day by Day" moment in the show was where Lamont's character caught on to what Jesus had been teaching. Prior to this scene, clowns acted out parables that referred to making peace with one's brother and forgiveness. Lamont says, "My goal was to try to communicate through the song a sense of 'aha' revelation, the first sense of 'Oh, wait a minute, this isn't just fun and games is it?! I get it!' And then the pleasure of receiving his acknowledgment that, 'Yes, that's right.'"

Paul Shaffer remembers the importance of the song in the context of the show as he experienced it in Toronto: "'Day by Day' was a key point in the show. Not only was it the most well-known song but it had such a strong and simple and beautiful message." His sense was that the show's first few songs had a fast-paced complexity to them, with the philosophers, baptism, and the audience getting comfortable with Jesus in a clown role. "Day by Day" was a turning point—the audience's heart was fully captured and everyone relaxed into the performance.

Most of the lyrics for "Day by Day" are from Richard of Chichester (1197-1253), who was the Bishop of Chichester in the United Kingdom. He was regarded as a saintly man who was canonized by Pope Urban IV in 1262.

Chichester wrote the original version in Latin without the beginning and ending words "day by day." By the time it was published as hymn 429 in the Episcopal hymnal of 1940, it was in English with several rhyming lines:

> *Day by day*
> *Dear Lord, of thee three things I pray:*
> *To see thee more clearly,*
> *Love thee more dearly,*
> *Follow thee more nearly,*
> *Day by day.*

When Schwartz adapted the lyrics for the Cherry Lane Theatre production of *Godspell*, he changed them slightly, removing "of thee" to make it the simpler: "Oh Dear Lord, three things I pray." He also added some repetition.

Musical Nuances

As simple as it is, "Day by Day" has several sections because of what's happening during the song. Schwartz explains, "It started out as the Robin character's statement to Jesus. So it was simple and sincere and there were 'aaahhs' behind it (from the other clowns)." For that section of the song, Schwartz believes he was influenced by songwriter Burt Bacharach. He says, "The beginning is sort of a Burt Bacharachy jazz waltz that has the feel of 'What the World Needs Now' [a Hal David/Burt Bacharach pop hit from the mid 1960s]. Then it goes into the 4/4, which is more straightforward pop."

The harmonic structure is technically called a circle of fifths. For this, Schwartz reflects that he was somewhat unconsciously influenced by folk-rock writers like Janis Ian, or even George Harrison's "My Sweet Lord."

"The harmonic progression is a little unusual," Schwartz explains. "You start in F, then suddenly you're in G for a little while, then you arrive at C major, which happens to be the fifth of F, so you're back to F. So it's a little bit of a circle of fifths journey. Now I can analyze it, but I certainly wasn't thinking of this in any way when I wrote it. I just put the lyric in front of me and started playing along, and this is what happened."

"Day by Day" through Time

Tebelak's way of staging the song was to have each cast member come up with a daily activity they could mime during one or two of the repetitions. Over the years directors have found creative ways to vary what the actors do on stage during the piece, including using American Sign Language gestures for the lyrics, to add an interesting and touching movement for the audience to watch.

Could the song lyrics have been more varied? Schwartz didn't think so. After the show opened, he was questioned about the paucity of lyrics. He recalls, "The publisher Tommy Valando asked me to write more words to it because he thought it had the potential to be a hit, but he felt it could never be a hit with just these six lines. And I just said, 'What can I tell you? That's what the song is. If it's not a hit, it's not a hit.'" The song went on to become one of his all-time most popular pieces.

Lamont suggests several reasons for the song's success: "I think it's like any hit song. It's memorable in its simplicity, it's easy to hum, and it's easy to sing. It's not a simplistic tune at all. Musically, it is complex. But that's Stephen's brilliance; he writes fabulous tunes and that was one of his most fabulous."

LYRICS

"Day by Day"

ROBIN (sings 2 x)
 Day by day
 Day by day
 Oh, dear Lord, three things I pray
 To see Thee more clearly,
 Love Thee more dearly
 Follow Thee more nearly
 Day by day

ALL (sing 4 x; last time with altered ending)
 Day by day
 Day by day
 Oh, dear Lord, three things I pray
 To see Thee more clearly,
 Love Thee more dearly
 Follow Thee more nearly
 Day by day

[Final ending]
 Day by day by day by day
 By day

The Godspell Experience

John-Michael Tebelak holds up the framed Gold record for *Godspell*. Sales of the album were aided by the popularity of the "Day by Day" single. (Photo by Bill Phillips, 1983)

CHAPTER 21

"Learn Your Lessons Well"
A Flexible Song

"Learn Your Lessons Well" is simple and direct, yet performances of it have probably varied more than for any other song in the show, with styles ranging from ukulele-accompanied folk to high-speed rock.

Schwartz pulled the piece out of his creative hat just before previews in 1971. He and Tebelak noticed a section of Act I that seemed long on proverbs and short on music. *Godspell*'s first previews were fast approaching. Tebelak didn't have any hymns on hand to adapt, but Schwartz decided to go ahead and write new lyrics as well as music. He was mainly writing songs in his Manhattan apartment, but he had to work on this song on the fly. "I remember being in the 79th Street subway station, waiting to go down to rehearsal. I was figuring out lyrics for this in my head, and just sort of scribbling them down." Fortunately, the song came quickly.

Schwartz instinctively felt that the new piece could relate to the cautionary tale of Lazarus and Abraham. He explains that the lyric ideas for "Learn Your Lessons Well" came out of what was happening in the previous scene: "Gilmer says, 'If they don't listen to Moses and the prophets, they ain't going to listen to anybody.' And that was where she had to sing, so it was about you should learn your lessons. It was pretty clearly indicated by the foregoing material."

The lyrics are a bit reminiscent of an old fashioned Sunday school lesson. Schwartz set them to music in the style of a 20th century American honky-tonk song.

From Schwartz's standpoint, it seemed easy to sing and remember, but McCormick only had about four days to learn it. She recalls, "I completely panicked to suddenly have a song with the tongue twisters: 'I can see a swath of sinners sittin'...' Steve said, 'I tried to write it easy with a lot of esses.' But I remember going on opening night with that written in my hand."

After McCormick had been performing "Learn Your Lessons Well" in front of an audience for a while, she felt it wasn't charming the audience as much as other numbers, so she and Lamar Alford tried a more comedic approach: McCormick mouthed the words while Alford sang them, only his head remained hidden under a bucket. To the audience it appeared that a huge male voice was coming from her. "We brought the house down, so that's the way it was kept," says McCormick.

Having Alford sing "Learn Your Lessons Well" was so effective that toward the end of the intermission, he came out and sang it again but in a holy roller, religious revival style, while accompanying himself on piano. That, too, pleased the crowds, who were drawn back to their seats with entertainment before Act II officially began.

For the 2011 Broadway revival, actor Telly Leung (with encouragement from the show's director) settled onto the piano bench after intermission and started playing as he would if he was hanging out with friends at a piano bar. After a brief medley of Schwartz tunes, he launched into "Learn Your Lessons Well," holding very long notes and riffing on them, to the audience's delight. Several other cast members joined him, showing off their stunning vocal prowess. *The Godspell* New Broadway Cast album records their approach to the intermission version as a bonus track titled, "Learn Your Lessons Well (after hours)." Leung comments, "I always like to think of it as 'my idea of heaven.' I love theater. I love Broadway. I love show tunes. My idea of heaven is a piano bar, like Marie's Crisis or The Duplex, where it's an endless night of gathering around the piano, drinking cocktails, and singing songs with good friends."

LYRICS

"Learn Your Lessons Well"

GILMER

I can see a swath of sinners sittin' yonder
 And they're actin' like a pack of fools
 Gazing into space, they let their minds wander
 'stead of studyin' the good Lord's rules
 You better pay attention
 Build your comprehension
 There's gonna be a quiz at your ascension
 Not to mention any threat of hell
 But if you're smart, you'll learn your lessons well.

Ev'ry bright description of the Promised Land meant
You can reach it if you keep alert
Learning every line and every last commandment
May not help you, but it couldn't hurt
First you gotta read 'em
Then you gotta heed 'em
You never know when you're gonna need 'em
Just as old Elijah said to Jezebel:
You better start to learn your lessons well!

[New version]
JESUS: The lamp...
OTHERS: ... lamp…..lamp…
JESUS: ...of the body...
OTHERS:…body, body….
JESUS: Is the eye.
OTHERS: …eye…eye…eye…eye…eye…
JESUS: If your eye…
OTHERS: …eye…eye… eye…

The Godspell Experience

JESUS: ...is bad...
OTHERS: ...baddy...baddy...
JESUS: ...your whole body will be darkness.
OTHERS: ...whole body will be darkness-ness-ness-ness-ness-ness...
JESUS: And if darkness is all around....
OTHERS: Darkness all around....
JESUS: ...your soul....
OTHERS: ...soul...soul...soul...
JESUS: ...will be doubly unbright.
OTHERS: ....doubly unbright...
JESUS: But...
OTHERS: ...but...but...but...
JESUS: ...if your eye...
OTHERS: ...eye is sound...sound...
JESUS: ...your whole...
OTHERS: ... whole...
JESUS: ...body will be...
OTHERS: ...body will be...
JESUS: ...filled with light.
OTHERS: ...with light...
JESUS: Your whole body will be filled with light.
OTHERS: ...whole body will be filled with light.
JESUS: Your whole body will be filled......
OTHERS: ...filled, filled, filled, filled, filled,
Filled, filled, filled, filled, filled,
Filled, filled, filled, filled, filled...
JESUS: With light.
OTHERS: ...light, light, light, light, light, light, light, light,
Light, light, light, light, light, light..

[GILMER repeats her previous verse.]

New Music for the Lamp of the Body

Until recently, the song's two verses had been separated by a spoken section that was a variation of Matthew 6:22-23. "The lamp of the body is the eye. If therefore your eye is good, your whole body will be full of light. But if your eye is bad, your whole body will be full of darkness. If therefore the light that is in you is darkness, how great is that darkness!" (From the King James version.)

Then, while preparing for a Broadway revival scheduled for 2008 (and later cancelled), the show's director asked for a bigger musical number. Schwartz wrote music for the "lamp of the body" section so that it became a bridge for the song. He rewrote the bridge for the 2011 Broadway revival where it was staged in darkness while actors danced with tiny, flickering, battery-operated candle lights. The effect was like fireflies on a summer night. The new music can be heard on the revival's cast album.

The Godspell Experience

Stephen Schwartz wrote out new music for the bridge section of "Learn Your Lessons Well." It was recorded on the Broadway revival cast album. This music is courtesy of Stephen Schwartz, who holds the copyright.

"Learn Your Lessons Well"

The Godspell Experience

ABOVE: Original *Godspell* cast members gather around Gilmer McCormick who leads "Learn Your Lessons Well." (Photo by Martha Swope/©The New York Public Library). BELOW: Telly Leung performs a piano bar version of "Learn Your Lessons Well" after intermission at the Circle in the Square Theatre during the Broadway revival. (Photo by Jeremy Daniel)

CHAPTER 22

Bless the Lord My Burst of Energy

When Schwartz reviewed the song sequence for *Godspell*, he decided it needed an energy burst in the middle of Act I to help sustain the show's momentum. "We needed that big musical number that would get a big hand, basically stop the show, and just pick up the energy musically," he comments. "I was very clear that that's what I was trying to accomplish. And I basically used my summer stock experience for how to build a number."

The original "Bless the Lord" for Carnegie and La MaMa was an up-tempo blues/rock number performed by the whole cast with a heavy electronic organ accompaniment and percussion. As with most of the other *Godspell* songs, Schwartz wanted his version to be led by one really strong singer and to have some sense of development as the song progressed.

"Bless the Lord" is rhythmically varied, but the shifts weren't something that Schwartz mentally calculated in advance. Rather, they emerged spontaneously as he brought to mind the work of singer-songwriter Laura Nyro. He says, "'O bless the Lord my soul' is a very celebratory idea and I always found Laura Nyro's music so exciting."

Nyro was Schwartz's contemporary, born about six months before him in 1947. Her father was a jazz trumpet player. For her own songwriting she drew from diverse influences such as John Coltrane and Bob Dylan. Her songs became top 40 pop hits in the 1960s when covered by groups like Blood, Sweat, and Tears ("And When I Die"), the 5th Dimension ("Wedding Bell Blues"; "Stoned Soul Picnic"), and Three Dog Night ("Eli's Comin'").

Once described as having a three octave range of emotions, Nyro would invest her feelings in unusual chord combinations and shifting rhythms—something Schwartz hadn't heard much of before listening to her. He was enamored of her combinations of piano chords for the left and right hands. "All of a sudden she would do G over A [instead of G over G]." He also liked the way she broke the mold in her rhythms. He comments, "Pop music was about hitting a groove and absolutely sticking with it, and she did really radical things," such as in "Save the Country," and "Eli's Comin'," two pieces that particularly inspired the music of *Godspell*.

About the music, Paul Shaffer suggests a reason that the energy and speed rev up over the course of the song. In older gospel music, a standard trick was to speed up the song tempo over time, and then include a shout chorus toward the end; then the preacher, leading the song, could just go wild. Laura Nyro seems to have borrowed the style for the climax for songs like "Eli's Comin'", and then Schwartz took his inspiration from her.

Michael Holland, who orchestrated the Broadway revival score for *Godspell*, notes that this piece has three different musical moods: "The first feel is like a shuffle that accompanies the verse. The choruses go into a four-on-the-floor rock beat. Then, at the end, it does a gospel music turn."

"Bless the Lord" is one of the most vocally demanding pieces of the show. It requires the talents of someone like Joanne Jonas from the original production or Lindsay Mendez from the 2011 Broadway revival.

Jonas contributed the high note on the word "soul" toward the end of the piece that is heard on some of the recordings. "It wasn't written that way," she recalls. "It was written another way but quite spontaneously, excited by the sheer joy of appreciation I felt in the gifts I was getting, I just went up into my upper range." It serves as an expression of transformation for the character Joanne.

Joanne and company sing "Bless the Lord" following a parable from Luke 12:16-20 about a wealthy landowner whose crops are abundant. In the parable, this landowner decides he will build bigger storehouses, but then God calls to him and says he is a fool, for tomorrow he will die. Right after the song, the parable lesson is completed when Jesus says, "Therefore I bid you: Put away anxious thoughts of food and clothes to cover your body."

"Bless the Lord" fits right in. Lyric lines like "He clothes thee with his love" emphasize the benefit of grace over material accumulation.

Tebelak had found hymn 293, dated 1819 and attributed to British poet James Montgomery. Montgomery had adapted Psalm 103 into rhyming lyrics.

LYRICS

"Bless the Lord"

JOANNE
O bless the Lord, my soul
His grace to thee proclaim
And all that is within me join
To bless his holy name
Oh, yeah

O bless the Lord my soul
His mercies bear in mind
Forget not all his benefits
The Lord to thee is kind

JOANNE AND GIRLS
He will not always chide
He will with patience wait

His wrath is ever slow to rise...

WOMEN/MEN
And ready to abate.../O bless the Lord
And ready to abate.../ O bless the Lord
And ready to .../ O bless the Lord
And ready to .../and ready to...

JOANNE
And ready to abate!
Oh, yeah!

ALL
He pardons all thy sins
Prolongs thy feeble breath
He healeth thine infirmities...

JOANNE
And ransoms thee from death!

WOMEN
O bless the Lord my soul...

JOANNE
Oh, yeah!

MEN
O bless the Lord my soul...

ALL
He clothes thee with His love
Upholds thee with His truth
And like the eagle He renews...

JOANNE
The vigor of thy youth!

JOANNE AND WOMEN
Then bless his holy name
Whose grace hath made thee whole

Whose loving kindness crowns thy days...

WOMEN/MEN
O bless the Lord, my soul/O bless the Lord
O bless the Lord, my soul/O bless the Lord

JOANNE
O bless the Lord

WOMEN
O bless the Lord my soul

MEN
O bless the Lord my soul

JOANNE
O bless the Lord my soul!

ALL
O bless the Lord my soul! (etc.)

JOANNE
Oh bless the Lord...

ALL
O bless the Lord my soul

JOANNE
Bless the Lord my soul!

The Godspell Experience

ABOVE: Lindsay Mendez and the Broadway revival cast of *Godspell* perform "Bless the Lord" at the Circle in the Square in 2011. (Photo by Jeremy Daniel) BELOW: Whitney Players *Godspell Jr.* cast sings "Bless the Lord" in Hamden, Connecticut, March, 2013. From left to right: Clare Kaye, Grace McGovern, Stella DeAngelis, Mia Laguna. (Photo by Kami Parisella)

Chapter 23

"All for the Best"
The Friendship Duet

"All for the Best" is *Godspell*'s homage to vaudeville soft-shoe duet routines of the past, using a fresh approach that always seems to please a crowd. The new spin is not only the unexpected coupling of Jesus and Judas in the routine, but also the opposite values expressed in both the music and the lyrics.

Why include a duet at all at this point in the show? Schwartz remembers suggesting to John-Michael Tebelak that Jesus and Judas needed to connect emotionally in order to make the show work dramatically. He knew that having Jesus and Judas perform a piece like this together would layer in a message about their relationship, and be funny to boot.

Schwartz comments, "I hadn't been brought up Christian, and so I was not someone coming in with reverence. I was coming in thinking if you're going to tell this story, how do you make it work? How do you actually care about these people if you don't come in already caring about them? Since the central personal relationship was for Jesus and Judas, I said, 'John-Michael, if Judas is going to betray Jesus in the second act, you have to see that they're friends and allies in the first act, so they need to do a musical number together.' He agreed."

Schwartz had another dramaturgical reason for this type of number. For an audience to admire a teacher in a musical, it wasn't enough that the character spoke wisely. He must also amuse and delight. "A man who does a soft-shoe, tells jokes, and cheers people up when they are depressed" captures our hearts.

The Godspell Experience

Contrast in Music

The feel and musical accompaniment for the piece is reminiscent of the vaudeville period. But for the structure of the piece, Schwartz found inspiration in a song that he heard while growing up in the 1950s: Irving Berlin's "You're Just in Love" from *Call Me Madam*. He explains: "A man sings, 'I hear music and there's no one there,' then Ethel Merman sings, 'You don't need analyzing,' and then they sing the two sections simultaneously. I loved it." Schwartz notes that Berlin's "Old Fashioned Wedding" from *Annie Get Your Gun* also employs this contrapuntal device. So while writing the "All for the Best" duet for *Godspell*, Schwartz decided to pay homage to Berlin by creating his own dual melody lines.

The second half of the song is performed as rapid-fire patter—a style the composer admired in Rossini's famous Figaro aria from *The Barber of Seville*, and similar works. By using it in *Godspell*, he enhanced the comedic value of the moment.

Context and Contrast in Lyrics

In "All for the Best," the lyrics playfully duel with each other, in part because of the context of the song.

Leading up to the song, Jesus has offered uplifting spiritual messages in the Beatitudes. Then Judas darkens the mood with a line from Matthew 5:11 that presages traumatic times to come: Blessed are you, when all men shall revile you and persecute you…. Schwartz comments, "It is too soon for the other disciples to know this, so Jesus lightens the mood again and distracts them with his soft-shoe routine."

The song begins after Jesus completes the Beatitudes with the line: "Rejoice and be exceedingly glad, because great is your reward in the kingdom of heaven (Matthew 5:12). This line from Matthew inspired the Jesus lyrics. Schwartz explains that the Jesus character presents a realistic or sympathetic view of life's woes and offers something positive at the end. Judas does the opposite.

> *"By having Jesus and Judas be at odds with one another philosophically in the song's lyrics, and yet performing and dancing together as a team, it helps to illustrate the paradox in their relationship in a way dialogue never could."*
> — Stephen Schwartz

"All for the Best" is a "list" song, like Cole Porter's "You're the Top." Jesus' list includes your wife crying, olive tree dying, temples graying, and so on. By contrast, Judas' list mentions making mountains of money and houses on the street where it's sunny.

Schwartz describes this as Judas' cynical counterpoint. Only those who are "the best" in society's view get the good life. Schwartz explains, "Judas is talking about how life is on earth, and how unfair it is. The lyric is a little confusing, admittedly, but what I tried to do was have him say that the rich people and the lucky get all the stuff, and they're the best at this, best in town. Therefore, at the end when he says 'It's all for the best,' he's referring to them." It presents the image of the self-interested "best" hanging onto their mountains of money without a care for the rest of humanity.

Actor Bob Garrett, who performed the John/Judas role for a while in the New York City production, kept these divergent perspectives on life in mind. "Ultimately, the intention was, 'Let's just agree to disagree at this point, and have fun.' And that's basically what they do. They agree to disagree until ultimately they don't. And that was my concept for it."

A Little Story about the "All for the Best" Dance

After *Godspell* had been running in New York with Stephen Nathan and David Haskell, new productions opened around the country. Nathan remembers that he was called to play Jesus in the ongoing San Francisco production. "I had a day to get into the show. So the cast was called in and we were doing a run-through. I did 'All for the Best' and at the end, everyone said that was hilarious. And the rehearsal stopped and the stage manager said, 'That was a lot of fun, now let's do it again, and do it the way you're really going to do it in the show tonight.' I said, 'That's it, that's how I dance. That's as good as it gets.' I guess some of the productions had people who were terrific dancers but I always did my little goofy dance."

LYRICS

"All for the Best"

JESUS
When you feel sad
Or under a curse
Your life is bad
Your prospects are worse ...
Your wife is sighing, crying,
And your olive tree is dying
Temples are graying
And teeth are decaying
And creditors weighing your purse ...
Your mood and your robe
Are both a deep blue
You'd bet that Job
Had nothing on you
Don't forget that
When you get to heaven you'll be blest
Yes, it's all for the best

"All for the Best"

JUDAS
 Some men are born to live at ease
 Doing what they please
 Richer than the bees are in honey
 Never growing old
 Never feeling cold
 Pulling pots of gold from thin air
 The best in ev'ry town
 Best at shaking down
 Best at making mountains of money --
 They can't take it with them
 But what do they care?
 They get the center of the meat
 Cushions on the seat
 Houses on a street where it's sunny
 Summers at the sea
 Winters warm and free
 All of this, and we get the rest
 But who is the land for?
 The sun and the sand for?
 You guessed --
 It's all for the best

JESUS AND JUDAS (Jesus sings his verse again while Judas sings his at the same time. Then there's a spoken section about the speck of sawdust.)

ALL: (The cast joins JESUS AND JUDAS in singing the two versions simultaneously. The final "It's all for the best" is replaced by what follows:)

ALL
 Yes, it's all for the….

JESUS
 You must never be distressed! [spoken]

ALL EXCEPT JESUS AND JUDAS
 Yes, it's all for the….

The Godspell Experience

JESUS
　All your wrongs will be redressed! [spoken]

ALL
　Yes, it's all for the….

JUDAS
　Someone's got to be oppressed! [spoken]

ALL
　Yes, it's all for the best!

Bart Braverman (Judas) and Andy Rohrer (Jesus) perform a soft-shoe dance while singing "All for the Best." (Photo by Sam Freed)

Chapter 24
"All Good Gifts"
Godspell's Thanksgiving

"All Good Gifts" fits into the show's storyline after an enactment of the Parable of the Seed from the Gospel of Mark chapter four. There's a natural segue into the song with its lyric about scattering seeds on newly plowed land.

For the Cherry Lane Theatre production, "All Good Gifts" was Lamar Alford's song. Lamar's character emerged from the seed parable, where he was rather slow on waking up to what was happening around him and had to be poked.

"Lamar as a person was the brightest, funniest, fastest person in the world," Peggy Gordon comments. "But he chose a clown persona that was the opposite." His rationale was that his clown's moment of revelation came so late in Act I, during his pantomime of the seed in good soil. "He finally figures out what's happening, and Stephen Nathan would hand him the microphone and he would sing, 'All Good Gifts'—it was such a beautiful moment," she recalls.

Song Development

When Tebelak was first piecing together the material for *Godspell*, he remembered this harvest song in the Episcopal hymnal that is sometimes performed at Thanksgiving services with other music. For the first version of the score, Duane Bolick wrote a choral ballad to go with the words. When Schwartz prepared his version of the music, also a choral ballad, he knew that Lamar Alford had the vocal range to sing the part he was composing for him.

Hymn 138, "We Plow the Fields, and Scatter," started as a German poem written by Matthias Claudius. This "Wir pflügen und wir streuen" was published in 1782. When Jane Montgomery Campbell translated it in the 19th century, she included three verses.

In his adaptation, Schwartz replaced the second verse with an instrumental break. He asked Jeffrey Mylett to play his recorder live on stage rather than have a band member perform it. The quiet recorder music provided the ideal background accompaniment for an essential piece of spoken text.

Rhythmically speaking, Schwartz says that the song is an amalgamation of James Taylor's 1970 hit ballad "Fire and Rain" and Elton John's "Your Song." Some of the chords are also similar and have a bit of a Protestant church hymn feeling that Schwartz associates with one aspect of James Taylor's style.

The Gifts of "All Good Gifts"

The composer is pleased with how "All Good Gifts" turned out. He once commented, "The song that struck home the most was 'All Good Gifts.' Musically, I hooked into something very heartfelt for me. It's the *Godspell* song for which I have the most passion."

"The song has so many levels," comments Bill Thomas, who played Lamar at the Promenade Theatre. "It's a love song to God that becomes a big choral power ballad, yet also remains a real, personal moment between the gentle, clumsy Lamar and Jesus."

For Thomas, it was especially meaningful that this was Lamar's song . "As I look back on 'All Good Gifts' I realize now that it is the Lamar character who is the most meek, who probably has the least dialogue in the show, nevertheless has the song that ushers in the company's collective mature discovery of who Jesus is. I replaced the original 'Lamar'—Lamar Alford in the New York Company. I thrilled to his full operatic delivery. I grew up singing in a little church in Columbus, Ohio. For me, delivering 'All Good Gifts' on the New York stage was very emotional. As I said, the largely silent character, Lamar, gave voice to the collective growing consciousness. Lamar's 'aha' had to start from his timidity. Yes, there are those wonderful big notes that come, soaring over the ensemble, but the beginning is so naked, so exposed, so vulnerable, that many nights it was difficult not to cry. Harpo got to speak."

The song is often performed as an expression of gratitude out of context of the musical on special occasions such as Thanksgiving celebrations. It has been a favorite for actors from *Godspell* casts who have met up in later years. Paul Kreppel says, "If someone passed away or if we had a reunion or a gathering, we'd hold hands and walk around in a circle singing 'All Good Gifts.'"

Additional Verses

An actor once wrote to Stephen Schwartz about using additional hymn verses. He asked, "Those who have looked up the original version or found it in their hymnals have noticed that there is an unused second verse that is replaced in the script by the recorder solo and 'treasures in heaven' monologue. I wish to know if Mr. Schwartz was even aware of this set of lyrics and also if these may be included in a future *Godspell* licensing package for potential use by more faith-based groups aiming to perform this musical."

Schwartz answered, "Virtually all the Episcopal hymns used in *Godspell* have additional verses that were not used in the show. The length of the songs and the verses to be used were decided upon by John-Michael Tebelak and myself, based on what we thought would work best for the show. Therefore, I wouldn't want, nor would I authorize, any changes to lyrics used within a production of the show.

"In 'All Good Gifts,' the instrumental accompaniment gives time for Jesus to do his 'Don't store up your treasures …' monologue, which is an important part of the content of *Godspell*. However, for performances of the song outside the context of the show (in a concert or church, for instance), I actually wouldn't object to the performers singing the additional lyrics you cite in place of the instrumental, as long as the arrangement was interesting enough that the tune didn't seem redundant…."

LYRICS

"All Good Gifts"

LAMAR
We plow the fields and scatter
The good seed on the land
But it is fed and watered
By God's almighty hand
He sends the snow in winter
The warmth to swell the grain
The breezes and the sunshine
And soft, refreshing rain …

All good gifts around us
Are sent from heaven above
So thank the Lord, O thank the Lord
For all his love…

JESUS (spoken)
So don't store up your treasure on earth, where it grows rusty and moth-eaten, and thieves break in to steal it. No, store up your treasure in Heaven, where there is no moth and no rust and no thief. For where your treasure is, there will your heart be also.

ALL (except JESUS)
We thank Thee then, O Father,
For all things bright and good
The seed time and the harvest
Our life, our health, our food
No gifts have we to offer
For all Thy love imparts
But that which Thou desirest:
Our humble thankful hearts ...

ALL WITH JESUS
All good gifts around us
Are sent from heaven above
So thank the Lord, O thank the Lord
For all his love ...

LAMAR (while others repeat the chorus)
I really want to thank you, Lord
I want to thank you, Lord
Thank you for all of your love
I want to thank you, Lord
I want to thank you, Lord
O, thank you, Lord

The Godspell Experience

The original cast of *Godspell* performs "All Good Gifts" at the Cherry Lane Theatre. Jeffrey Mylett sits in front holding his recorder that he plays during the song's instrumental breaks. Stephen Nathan (Jesus) is on the far right, observing. Front row behind Mylett, from left: Robin Lamont, Gilmer McCormick, Peggy Gordon, Sonia Manzano. Second row: David Haskell. Third row, from left: Joanne Jonas, Lamar Alford, Herb Braha. (Photo by Kenn Duncan/©The New York Public Library).

CHAPTER 25

"Light of the World" Rhymes for Matthew 5:13-16

To generate song lyric lines for "Light of the World," Stephen Schwartz adapted an unrhymed passage from Matthew 5:13-16 that Tebelak had included in the early script. In the Matthew text, for example, Schwartz read the line: "But if the salt has lost its flavor, what can make it salty again?" He transformed the expression with rhythm and rhyme: "If that salt has lost its flavor, it ain't got much in its favor."

The *Godspell* movie plays off of some of the visual images in the lyrics. "Light of the World" is performed on a tugboat as it streams toward the Statue of Liberty. When Gilmer McCormick sings the line about salty flavor, the camera captures her tasting and rejecting a bit of harbor water. When Robin Lamont sings "the tallest candlestick ain't much good without a wick," the audience sees a silhouette of Robin with Lady Liberty in the background holding her torch.

In the stage production, this musical number follows the parable of the Prodigal Son that is narrated and acted out by Herb and several others. After a mini-rap, the Herb clown begins "Light of the World," usually in a speak-sing style on the order of Rex Harrison's song performance in *My Fair Lady*. Schwartz wrote it that way specifically for Herb Braha, who wasn't a singer.

Musically, "Light of the World" is a mix of styles. To launch into the piece, Schwartz took inspiration from the opening chords of The Mamas and the Papas song, "Gemini Childe." Stephen Reinhardt comments about the music, "'Light of the World' is a rock 'n' roll blues song [until] you get to the break 'let your light so shine.' That gets into more of a pop showtune kind of thing, which at the time was a new genre."

The song is structured in the call-and-response format of a joyful gospel number, with Herb, Jeffrey, Robin, and Peggy each performing one of the "calls." At Café La MaMa, this section of the show was a spoken rhythmic group number, with Stephen Nathan rapping the lead. Peggy Gordon notes that for the Cherry Lane Theatre version, "Steve Schwartz reconceived it as a musical number with Jeffrey, Robin and I each singing lead because we could wail!"

For the 2011 Broadway revival, rather than divide up the "call" lines, the director gave the entire song to their Herb clown, George Salazar, a talented vocalist. This allowed for the other actors to sing in the aisles while Salazar led the song from the stage. They took advantage of the theater-in-the-round style venue. "For the whole first act we were surrounded by the audience," Salazar explains. "At the end of that, during 'Light of the World,' we tried to surround them and then invite them on stage to become one with us."

In Salazar's mind the "you" in "You are the light of the world" was the audience. "The audience had watched us perform the lessons and parables, and at that point we were able to turn it around and say you're all with us on this journey."

For Salazar, as for other actors, the message of this song and other parts of the show impacted his life. "You can't say these words, you can't sing these songs, and you can't tell these stories and not be affected by them. Through doing *Godspell* I realized the themes are universal: be respectful to your fellow man, lend a helping hand, be a light in the world, and be a source of light for other people… My life has been better for it."

LYRICS

"Light of the World"

HERB (To audience)
 You are the light of the world!

ALL
 You are the light of the world

HERB
 But if that light's under a bushel
 It's lost something kind of crucial

ALL
 You've gotta stay bright
 To be the light of the world

PEGGY
 You are the salt of the earth

ALL
 You are the salt of the earth

PEGGY
 But if that salt has lost its flavor
 It ain't got much in its favor

ALL
 You can't have that fault and be the salt of the earth
 So let your light so shine before men
 Let your light so shine
 So that they might know some kindness again
 We all need help to feel fine

JUDAS (To audience)
 Let's have some wine!

JEFFREY
 You are the city of God

ALL
You are the city of God

JEFFREY
But if that city's on a hill
It's kinda hard to hide it well

ALL
You gotta stay pretty in the city of God
So let your light so shine before men
Let your light so shine
So that they might know some kindness again
We all need help to feel fine
Let's have some wine!

ROBIN
You are the light of the world

ALL
You are the light of the world

ROBIN
But the tallest candlestick
Ain't much good without a wick

ALL
You gotta live right to be the light of the world

"Light of the World" Leading into Intermission

"Light of the World" comes just before intermission, when the audience is invited to join the community, literally. In many productions, the actors welcome their audience onto the stage to share wine or grape juice with them before they go off for a break.

The tradition of sharing food and/or drink during *Godspell* intermissions started with the first Off-Broadway production. Robin Lamont recalls, "In the original company we always served a little bit of Matzo and real wine. Joe Beruh would spring for a jug of Gallo wine once a week and we would pour it out into little tiny cups. I always enjoyed intermission a lot, both because I got to drink a couple of little cups of wine and because it was fun. We [cast members] didn't always stay out the entire time. It was up to us when we wanted to go backstage and freshen up or stay on stage the whole time and talk to people."

There is usually some music in the air at this time. Schwartz explains, "One of the concepts for *Godspell* for me was that there was no finite moment where you took your intermission; you just leak in and out of it. You couldn't actually say, 'Oh, this is the end of Act One and this is the beginning of Act Two,' rather that it was sort of all going on, and therefore 'Light of the World' ended with this jam session as the audience was leaving. Meanwhile, the band continued to play and the audience was invited on stage for wine or grape juice. And again, after intermission, the cast just started to do some version of 'Learn Your Lessons Well' and we sort of leaked out of intermission into the second act."

The Godspell Experience

Sonia Manzano sang "Turn Back, O Man" in the Cherry Lane Theatre production of *Godspell* and on the first cast album. This photograph is from the costume review at Carnegie Mellon University the previous fall.

Chapter 26
"Turn Back, O Man"
An Invitation to Act II

For the student production of *Godspell* in 1970, Tebelak had inserted the "Turn Back, O Man" lyrics from Episcopal hymn 536 in the middle of his first script. After intermission, Robin Lamont, with her long straight hair and hearty voice, belted this minor key number as if was a 1960s protest song. Bob Ari sang harmony.

When John-Michael Tebelak and Stephen Schwartz met to discuss song placements, they realized that "Turn Back, O Man" was, in fact, an ideal second act opener. By using it at the top of Act II, the song would emphasize the contrast between, as Schwartz phrases it, the "slightly ribald and innocent fun" of Act I and Jesus' mood when facing his demise.

Hymn writer Clifford Bax originally wrote the piece in response to World War I. It was first published in 1919.

In Schwartz's recollection, this is the first piece he wrote for the show; he had in mind Sonia Manzano's performance at La MaMa when he composed it. He limited the melodic range to suit Manzano's voice and also styled it to suit her on-stage persona. When she performed at Café La MaMa, Schwartz noted her approach as a funny vixen. It reminded him of Mae West from 1930s movies, as when she delivered her notorious one-liner from *She Done Him Wrong*, "Why don't you come up sometime 'n see me?" (The line is often misquoted as "Why don't you come up and see me sometime?") Only Manzano's version was faux sexy rather than authentically seductive.

Schwartz had accompanied silent films in college and knew how to create a honky-tonk sound. For "Turn Back, O Man" he developed a vampy tune that might remind audiences of early films or vaudeville halls. "It's what I call hootchy-kootchy music," Schwartz says.

Manzano learned the piece, and for her performance at the Cherry Lane Theatre, she would do a fake strip tease. "I would do this seductive thing of peeling off my stocking, only it wasn't a stocking, it was a sweat sock." Underneath one sweat sock was another sock, which added to the humor of the situation.

She remembers being inspired by a specific Charlie Chaplin scene. "When he eats a shoe in the movie *Goldrush*, he eats it as if it was filet mignon and spaghetti, and that's why it's so funny. He's acting as if it's a fancy meal. So if I treated a sweat sock as if it was a silk stocking, it was the same thing. So that's how I transposed it."

Manzano sauntered down the center aisle as she sang, making up asides as she went along, on the order of "Whatcha doin' after the show?" or "Can ya see from where you're sittin'?"

Before Act II she would find out from the box office who was in the audience and sometimes keep them in mind for her ad libs. Once, when Leonard Bernstein was attending the show, she came up to him and said seductively, "When you're a Jet, you're a Jet all the way," a lyric line from the maestro's musical *West Side Story*.

The song includes a solemn section with lyrics from Clifford Bax's hymn. *Godspell*'s writers also decided to have Jesus sing the part that didn't seem to fit with Manzano's character. Schwartz comments, "Thus he sings a more serious third verse of the song ['Earth shall be fair...'], then gets caught up in a little of the fun. But as soon as the song finishes, he quiets the rest of the celebrating cast members and tells them, 'This is the beginning.' And we are into the second act."

LYRICS

"Turn Back, O Man"

SONIA
Turn back, O man
Forswear thy foolish ways
Old now is earth, and none may count her days
Da-da-da-da-da
Yet thou, her child
Whose head is crowned with flame
Still wilt not hear thine inner God proclaim:
Turn back, O man
Turn back, O man
Turn back, O man
Forswear thy foolish ways

Earth might be fair
And all men glad and wise
Age after age their tragic empires rise
Da da da da da
Built while they dream
And in that dreaming weep:
Would man but wake from out his haunted sleep
Turn back, O man
Turn back, O man
Turn back, O man
Forswear thy foolish ways...

JESUS
Earth shall be fair
And all her people one
Not till that hour shall God's whole will be done
Now, even now
Once more from earth to sky
Peals forth in joy man's old, undaunted cry

Earth shall be fair
And all her people one…

ALL
Turn back, O man
Forswear thy foolish ways
Old now is earth and none may count her days …

SONIA
Da da da da da …

ALL
Yet thou, her child
Whose head is crowned with flame
Still wilt not hear thine inner God proclaim
Turn back, O man
Turn back, O man
Turn back, O man
Forswear thy foolish ways

Chapter 27

"Alas for You"
Song of Frustration

Early in Act II, Jesus sings the dramatic piece "Alas for You." Tebelak's original concept for the scene was for the actor playing Jesus to orate a passage from Matthew 23:13-37 that depicts Jesus' annoyance at hypocritical behavior of leaders of his day.

In the first rehearsals of *The Godspell* at Carnegie, Andy Rohrer memorized and delivered that monologue. "It was a horribly long speech that John-Michael insisted on," he recalls. "And that cost me my voice. It went on for five minutes while other cast members were just sitting around. It was really bad. That's why I say John-Michael did not have a lot of theatrical chops. He let it sit right there. He somehow thought one voice could carry this five-minute speech to some great oratorical climax. It wasn't possible."

When Schwartz saw the performance at Café La MaMa and met with Tebelak, he said, "I think I can musicalize that." Shortly thereafter he began adapting text from the Bible.

Along with a rhyming dictionary, he kept a blue hardcover edition of the King James Version near his piano. He says, "I remember sitting with the Bible and going through that section and turning it into lyrics." He found passages in Matthew in non-rhyming sentences, like "Woe unto you, scribes and Pharisees, hypocrites! for ye compass sea and land to make one proselyte, and when he is made, ye make him twofold more the child of hell than yourselves." (Matthew 23:15)

Schwartz set up new rhythms, rhymes, and phrases. "All I did was take what was there, paraphrase it, and make it singable," he says.

Stephen Nathan, who had been required to perform the long speech version at La MaMa, says, "I was very happy that it became a song!"

A Musical Rant

Dramatists like Schwartz love characters who can rant. "I think anger is very theatrical," he comments. Among the most popular songs of Schwartz's career have been these outburst pieces. He wrote "West End Avenue" for *The Magic Show,* "Lost in the Wilderness" for *Children of Eden,* and "No Good Deed" for *Wicked*—all songs that vent. The singer describes his or her internal tension while the driving rhythms of the music evoke frustration.

The scene with "Alas for You" was perfect for this type of piece. It was a moment when Jesus' emotions rose so much that, in a musical, it would be natural for him to sing. Schwartz says, "If you were adapting a play into a musical, that was an obvious place for musicalization. It was a very dramatic scene; to me, as a musical theater person, it's an obligatory number." He adds, "It's the most 'musical theater' of the songs in the show, although it's orchestrated for a rock band." Writing it gave him a chance to use his college acting training; he stepped into the character to feel what he was feeling, and tried to express that through music.

Schwartz likes to associate this scene with the Biblical story about driving the money changers from the temple described slightly earlier in Matthew (chapter 21:12). "I felt this [section of the musical] was the place where Jesus got angry and you saw the revolutionary that he could have been if that's what he chose to be. Remember, this was the time just after the Vietnam War protests, the Students for a Democratic Society and the yuppies, and people sitting in at universities and throwing desks out windows, really uprising against the establishment. And this is him being that."

Schwartz took inspiration for the music from one of his favorite composers, Leonard Bernstein. Schwartz comments, "'Alas for You' is very pianistic, very Leonard Bernstein, because of its shifting rhythms."

Reflecting on the lyrics of this piece forty years after he wrote it, Schwartz notes: "'Alas for You' is also one of the songs that betray my youngness as a lyricist. I would never make a bad pun like 'You cannot escape being devil's food' in an impassioned song like this now."

> *"I loved that song. It was one of my favorite things to do in the show. I loved belting it out. It was so strong.... I always loved taking a character who was a fool and then all of a sudden you saw this other side of him where he was angry and real and in agony himself."*
>
> —Stephen Nathan

LYRICS

"Alas for You"

JESUS
Alas, alas for you
Lawyers and Pharisees
Hypocrites that you be
Searching for souls and fools to forsake them
You travel the land, you scour the sea
Then when you've got your converts, you make them
Twice as fit for hell
As you are yourselves

Alas, alas for you

Lawyers and Pharisees
Hypocrites that you are
Sure that the kingdom of heaven awaits you
You will not venture half so far
Other men who might enter the gates you
Keep from passing through
Drag them down with you

You snakes, you viper's brood
You cannot escape being devil's food
I send you prophets and I send you preachers
Sages in rages and ages of teachers
Nothing can mar your mood

Alas, alas for you
Lawyers and Pharisees
Hypocrites to a man
Sons of the dogs who murdered the prophets
Finishing off what your fathers began
You don't have time to scorn or to scoff, it's
Getting very late
Vengeance doesn't wait

You snakes, you viper's brood
You cannot escape being devil's food
I send you prophets and I send you preachers
Sages in rages and ages of teachers
Nothing can mar your mood…

Blind guides! Blind fools!
The blood you've spilt
On you will fall
This nation, this generation
Shall bear the guilt
Of it all!

Alas, alas, alas
For you
Blind fools!

CHAPTER 28

"By My Side"
Songwriters and the Pebble "Dare"

Interestingly enough, "By My Side" fits into Act II of *Godspell* as if it was developed for the show, and yet it was written by Jay Hamburger (lyrics) and Peggy Gordon (music) for an entirely different play many years earlier. That the song suits the new usage perfectly is a testament to the poetical power of the lyrics, the emotional strength of the music, and the wisdom of the song placement. It provides a haunting, folk song-like moment within the second act of the show. The song's development is a complex tale that illuminates its meaning and power.

Song Development

Jay Hamburger, the son of two New Yorker magazine journalists, recognized in his teens that he had a flair for writing as well as drama. Before enrolling in the Carnegie Mellon University drama program, he attended a boarding school in Vermont where he studied literature, including Shakespeare. When he read *Romeo and Juliet*, Hamburger was touched by its story of love in the context of a family feud. That served as the initial creative spark for a play he'd write in college.

Hamburger's passion for theater led him to CMU where he met Gordon (whose singing voice he found most inspirational). On a break after his third semester, he started writing a play called *Marigold and Elkin* that was inspired by an earlier engagement with a small travelling theater troupe that resided for the summer in rural West Virginia. "I was just trying to upgrade *Romeo and Juliet* because I'd been down in West Virginia and there was this whole famous feud between the hillbilly families, the Hatfields and McCoys. And I said to myself, there's a play here." Sitting at his small desk in his room at his parents' apartment on Manhattan's Upper East Side, he wrote about an unlikely romance between two characters from different sides of feuding families. One of the last things he penned before returning to Carnegie was a speech for Marigold to express her feelings to Elkin.

Back at Carnegie, Hamburger and his fellow drama student friends Peggy Gordon, Stephen Nathan, and others decided to travel over the summer as an acting troupe they named the Open Players. They would perform *Marigold and Elkin* and other shows.

Gordon says, "I remember that I was sitting, ready for rehearsal, when Jay handed me a poem [Marigold's monologue] and asked, 'Could you write music to this? I think this would be a great song for Marigold to sing to Elkin.' I looked at it and said 'Sure,' even though it wasn't in song structure."

Before the semester ended, the Open Players fell apart. Gordon went off to San Francisco and life moved on. Three years later, while rehearsing for *The Godspell* at Café La MaMa, Gordon remembered that "Marigold's Song" was still in her guitar case. She played it for Gilmer McCormick, who quickly came up with a harmony for it, and the two of them performed it for Tebelak and other company members during a "show-and-tell" session.

Tebelak liked the piece and asked them to perform it in the show. Later, when Schwartz heard Gordon and McCormick perform it at La MaMa, he liked the song as well and thought it should be included in the final *Godspell* score.

New Title, New Context

Once it was accepted into *Godspell*, Gordon named Marigold's piece "By My Side" to suit the situation. Except for one verse that was cut during rehearsals at the Cherry Lane Theatre, the lyrics remained almost exactly what Hamburger wrote for *Marigold and Elkin*.

Where would it fit in the show? Tebelak found the perfect spot. Previously, when he pieced together parables for *Godspell*, he included a story from John 8:1-11. In this reported event in Jesus' life, Scribes and Pharisees bring a woman accused of adultery into the temple area where Jesus was teaching. They remind Jesus that according to the law of Moses, such women are to be stoned. Jesus suggests that only a faultless person (in other words, no one) could dare cast a stone. In effect, he holds up a mirror to the crowd so they can clearly see their own faults and hypocrisy, and they leave the woman unharmed.

In an early *Godspell* script, several clowns briefly narrated this parable. When Gordon and McCormick brought in Marigold's song, it seemed to fit right into this moment. The song begins with the lines "Where are you going? Where are you going? Can you take me with you?" Tebelak realized that it could express the feelings of the woman Jesus saves from being stoned. He concluded that Gordon should perform the role of the woman in this parable, and then sing the song with McCormick.

The Mellow Blueness Story

One of the problems Gordon had in writing the song was reading Jay's handwriting. She recalls, "Jay's handwriting was so tiny I couldn't make out the words in the line. I thought the song went:

Far beyond where the horizon lies, where the horizon lies,

And the gulls are flying into youness

So when Jay came to the production at Café La MaMa he said to Gordon afterward, "The gulls are flying into youness? That isn't what I wrote."

She said, "Well, what did you write? I don't know what you wrote." And he explained that it was:

Far beyond where the horizon lies, where the horizon lies,
Where the land sinks into mellow blueness

So the song was corrected. Jay also explained to Peggy that when he wrote that lyric, he was thinking of the hills of Vermont where he went to school. She used that image while performing. "It made that entire section work because I was able to take Jay's visual memory of Vermont and use it to visualize the place Steve Nathan's clown would lead me: into this beautiful place of mellowness, if I could only dare myself to follow."

The Pebble Dare

As he was writing "Marigold's Song," Hamburger came up with an image about a pebble in the shoe. For that image, he was specifically inspired by another part of his personal life experience in the 1960s. While still in high school, he had traveled to Tennessee for a school report. He wanted to experience civil rights efforts first hand, as he was impressed by courageous acts that defied segregation laws and expectations. He remembers witnessing poor African-American sharecroppers struggle, seeking their voting rights. He was also stirred by Martin Luther King, Jr., and the whole civil rights movement: with "the complex and difficult, yet inspiring nonviolent protests and marches."

He felt personally emboldened to walk a more difficult road. "I can accept difficulty. I can get involved in the civil rights movement. I can get involved in the environmental movement.

I don't have to take the easy way out of life. I can get involved in human struggles."

In *Marigold and Elkin*, Marigold needed to be courageous to love who she loves. She dared herself to place the pebble in her shoe and keep going. Hamburger wrote, "I'll put a pebble in my shoe/and watch me walk/I can walk and walk."

Interpolated into the *Godspell* story, a woman musters her courage to inquire if she can journey with Jesus. She feels she must test herself to do it. She even labels a pebble by her emotional state: "Dare." She puts it in her shoe and walks.

Gordon feels the entire lyric carries a rich meaning. "Walking with a pebble is a test of will. While she walks she gains strength" and is eventually able to remove the pebble and let someone else be tested.

Finalizing Permission for Use; Dare vs. Death Debate

To get final permission to use the newly titled "By My Side" in *Godspell*, Tebelak and Schwartz invited Hamburger to a rehearsal at the Cherry Lane Theatre where he watched the show and heard the song in the new context. He agreed to allow it in the show as long as credit was given. He recalls that the conversation continued:

"We have one request, Jay," Tebelak added. "This line, 'I shall call the pebble dare,' we'd like that to be changed to 'I shall call the pebble death.'"

"What are you talking about? No, the word is 'dare,'" insisted Hamburger.

"You don't understand," continued Tebelak. "We would like this word changed to 'death.' It should be 'death.' It's much more in line with what's coming – that Jesus dies."

Hamburger wouldn't budge: "If you change the word to 'death' then I want that song pulled from the show. The word is 'dare.'"

He telephoned Peggy Gordon and said, "You can't believe what they are doing. They want to change the word 'dare' to 'death.' It will destroy the entire song."

So they used the song as it was.

Hamburger later reflected, "I actually think it would have really wrecked the show because 'I shall call the pebble dare' sets up a whole new outlook on Jesus being crucified. It's always the most daring—the whole situation. [It's like Jesus is saying] 'Go ahead, crucify me. See what happens.' Also, if the word was 'death,' the line would have one meaning, whereas 'dare' has many. You can dare yourself into death, you can dare yourself into reincarnation, and you can dare yourself onto the next step in life."

Gordon elaborates: "It was about my clown having to dare herself to go with him, but also about all of us as a community daring to follow him.... His journey was going to be so intense and full of peril, and [so it was a reminder] for us to challenge ourselves as a group."

Stephen Schwartz's version of the story is that back when the group was first rehearsing *Godspell*, he mistakenly heard "dare" as "death." He posited that the song would work better if this was the wording. "'Death shall be carried,' is a bigger idea," says Schwartz, "and truer to what a belief in Jesus meant.... That's why there's Christianity—this guy said that he would conquer death. That's what people really care about. Peggy disagreed, but I still think I was right."

In any case, "By My Side" stayed in the show and is included on all of the cast albums.

Schwartz adds, "What really pleased me about being able to work on 'By My Side' was that I could do vocal arrangements. Because I loved the song so much, that was sort of my way of giving to the song."

"By My Side" Through Time

The song and scene related to "By My Side" has remained unchanged over the decades, except for variations in arrangements. Gordon notes, "This moment is always left intact by *Godspell* directors exactly the way it's written in our libretto because the simple spiritual intent of the scene and song clearly translates. The Jesus clown saves the woman's life, imperiling his own when he goes against the law that Moses has laid down. She is transformed by his selfless act and commits to following him. And this proves John-Michael's assertion that the parables do not need either a contemporary context or contemporary commentary to make relevant their simple, timeless spiritual message."

By Whose Side?

Is Jesus standing by the Peggy clown's side or is the Peggy clown by Jesus' side? It may appear to be immaterial because they are ultimately standing by each other. But for Peggy Gordon, the nuanced differences between points of view in this song are important to consider, both in the main singer's line and in the harmony line.

Originally, Marigold wanted to be emotionally and physically close to Elkin. Addressing him, she sang that she was "finally glad to be here by your side."

This was how Peggy sang it to her friend, Gilmer. When Gilmer made up a harmony line, she imagined herself to be voicing Jesus' response. Thus when Peggy sang "I am here...by your side," Gilmer sang "that you are here…by my side" as if Jesus was responding.

When Tebelak approved the song for *The Godspell* at La MaMa, it needed a suitable title. Gordon decided to use "By My Side," based on the line sung from Jesus' point of view instead of on her melody line with the words: "By your side."

For the final version of *Godspell*, Schwartz kept the song and its title, "By My Side." Peggy and Gilmer continued singing the last two stanzas this way, in the show and on the cast album:

> *Then I'll take your hand*
> *Finally glad (finally glad)*
> *That I am here (that you are here)*
> *By your side (by my side)*
> *By your side (by my side)*
> *By your side (by my side)*
> *That you are here by my side (Gilmer's line)*
>
> *[Spoken section]*
>
> *By my side (by my side)*
> *By my side (by my side)*
> *By my side (by my side)*
> *That you are here by my side*

At some point the second to the last stanza was changed in the official materials so that the "my" and "your" were switched. Gordon considers this to be incorrect.

LYRICS

"By My Side"

PEGGY:
 Where are you going?
 Where are you going?
 Can you take me with you?
 For my hand is cold and needs warmth
 Where are you going?

PEGGY AND GILMER
(AND OTHERS GRADUALLY JOINING WITH HARMONY)

 Far beyond where the horizon lies
 Where the horizon lies
 And the land sinks into mellow blueness
 O please, take me with you

 Let me skip the road with you
 I can dare myself, (I can dare myself)
 I can dare myself
 I'll put a pebble in my shoe
 And watch me walk (watch me walk)
 I can walk and walk…

 I shall call the pebble dare (I shall call the pebble dare)
 We will talk together about walking
 Dare shall be carried
 And when we both have had enough
 I will take him from my shoe, singing:
 Meet your new road…

 Then I'll take your hand
 Finally glad (finally glad)
 That you are here (that you are here)
 By my side (by my side)
 By my side (by my side)
 By my side (by my side)
 That you are here by my side…

[Spoken section]

By my side (by my side)
By my side (by my side)
By my side (by my side)
That you are here by my side…

CUT VERSE that followed "O please, take me with you."

For I fear I shall weep
And never laugh again
I do want to laugh again and again.
I want to smile inside
And put my eye in every flower
Please take my hand

LEFT: Peggy Gordon sings "By My Side" about forty years after the original production, during an event in 2008 for the author's book, *Defying Gravity*. RIGHT: "By My Side" lyricist, Jay Hamburger, performs in a play for his Theatre in the Raw company in 2009.

CHAPTER 29

"We Beseech Thee"
Come Sing about Love

As Schwartz applied his musical theater background to *Godspell* for the Cherry Lane Theatre production, he realized that Act II needed a new song in order for Jeffrey to have a piece to sing and also to fulfill a tradition.

Most musicals, in Schwartz's experience, include a show stopping number at a climactic moment near the end of Act II. This song is often labeled the "Eleven O'clock" number because that's about the time it would appear in an evening performance in the days when shows started about 8:30 p.m.

Robin Lamont recalls a little scuffle about this when Schwartz brought it up in front of Tebelak and the group of actors. "I remember Stephen saying, 'At this point in the second act, about two-thirds of the way through, one always does an up-tempo number.' John-Michael was saying, 'What? That's musical theater [structure]; I want to create a personal experience for people.' And Stephen was saying, 'We've got to get the up-tempo number in here because that's what makes the show,' and Stephen was right."

That's when Tebelak came up with hymn 229 as something that would work in this spot. The lyrics are attributed to Thomas Benson Pollock, a graduate of Trinity College in Dublin. He took holy orders in 1870, and in 1871 wrote this particular piece, then titled "Father Hear Thy Children's Call." One hundred years later, Schwartz put the lyrics on the piano stand, brought Jeffrey Mylett to mind, and played around with ways to musically enter the song.

Mylett had a bouncy personality. "Jeffrey made the energizer bunny look lethargic," comments Lamont. "He was quick and nimble." Schwartz says, "He was the highest energy character. Jeffrey was almost elfin. He was small and sprightly and Irish. There was something very leprechauny about Jeffrey, and playful." The song's lively pace and cheerful tune reflects his energy and personality.

About the style of the piece, Schwartz recalls his musical diving board. "The jumping off point was 'You Can't Hurry Love,' the 1966 chart-topping single by the songwriting team of Holland-Dozier-Holland, recorded by The Supremes. I was so influenced by Motown and the Supremes. 'We Beseech Thee' is derived from that and then it became a sort of country hoedown."

"We Beseech Thee" in Context

Within the whole structure of *Godspell*, this particular Eleven O'clock number satisfies the needs of the show in terms of emotional swings. The song brings cheer to the otherwise solemn second half of Act II as the musical approaches the Crucifixion scene. "In the context of *Godspell*'s second act," Schwartz explains, "'We Beseech Thee' is the last unalloyed celebratory moment."

A downturn of events has already been set in motion during the previous song, because while others are singing "By My Side," we are told that Judas has gone to the chief priests and accepted 30 pieces of silver to betray his teacher.

The show starts shifting out of comic mode as Act II proceeds. Schwartz suggests, "The emotional transition is aided by the fact that Jesus, having recognized that things have begun getting a little dire, has picked up the mood with the sheep and goats parable. And in that parable, he promises his faithful followers 'eternal life.'" Consequently, Jeffrey's character reacts to the happy promise. He sings about love in "We Beseech Thee."

> *"When you go to a funeral, there's often a meal at the house where you try to get your mind off it. 'We Beseech Thee' functioned in that way. It just gave the audience a chance to laugh and forget the building tension and the sense of foreboding as the second act neared its climax."*
> —Music director Stephen Reinhardt

As Schwartz adapted the hymn lyric, he added the "Come sing about love" refrain that captures the *Godspell* experience as a whole. Sung two-thirds of the way through Act II, it reinforces the meaning of what has transpired.

LYRICS

"We Beseech Thee"

JEFFREY
 Father, hear Thy children's call
 Humbly at Thy feet we fall
 Prodigals, confessing all

ALL
 We beseech Thee, hear us!

JEFFREY
 We Thy call have disobeyed
 Into paths of sin have strayed
 And repentance have delayed

ALL
 We beseech Thee, hear us!

JEFFREY

Come sing about love
That caused us first to be
Come sing about love
That made the stone and tree
Come sing about love
That draws us lovingly

ALL
We beseech Thee, hear us!

Sick!

JEFFREY
We come to Thee for cure

ALL
Guilty!

JEFFREY
We seek Thy mercy sure

ALL
Evil!

JEFFREY
We long to be made pure

ALL
We beseech Thee, hear us!

Blind!

JEFFREY
We pray that we may see

ALL
Bound!

JEFFREY
We pray to be made free

ALL
 Stained!

JEFFREY
 We pray for sanctity

ALL
 We beseech Thee, hear us!

JEFFREY/ALL
 Come sing about love/love!
 That caused us first to be
 Come sing about love/love!
 That made the stone and tree
 Come sing about love/love! Love!
 That draws us lovingly

ALL
 We beseech Thee, hear us!

 By the gracious saving call
 Spoken tenderly to all
 Who have shared man's guilt and fall
 We beseech thee, hear us!

 By the love that longs to bless
 Pitying our sore distress
 Leading us to holiness
 We beseech Thee, hear us!

 Boom-chicka-chicka-chicka-boom-chick-chick
 Chicka-booma-chicka-booma-chicka-boom-chick-chick ...

 Grant us hope from earth to rise
 And to strain with eager eyes
 Towards the promised heavenly prize
 We beseech Thee, hear us!

 Come sing about love/love!

The Godspell Experience

That caused us first to be
Come sing about love/love!
That made the stone and tree
Come sing about love/love! Love! Love!
Come on sing about love/love! Love! Love!
Come on sing about love/love! Love!
That draws us lovingly
We beseech thee, hear us!

Boom-chicka-chicka-chicka-boom-chick-chick
Chicka-booma-chicka-booma-chicka-boom-chick-chick!
Chick chick!
Boom chick!

The Broadway revival cast bounce on mini-trampolines during "We Beseech Thee." (Photo by Jeremy Daniel)

Chapter 30
"On the Willows"
The Ballad of Psalm 137

"On the Willows" is performed right after the Last Supper and accompanies the characters' goodbyes to Jesus. Schwartz intended the song to "serve as sort of movie-like scoring to the action," which is why it is usually sung by the band rather than by the cast while they are involved in the transitional moment with their leader.

Psalm 137, with its well-known line about a group of captives being requested to "sing the Lord's song in a foreign land," is said to describe the sadness of the Israelites who were in exile following the Babylonian conquest of Jerusalem in 586 BCE. Tebelak may have wanted to use this psalm because the word "captor" seemed relevant to the moments before Jesus would be captive, or simply because the psalm has been used as an after-supper Passover hymn.

Duane Bolick's original music for this piece was a gentle, slightly mournful ballad. Schwartz also wrote "On the Willows" as a ballad, and remembers taking a stylistic hint from John-Michael Tebelak that it be oceanic. The comment triggered the songwriter's memory of an arrangement he'd heard for a Judy Collins piece—an adaptation of a William Butler Yeats poem, "Golden Apples of the Sun." With that in mind, a lilting new tune came to life.

In the original production and on the album, Stephen Reinhardt sang lead vocal, Rich La Bonte sang the higher harmony line and Jesse Cutler the lower. For a musical interlude, Cutler improvised an acoustic guitar solo on the spot during a band rehearsal. It pleased the composer, so that became part of the music for future performances.

David Lewis, who served as *Godspell*'s music director and keyboard player at the Promenade Theatre for two years, loved the "On the Willows" song moment. He comments, "The cast is getting ready to understand what's going to happen. It's at the beginning of the dark period of *Godspell*. I thought of it as pure love and harmony getting ruined by social divisions and religious friction.... It's a beautiful, sad, regretful, meditative song."

Schwartz describes the song's mood as melancholy and wistful. "'On the Willows' is a song about loss, both in the original psalm and here," he explains. "In *Godspell* the group is losing their leader—this person that they all love, so it's a song of advanced mourning."

Lyre or Lives

Schwartz and Tebelak did discuss whether or not they should use the word "lyres" or "lives." For the licensed script, the word "lyres," found in the original psalm, was changed to "lives."

> *On the willows there*
> *We hung up our lives*

In answer to a performer's question about it, Schwartz once commented, "The adaptation of the lyric, with the change of words, was suggested by the conceiver and original director of the show, John-Michael Tebelak. I'm not sure I would make the same change today, but the reasoning behind it was that we wanted to be clear it was their entire life that had changed for each of the disciples, and we weren't sure the metaphor of the lyres would be clear enough, particularly since we don't get to the explanatory line about singing the Lord's song in a foreign land until much later in the song."

LYRICS

"On the Willows"

BAND
On the willows there
We hung up our lives [lyres]
For our captors there
Required
Of us songs
And our tormentors mirth

On the willows there
We hung up our lives [lyres]
For our captors there
Required
Of us songs
And our tormentors mirth

Saying:
"sing us one of the songs of Zion"
"sing us one of the songs of Zion"
"sing us one of the songs of Zion"
But how can we sing
Sing the Lord's song
In a foreign land...?

On the willows there
We hung up our lives [lyres]

The Godspell Experience

Andy Rohrer (Jesus) and his followers gather for the Last Supper/seder in the production at the Promenade Theatre. Actors from left to right: Judy Kahan, Marley Sims, Bill Thomas, Elizabeth Lathram, Andy Rohrer, Herb Braha, Bob Garrett, Linda Sherwood, Jeanne Lange. (Photo by Sam Freed)

In *Godspell* Jesus says a traditional prayer in Hebrew. Here are two different transliterations:

Over bread: *"Boruch atoh Adonoy, Elohaynu melech ho-olum, Ha-mo-tzi lechem min ho-o-retz."*

Over wine: *"Boruch atoh Adonoy, Elohaynu melech ho-olum, boray p'ri hagofen."*

OR

Over bread: *"Baruch atah Adonai, elohaynu melech ha'olam hamotzi lechem min ha'aretz."* (Praised are You, Adonai our God, Sovereign of the Universe, who brings forth bread from the earth.)

Over wine: *Baruch atah Adonai, elohaynu melech ha'olam boray pri ha'gafen. (Praised are You, Adonai our God, Sovereign of the Universe, who creates the fruit of the vine.)*

Chapter 31

"Finale"
Long Live God Counterpoint

Can the followers survive the earthly departure of their charismatic leader? The "Finale" conveys their emotional journey as they listen to Jesus' last words, mourn his passing by slowly carrying him away on their shoulders, and then celebrate their willingness to carry on.

In the original production, the actor playing Jesus stood up against the chain link fence while John/Judas tied his hands to the fence with red ribbons. It wasn't meant to be an elaborate scene or a literal scene. Tebelak never used a cross. Jesus slowly sings "Oh God, I'm bleeding," then "Oh God, I'm dying," and "Oh God, I'm dead" (with each line echoed by disciples around him). Slowly, the disciples begin to sing "Long live God."

Schwartz recalls that "Long live God" existed in the early script. "In the script that I got from John-Michael, at the end they sang 'Long live God, long live God, long live God.' There was this one line repeated over and over again, and I thought, 'I should do something with that and then have 'Prepare Ye' come in on top of it.' It was just one of those things that suggests itself, because they seemed similar in structure." So he wrote the music so that a few actors sing "Long live God" quietly while a second group brings in "Prepare ye the way of the Lord" in counterpoint.

The song's opening measures feature an electric guitar riff typical of the period. Schwartz says, "It's sort of Vanilla Fudge or Jefferson Airplane or one of those electric guitar dominated groups." Then it smoothes out and a lullaby-like tune is sung in counterpoint with "Prepare Ye."

The Godspell Experience

For the 2011 Broadway revival, arranger Michael Holland, who was known around New York City for his mash-ups of pop songs, started working on a blend of multiple pieces for the ending of the *Godspell* "Finale." Then Stephen Schwartz had the idea to layer in "Beautiful City," with its lyrics about building a beautiful community together. So Schwartz went to Holland's apartment, and they fiddled with the piece until they had a blend that worked. It included the "Long live God" section of the "Finale," "Prepare Ye," "Save the People," and "Beautiful City."

Holland comments, "It basically says what the show is saying. These people who came from all different corners are now all together. It really does sum it up. And I think it does so really eloquently in that musical moment."

Lamar Alford and David Haskell carry Andy Rohrer during *Godspell*'s "Finale." (Photo by Martha Swope/©The New York Public Library)

LYRICS

"Finale"

JESUS
Oh, God, I'm bleeding!
Oh, God, I'm bleeding!

ALL
Oh, God, you're bleeding!

JESUS
Oh, God, I'm dying!

ALL
Oh, God, you're dying!

JESUS
Oh, God, I'm dying!
Oh, God, I'm dead…

ALL BUT JESUS
Oh, God, you're dead
Oh, God, you're dead
Oh, God, you're dead …

Long live God (12 x)

[counterpoint]
Long live God/Prepare ye
Long live God/the way of the lord
Long live God/Prepare ye
Long live God/the way of the lord

Prepare Ye the way of the Lord (4 x)

The Godspell Experience

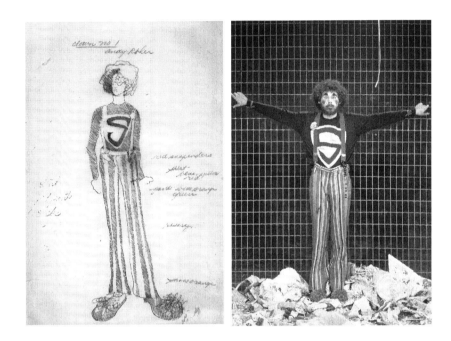

Above left: Jesus costume sketch by Susan Tsu. Above right: Andy Rohrer as Jesus in the CMU production.

CHAPTER 32

"Beautiful City"
The Lasting Tribute

Stephen Schwartz originally wrote this song for the 1973 *Godspell* movie at the request of the film's director, David Greene. Greene believed that "We Beseech Thee" from the stage version was "too theatrical" to work effectively in the film medium.

Schwartz elaborates, "We had this idea for a song called 'Beautiful City,' since the movie was set in a magically emptied New York City. And it was very sort of flower child like; the cast went skipping through the streets and sang these sweet words. I have to admit, I always felt that [the movie version of] the song was a little too sweet for its own good."

However, he decided to rewrite the lyrics years later when someone organized a one-night benefit production of *Godspell* in South Central Los Angeles. It was shortly after the 1991 Rodney King riots. Schwartz remembers, "I suggested that I rewrite the words, because I felt I could come up with something more appropriate for this particular situation."

So he supplied new lyrics and kept the tune essentially intact, although he made the music starker. The revised lines, influenced by the aftermath of the riots in L.A., reflected a more thoughtful, practical approach to rebuilding community spirit in contemporary society. At the same time, they suggested metaphorical construction, or reconstruction, of community spirit, as was the case for the followers of Jesus in *Godspell*.

Using "Beautiful City" is optional for performance within *Godspell*. Some productions include it right before the Last Supper, and others use it to open the second act, or in place of "Long live God" at the end of the show.

The Godspell Experience

After the September 11, 2001 destruction of the World Trade Center in New York, the song was used in many memorial services and benefit performances.

LYRICS

"Beautiful City"

JESUS
Out of the ruins and rubble,
Out of the smoke,
Out of our night of struggle,
Can we see a ray of hope?
One pale, thin ray reaching for the day
We can build a beautiful city,
Yes, we can; yes, we can.
We can build a beautiful city.
Not a city of angels,
But we can build a city of man.

We may not reach the ending,
But we can start
Slowly but truly mending
Brick by brick,
Heart by heart.
Now, maybe now
We start learning how
We can build a beautiful city,
Yes, we can; yes, we can.
We can build a beautiful city.
Not a city of angels,
But we can build a city of man.

When your trust is all but shattered,
When your faith is all but killed,
You can give up, bitter and battered,
Or you can slowly start to build...

A beautiful city,

Yes, we can; yes, we can.
We can build a beautiful city.
Not a city of angels,
But finally, a city of man.
A city of man.

Additional Reflections on the *Godspell* Score

The *Godspell* score stands out in musical theater history as one of the first of its kind. Musicologist Paul Laird comments, "*Godspell* showed Schwartz to be one of the early composers to embrace popular styles so fully in a theatrical score, a prescient stance that helped show the way for many composers who followed him…The confidence of his melodic expression and wholesale embrace of pop syncopation in this score superbly placed it within its time and ensured its long-term popularity."

As *Godspell* recordings and show performances reached a large audience, they helped create a demand for musicals with this composer's scores. One of the millions of people touched by *Godspell*'s music was movie and stage producer Marc Platt, who often listened to the *Godspell* and *Pippin* albums in his youth. Platt's familiarity with Schwartz's music was a key factor in his decision that the novel *Wicked*, for which Platt's company had acquired production rights, could be adapted as a musical with a Stephen Schwartz score. "The wonderful thing about music is that it has no filter for people," says Platt. "Music seeps into you somehow. And Stephen's music, however you want to label it, is music that people love. It is emotional music and it wears its emotion on its sleeve."

The Godspell Experience

One of the Toronto cast groups sings at the Royal Alexandra Theatre. Front: Andrea Martin; second row: Valda Aviks, Gilda Radner, Avril Chown; third row: Eugene Levy, Martin Short, Rudy Webb; in back: Jayne Eastwood, Don Scardino (Jesus), Gerry Salsberg.

"Beautiful City"

PART IV
A *Godspell* Grab Bag

The New Zealand cast of *Godspell* performs "Save the People." This photo shows the tableau that the cast members formed at the end of the song, in the professional productions of the 1970s. Jesus conducted the choral section with his back to the audience and then, at the last minute, leapt onto the platform to join the scene.

A *Godspell* Grab Bag

With over forty years of *Godspell* history as a background for this book, there are countless tales and details that could be shared. This "Grab Bag" touches on a few aspects of the legacy that deserve attention—the worldwide interest in the show, the recent Broadway revival, the movie adaptation, colorful costume details, and a report on what has happened in the lives of *Godspell*'s pioneers.

The book ends with reflections on the subtitle: What else does it mean to be "Inside a Transformative Musical."

David Essex as Jesus in the original London cast.

CHAPTER 33

Godspell Worldwide: The Stories Continue

American Productions, 1971 to 1977

In New York City a professional production of *Godspell* ran continuously for six full years, from the Off-Broadway opening on May 17, 1971 through the closing of the Broadway version on September 4, 1977. The show attracted audiences of all ages and types, and seemed to serve as an antidote to some of the turmoil of the Watergate era.

It was a time when the so-called "generation gap" caused confusion and lack of trust between young people and older adults. Susan Tsu remembers when "grimy jeans and long hair" were a stereotype for the younger generation. "There were all these aspects in the world of youth that our elders really disapproved of," says Tsu. "And in the middle of all that, coming from young people, was a piece that actually had a good message—a piece that was more or less wholesome, honest, and down to earth. It could speak to people without appearing to be from the church lectern."

Many members of the clergy who were speaking from lecterns and altars took *Godspell* in stride. The publicists went out of their way to invite them to a performance. Gary Gunas believes that the Giffords' efforts contributed significantly to the show's success. For example, they worked with Rev. Rodney Kirk of St. John the Divine Episcopal Cathedral, who provided much needed support. Gunas comments about Rev. Kirk, "He got very much behind us and was very useful. [He said] 'You're doing a good thing and we support that.' So his name was very valuable to the Giffords in other marketing. They could say, 'Well we have this wonderful quote from Rodney Kirk and here's what he said, so we're not reviled by religious people in the least. On the contrary, here's what they are really saying about us.' So it was a great entry. He didn't do public appearances on behalf of *Godspell* or anything like that, but he gave support that he was very genuine about."

Godspell started Off Broadway as a little musical that could have gone unnoticed, especially in the shadow of the big Jesus-connected musical of the day: the rock opera *Jesus Christ Superstar*. The Andrew Lloyd Webber/Tim Rice musical was strongly promoted through a popular pre-production concept album (1970). The show was a huge hit when it ran in the U.K. *Superstar* also ran on Broadway from October 1971 through June 1973.

Godspell worked its way into public awareness, in part, through television appearances that brought pieces of the show into American living rooms. Audiences outside of New York City first sampled the show through the cast's appearances on Johnny Carson's *The Tonight Show*, *The Dick Cavett Show*, several regional TV shows, and *The Today Show*. Cast members also appeared later on CBS's weekend arts magazine *Camera Three*.

One of the show's biggest assets was the cast album, which picked up two Grammy Awards, one for best producer and the other for best composer. At the nationally televised Grammy Award ceremony in March of 1972, Andy Williams introduced the current New York cast. They performed part of "Prepare Ye" and "Day by Day."

Around Thanksgiving time in 1972, *Godspell* again reached a national audience in a PBS special produced by WGBH of Boston. WGBH filmed the Boston Company of *Godspell* visiting the Plimoth Plantation, an outdoor re-creation of the original

Pilgrim settlement established in the 17th century by English colonists (and named with the original spelling of Plimoth rather than Plymouth). During the special, a commentator read from William Bradford's diary as a set up for the performance of songs like "All Good Gifts," "Bless the Lord," and others. The actors, in their *Godspell* outfits, intermingled with costumed role players who were engaged in activities of early settlement life.

When *Godspell* toured and played regionally for several years, hundreds of local newspapers and other publications printed reviews or feature articles. Some national magazines mentioned it. *Life Magazine*'s reviewer declined to review it after seeing it early on (apparently after making a deal with the producers that if he didn't like it, he wouldn't review it). But the publicists convinced the critic to come back later, and in 1972 he did return. Andy Rohrer was playing Jesus and recalls, "He loved it. He wrote the review and it appeared in *Life Magazine* at that point…. The show had been up for awhile and here was this big national review that punched up our advance sales again." All this, and word of mouth, helped the show to thrive.

Wildness and Scares

While the audience response to *Godspell* was, for the most part, positive, over the years in some locations people disrupted the show by throwing religious leaflets or making noise.

Of the audiences Rex Knowles and Sherry Landrom encountered on tour, they do remember one challenging situation. During an evening performance in Memphis, Tennessee, a man from the audience walked on stage. Landrom recalls, "We had just finished 'By My Side' and we were doing the Sheep and Goats parable… He started in on us, saying we were going to Hell–just a stream of things. He said it to the audience too, and we were just sitting there in stunned silence. The stage manager came on stage and said, 'Sir, you have to leave the stage right now.' So finally the guy turned around and as he was walking off the stage…he yelled at the audience the whole way out. And we just continued the show. The audience attention was rapt after that—they were just focused on us. At the end, they erupted—they were on their feet to applaud the minute they had the opportunity and they went on and on applauding. So he actually had a cohesive effect."

Actor Don Scardino treasured his experience playing Jesus, both in Toronto and later in New York City. But he remembers a disruption at the Promenade Theatre in Manhattan that almost didn't have a happy ending. He'd already performed the role hundreds of times. "There was this one time when all through the play there was this weird, very paranoid feeling. And I got up on the fence singing, 'Oh God, I'm dying,' and I felt I was really going to be killed. I thought, 'I've been doing this too long.' I look over at Bill Thomas who was playing Lamar and he's looking at me with this terrified look on his face and I'm feeling paranoid and I sang, 'Oh God, I'm Dead' the fastest that I could, and I get off stage and I see Billy in the dressing room and he said, 'Are you okay?' And I said, 'You gave me this really weird look at the end,' and he said, 'I had this weird feeling that you were actually going to be killed.' And I said, 'I had the same feeling that someone was going to kill me. We've been doing the show too long, Billy; we've got to get out.'"

Their intuition was not as far off as they thought. Scardino continues, "I went to my dressing room that was under the tunnel of the theater there and the company manager came back and said, 'Is everything okay?' I said, 'Yeah, why are you asking?' He said, 'I guess I can tell you now. You know this used to be the welfare hotel. A woman came to the usher at intermission and said there is this guy sitting in front of her who said he was going to kill Jesus. And he had a gun. Someone from *Godspell* went to the guard from the Promenade hotel who came to watch. During the end of the play, the guy reached into his coat and pulled out a gun. They took him away and arrested him for having a hand weapon."

Oh, the Injuries

In this ensemble show, all the actors remained on stage through almost the entire performance. They often needed to kneel, dance, and jump onto or off the plank platform. The show became so physical that the actors added knee pads to their outfits and the producers added carpet on the stage floor (in a gray tone so that it resembled cement).

There were muscle injuries, sore knees, and even a few knee operations. "The show was so physical that we couldn't do it without knee pads even though they carpeted the stage," says Robin Lamont. "We were on our knees and up and down. And because it was an ensemble group, you were on stage the whole time. There was never a moment, except for intermission, when you got to leave the stage." The amount of motion itself would leave cast members sweating. Sonia Manzano recalls, "Some people would clock that you'd run ten miles during a show. It was really high energy."

There were other mishaps in the various locations *Godspell* played, even though precautions were taken. A few cast members were temporarily knocked out by improperly wielded wooden planks, or even had teeth knocked out by overly ambitious acrobatic dance moves performed by fellow cast members. Peggy Gordon recalls an accident at the Promenade. "There was one of the moments when instead of hearing thunderous applause, we heard the audience gasp and realized something had happened. One of the guys had accidently hit Joanne on the head with a plank and she was rushed to St. Vincent's. I had to sing 'Bless the Lord' in the next performance."

The aisles where actors walked up and down several times during the show could be hazardous for slipping on a fallen program, which did happen. The adage, "The show must go on!" was invoked often enough for *Godspell*.

From Off Broadway to Broadway

The producers believed that the production could run longer in New York City if it moved to the "Great White Way," attracting theatergoers to see it in one of the many Broadway theaters close to Times Square. *Godspell* had already proven itself in large venues in Boston and on the national tour, so the loss of intimacy afforded by a smaller venue wasn't their worry. On June 22, 1976, *Godspell* opened at the 1,200-seat Broadhurst Theatre after five previews.

Robin Lamont and Lamar Alford reprised their roles. New cast members all had experience with the New York or regional productions of the show. They included Laurie Faso, Lois Foraker, Elizabeth Lathram, Bobby Lee, Tom Rolfing, Don Scardino, Marley Sims, and Valerie Williams, with Bob Garrett and several others as understudies. Various other cast members slipped in and out during the run. Victor Garber, who was experienced in the role of Jesus from the Toronto production, remembers once visiting the show to see friends and being drafted to go on that night.

> *"People loved the show; it was of the times. There were people who would come from out of town on the weekends and see it over and over again."*
> —**Broadway cast member Marley Sims**

The show was successful enough to run for a little over a year, although it shifted venues when big budget shows wanted to move into the spaces. It played in a total of three theaters: at the Broadhurst Theatre, Plymouth Theatre, and Ambassador Theatre, for a total run of 527 performances.

London Production and Casting

Godspell thrived in Great Britain after it was introduced there by native Londoner, Edgar Lansbury, in 1971. To get *Godspell* off to a good start in the U.K. required ideal casting, and David Essex proved to be a significant draw. Originally, Schwartz and Tebelak had someone else in mind to play Jesus. "When we were going to do *Godspell* in London," Schwartz recalls, "there was this singer who had been on the *Jesus Christ Superstar* album [as Judas] named Murray Head....And it had just been decided that he was going to play Jesus in *Godspell*.

"We went over to London to look for the other performers, and David Essex had come in and auditioned. We liked him very much and we thought, well, maybe he'll be Judas. I remember even talking to him and asking him if he'd consider doing that and he would have. When we brought everyone in for the final call back, Murray Head was there and David Essex was there. And I'm sitting in one part of the theater and John-Michael was in another part, and we're both looking at the stage. And I'm watching the stage and realizing that wherever David Essex was, that's where I was watching. He had this inner glow, like someone was holding a spotlight on him wherever he went. After about fifteen minutes, I went over to John-Michael and I said, 'We've made a terrible mistake haven't we.' He said, 'Yes, I know, it's David Essex, isn't it? It has to be him.' And I said, 'Absolutely.'" So they cast Essex as Jesus.

Both Essex and Head enjoyed further success on the West End and elsewhere. Jeremy Irons, who has since starred in multiple film, television, and stage productions, was the original John/Judas in the London cast. Other cast members included Jacquie-Ann Carr, Julie Covington, Neil Fitzwilliam, Verity-Anne Meldrum, Deryk Parkin, Tom Saffery, Gay Soper, and Marti Webb.

Lansbury scheduled a West End house for *Godspell*, but the theater owner reneged on the arrangement. "We ended up going into the Roundhouse, an Off-West End theater, which turned out to be the luckiest thing that ever happened because it set the show in the right kind of atmosphere."

David Essex remembers the excitement of the opening. "We had a full house for the opening night, as religious zealots milled around outside with placards proclaiming us 'Sinners' who would 'Burn In Hell.' I guess it made a change from people saying 'Break a leg.'" He says the audience adored the show right away and remembers, "At one point they were laughing so much that I glanced behind me, convinced something must be going wrong, but no: it was sheer, spontaneous appreciation."

For the first two months of the run that opened November 17, 1971, the audience for the more intimate Roundhouse Theatre greeted the show with enthusiasm and spread the word. In January 1972 the musical moved to the West End where it ran for several years. Cameron Macintosh produced a *Godspell* tour starting in 1972 that ran almost five years.

Scottish writer Ian Bradley, in a book about musicals, contrasts *Godspell* with the Andrew Lloyd Webber/Tim Rice musical *Jesus Christ Superstar*, finding the American-born musical quite suited to the British sensibility. "In contrast to the Englishness of the cricket-mad Rice and the Victorian church enthusiast

Lloyd Webber, Tebelak and Schwartz were quintessentially American college boys. Yet ironically, it is *Godspell* which is the more 'British' musical in terms of being understated, gently humorous and not taking itself too seriously, while *Superstar* has the brash vulgarity that, rightly or wrongly, tends to be associated with American musicals."

Godspell in Toronto

Godspell opened at the Royal Alexandra Theatre in Toronto, Canada, in May 1972, and ran for over a year to cheering crowds and nightly standing ovations.

Martin Short, who won the role of Jeffrey, remembers the huge gathering of actors auditioning for the show before rehearsals began. He felt pity for one girl who seemed out of place wearing loose-fitting bib overalls and her hair in goofy pigtails. For her audition song, she performed "Zip-a-Dee-Doo-Dah." Short says that she sang "…like a demented child at the peak of a sugar rush." But when she finished, Schwartz and director Howard Sponseller jumped out of their seats to applaud the then unknown Gilda Radner. She had seen *Godspell* in New York, modeled her intentionally unpolished performance on the clown behavior she saw there, and won everyone's hearts with her humor and stage presence.

The Toronto production was the breakaway moment for many of these talented actors whose careers skyrocketed afterward. In addition to Martin Short (*Father of the Bride*) and Gilda Radner (*Saturday Night Live*), these included Victor Garber (*Titanic; Alias*), Andrea Martin (*My Big Fat Greek Wedding*), Eugene Levy (*American Pie*), and others. Don Scardino (*30 Rock* director) also played Jesus after Victor Garber left to do the *Godspell* movie.

Their musical director was Paul Shaffer of *The Late Show* with David Letterman fame, whose piano-playing talent Schwartz and Reinhardt recognized when Shaffer came in to play as audition pianist for several actors.

Paul Shaffer remembers a few protestors standing outside the theater for a while. "They were protesting the blasphemy that they thought was a part of *Godspell* portraying Jesus as a clown. Some of the cast members were asked and did go outside and speak to these people, give them a flower [and show them] that we're treating the subject matter with respect in our own way." For the most part, the Canadian crowds embraced the show and filled the theater night after night. Shaffer adds, "Clergymen loved this show. We did a number of promotional appearances in churches during this time. We would go and in the middle of the church service sing a song."

Unfortunately, no *Godspell* cast album was recorded for the Toronto group.

Australia

The story of *Godspell* coming to Australia begins with Nan Pearlman, who knew *Godspell*'s producers and later ran the Theatre Maximus licensing agency for the show. She remembers the day in 1971 that the prominent Australian theatrical producer Kenn Brodziak came to New York with an associate to make licensing arrangements for other shows. When she mentioned *Godspell*, he was skeptical that anything dealing with religion would interest him. But Pearlman was firm. "I'm telling you, this will be a good one for you; I will call the producers." At the time the show was still playing at Cherry Lane. She remembers, "They went down to Cherry Lane and he called me and said we loved it, you were right, how can we get it?"

Shortly thereafter, Australia was hopping with *Godspell* productions. In Melbourne (November 1971) and Sydney (April 1972), the show ran for about a year, with an Australian tour starting in 1973. *Godspell* was revived in Sydney in 1992 and 1998. Cast albums were created for all productions except the tour. Sammy Bayes, who also served as choreographer for the 1973 *Godspell* movie, directed the original Melbourne production. Colleen Hewett of the original Melbourne cast had already been a pop music star featured on the television production of *Bandstand*. Her single of "Day by Day" earned a gold record.

South Africa

In 1974, *Godspell* became the first show to break the color barrier in South Africa. Tebelak and Schwartz stipulated that as a condition for receiving performance rights, a production had to maintain a racially integrated cast and be performed before an integrated audience. Schwartz says: "When asked about my proudest moment in show business, I often cite what we were able to accomplish in South Africa—the small but real role we played in breaking the strict policy of apartheid."

Other Settings and Revivals

Godspell fared well in many other countries, including Spain, Scandinavian countries, a few in South America, and elsewhere. The producers called upon Nina Faso, who spoke French, to direct a production in Paris. Stephen Reinhardt produced the cast recording.

As mentioned in Chapter 10, *Godspell* spread around the U.S.A. by way of multiple residential ("sit down") companies and by several tours. In addition, there were special presentations. *The Godspell* cast offered a special production on August 14, 1977, in the sanctuary of the Cathedral of St. John the Divine in New York City, at the invitation of the Rt. Rev. Paul Moore Jr., Bishop of New York. There have been performances of parts of *Godspell* at the White House and in front of two popes. It has even been staged in prison.

Ten years after *Godspell* opened, a group of *Godspell* alumni gathered in a production in Los Angeles. The production was noteworthy in terms of who was involved and the length of the run. It started with the first *Godspell* couples: Gilmer McCormick and Stephen Reinhardt, along with Jeanne Lange and David Haskell. Both couples had moved to Los Angeles in the late 1970s and were involved in the First Christian Church of North Hollywood. The church building had a hall with a stage that could serve as a theater space. Jeanne Lange comments, "Gilmer and I produced the tenth anniversary show and it was huge. We set up ourselves for a two-week engagement seating four hundred people, and it ran for eight months."

The actors were now ten years older, but they still easily performed all the physical moves. "I was amazed at how energetic it was and how much people remembered," recalls cast member Marley Sims. "All we needed was a little rebooting to remember," and with the help of Stephen Reinhardt as music director, the memories of songs and scenes came back quickly.

A group of actors mounted the show again at Café La Mama about ten years after it first appeared there. Major New York City revivals have included two Off-Broadway productions: at the Lamb's Theatre (June 12 to December 31, 1988) and the York Theatre (August 2 to October 7, 2000). The Off-Broadway 2000 revival and the Broadway revival both have their own cast albums. In 1998 a production was mounted at Harlem's Victoria Theatre with an all-black professional cast.

Godspell was revived on Broadway in 2011-2012.

See Chapter 36 for the story of the Broadway revival of 2011-2012.

Scott Schwartz, the son of Stephen and Carole Schwartz, directed a *Godspell* production in 2001 that both toured the United States and resulted in a cast recording with DRG Records. Scott had a few advantages directing *Godspell*. He not only knew the show inside and out, but he was able to pick up the phone and consult with the composer any time.

For John-Michael Tebelak, one of the most personally important productions was the one he directed in the summer of 1971 back in Cleveland. His college professor, Larry Carra, had been leading a long-term summer program in Cleveland known as the Great Lakes Shakespeare Festival, with shows staged in a large school auditorium. Tebelak urged Carra, who had initially rejected the college version of *Godspell*, to leave room for the new version of the show in the schedule.

Bill Phillips recalls the moment Tebelak got the news that *Godspell* had been approved as one of the festival's summer shows. "I was at his parents' home at the time and John-Michael was so ecstatic, so over the moon. I'd just never seen him like that before–just radiating confidence the way he was walking around the room and was carrying himself because he'd gotten Larry Carra to agree to put *Godspell* in the festival." Although it was a nerve-racking process for Tebelak to direct an independent *Godspell* production on his own with Schwartz's music, and then have Schwartz come see it, the show was a success.

The Godspell Experience

ABOVE: *Godspell* tour cast members Sherry Landrom and Rex Knowles in Hawaii. BELOW: *Godspell* 10th anniversary (Los Angeles) cast members. Front: Peggy Gordon, Jeff Mylett. Second row, from left: Jeanne Lange, Patti Mariano, John-Michael Tebelak, David Haskell, Herb Braha. Top row, from left: Bob Garrett, Marley Sims, Steve Nathan, Gilmer McCormick.

Chapter 34
The *Godspell* Commune Company

In the early 1970s, the stage production of *Godspell* was a substantial commercial success, with millions of dollars flowing into the box offices. That meant an unusual career launch for men as young as Stephen Schwartz and John-Michael Tebelak, since a show's author royalties are based on the gross income. Through *Godspell*, they both reached a substantial level of financial security while in their early twenties. Schwartz and his wife bought a house in Connecticut not long after the show opened, as did Tebelak.

But the actors weren't part of the author's contract and were not well compensated, either for their eight performances every week or for their contribution to the script.

The business end of things for *Godspell*, including salaries, revolved around Lansbury and Beruh. Their personalities influenced the decision-making process. "Edgar was such a gentleman and such a role model in that respect," says Gary Gunas. "Joe was a tough, strong business manager. They had the 'good cop-bad cop' thing going."

As a person, people liked Joe Beruh, but he held the purse strings tightly. According to the actors, he pinched pennies by paying low salaries and not hiring understudies. (According to his friend and associate Nan Pearlman, it was because he cared about shows being financially successful for the investors.)

On multi-show weekends, he provided milk and cookies instead of dinner money between shows. All this was in violation of rules established by the actors' union. The Cherry Lane was an Equity house, so the actors expected more.

Gilmer McCormick recalls, "We weren't even getting Equity union minimum, and suddenly we became this big hit. I went to my agent, Clifford Stevens. He asked, 'How much are you making?' When I told him, he almost passed out on the floor. So he became our group agent."

Robin Lamont's memory of what transpired next is that the producers approached the group when they realized the new show might falter at the box office. "I guess they were concerned enough that they wouldn't make it. Joe said, 'Let's see if we can negotiate and give them a piece of the show.' Rather than us saying, 'Oh sure, whatever you want to give us is fine,' we realized this is serious business! We said to ourselves, 'Let's negotiate something.' That's when we got a group agent."

Edgar Lansbury's version of the story, remembering it more than 40 years later, is that everything was positive. "We had no obligation to do it, but they had worked with us to develop the musical. It was really Joe Beruh's idea—and it was a good one—that they should, in the communal spirit, have a piece of the proceeds."

There was no precedent for deciding a percentage of the box office that would be equitable. Meanwhile, the actors were working eight shows a week in a musical that required almost two solid hours of motion for minimal pay.

According to Peggy Gordon, the situation was unjust and necessitated action. "As much as I adored Joe Beruh, if you look up the word 'cheap' in the dictionary, you'll see his face. He was scarred by a poverty stricken childhood in Pittsburgh and would tell me story after story. I would listen and then say, 'Yeah, that was then, but now you're becoming a multi-millionaire because of this show and you're still cheap.'" So when the actors assessed the situation after the show had been running for a few weeks, they decided to band together to form a legal entity they called The Godspell Commune Company.

"We surreptitiously met with Gilmer's agent, Clifford Stevens," recalls Gordon. "He had this wonderful postage stamp-sized apartment in the West Village and we filled up the entire living room. He said, 'Here's the deal: you must sign this paper entitling me to act as your representative.' So in between two shows on a Saturday night, we ran out in our clown costumes to get that notarized because there was a notary public there. We were giggling our heads off. We go in and the notary public looked at ten people dressed as clowns and signed it. We gave it to Clifford. Clifford then had a meeting with Joe and Edgar. We were upstairs at Cherry Lane and heard Joe screaming for about three hours." Lamont only remembers a short rebuke, either because he didn't want to give them the percentage they were asking for or because they didn't trust him with the details.

In any case, the money that Stevens negotiated for The Godspell Commune Company was to come from the producers' share of the income, as if the cast members had been investors in the new musical's development. Each of the 10 cast members plus Nina Faso would split a full 15 percent of the producer income. They also received dinner money for multi-show days, and the producers paid for understudies.

Lansbury notes, "They did very well with it, and bought cars and houses. I think it was a very happy arrangement – a fair arrangement."

Traditionally, producers and investors keep a portion of the income during all the years a show receives a first-class production, and then for ten more years after that, at which time the income reverts to the authors. *Godspell* appeared in first-class productions through 1977, and under the new arrangements, the commune group received their 15 percent through 1987.

The story of The Godspell Commune Company is important because of the historical precedent it set. Actors, producers, and agents for other collaborative shows like *A Chorus Line* reviewed the contract as a possible model for their own. "I got requests for years from casts who were involved in the co-creation of their shows to see what the template was," recalls Gordon.

Authorship and the True Rewards

Even though the actors contributed many lines to the *Godspell* script, Tebelak was still considered the musical's book author. "We felt we were the arms and legs interpreting John-Michael's ideas," says Gordon. "The dialogue was from us and the characters were our characters. Nevertheless, we still felt that it came out of his mind. Without him, there's no *Godspell*."

Thirty years after *Godspell* opened, various early cast groups gathered in Los Angeles for a reunion, with Edgar Lansbury, and many others in attendance. Stephen Nathan spoke at the event, expressing what many of the actors felt about *Godspell*. "We were going to do it and we were going to be PAID! I remember the original salary, which was $47 a week. It doesn't seem like a lot, but in 2001 dollars that's $48 a week. [The audience laughs.] You can live pretty well in New York City on $48 a week! But the reality is, Edgar, if you had asked us to go for no money again, we all would have been there, because we weren't very bright then, and that worked out well for everybody. It was an amazing experience that changed everyone connected with it. The experience of doing that show every night and seeing people cry, and at the end seeing the audience stand up and applaud—and really seem changed—was something that obviously no amount of money could have given us. It was an incredible gift."

CHAPTER 35

The *Godspell* Movie

Not surprisingly, in late 1971 the idea of a movie adaptation rose out of affection for the stage musical. Producers Lansbury and Beruh hoped to receive option requests from major studios, but they didn't until John Van Eyssen, Columbia Pictures' representative in London, saw *Godspell* there. "He absolutely fell in love with it," recalls Lansbury. "He got his management to make a deal with us for the rights."

Producing partner Stuart Duncan helped secure funding of $1.3 million, a modest amount for a film but an amount that could work. Lansbury retained the main producing credit for the film, and the new project was listed as a Lansbury/Duncan/Beruh production. Pre-production started in May of 1972, only a year after the show opened at the Cherry Lane Theatre.

It wasn't obvious to everyone involved with *Godspell* that a movie could touch the power of the stage production. For Katie Hanley, who enjoyed performing in the show in New York, the experience of sharing the live show with a group had a special effect. "At the end of the night at the standing ovations, rabbis would be standing next to nuns, next to kids, next to older people. It was just this incredible group and there was a unity. It's pretty much impossible to take that intimate feeling and have it translate to film." Could a positive experience of a different kind be generated for moviegoers? Many were hopeful, including Hanley.

Key People: Lansbury, Greene, and More

Edgar Lansbury had been around show business all his life. His actress mother, Moyna Macgill, moved from London to America during World War II and brought daughter Angela and her twin boys, Edgar and Bruce. They first lived in New York and later relocated to the Los Angeles area, where Edgar remembers large parties at their house with Hollywood talent.

Although his preferred creative outlet of scenic design kept him busy in art departments, Lansbury felt comfortable around actors and other show people. He gradually made connections through his work on productions for film, television, and the stage in the U.S. and U.K. One of his friends was director David Greene, with whom he had worked on the television programs *Playhouse 90* and *Coronet Blue*.

Lansbury recalls considering Greene to be the movie director for *Godspell*. "He came to mind because I thought he would understand it and be compatible. He was in Paris doing some work, and I said, 'Come over to London and see this show. I'd like to see if it would be something you'd be interested in working on.' He fell in love with it and fell in love with John-Michael and everybody. So that's how that started."

Lansbury was pleased with his associate producer. "I got a very good associate producer/production manager, Kenny Utt, who I'd worked with in TV, and he eventually became a producer of major films, including *The Wiz*. He was a terrific guy. He kept the budget down." Utt recruited Alan Heim as editor. Richard G. Heimann came in as the daring cinematographer who ended up capturing scenes from challenging positions, such as by leaning out of a helicopter.

Since *Godspell* already had Tebelak and Schwartz as the legally contracted author team for the stage show, Lansbury brought them together with Greene to work on the movie concept and casting.

It was rumored that someone at Columbia wanted celebrity casting, with the Jesus role possibly being filled by David

Cassidy, who was starring in the popular TV show *The Partridge Family*.

When the existing cast members heard about the film, they began to either fantasize about being in it, or imagine who would be playing their role in the film. It didn't seem inevitable that the original cast would get the parts, especially when they found out that Greene, Schwartz, and Tebelak were traveling around to every production of the show, looking for a cast and for performance ideas.

The whole situation created some tension amongst *Godspell* actors. "It was an incredible bone of contention," recalls Jeanne Lange. "It was obvious that some of the original people were going to do the movie, but…there were a lot of battles that John-Michael put up for people and [still] they were going to look at all the casts to decide. That didn't set well with a lot of people." To blow it off in a playful way, her group changed the "Hear Us" banners used during the "We Beseech Thee" number in Act II. She reveals, "The first night we knew that David Greene was coming to the show, we made new banners that read 'Hire us.'" It didn't help.

Greene had, by then, worked in stage, television, and film, and had his own perspective on what type of acting and actor would suit the film medium. He was experienced enough with film to know that what worked under the close scrutiny of the camera was different from what worked on stage. At the same time, he valued the loving ensemble feeling that the *Godspell* groups had generated. Could the *Godspell*-like feelings be created with a newly gathered group? That was the risk and assumption.

Ultimately, it was up to Greene to finalize a film cast in agreement with the actors and their agents. Some actors were not going to be available. Of the women, Sonia Manzano had already been offered a part in *Sesame Street*.

Greene was especially interested in having Joanne work with the newly hired choreographer, Sammy Bayes, as his assistant. When Greene saw Lynne Thigpen in the "Joanne" role in Washington, D.C., he concluded that Thigpen would be perfect for the film. Joanne Jonas recalls, "I was asked by the producers if I was willing to split the role of Joanne and Sonia. Lynne sang the heck out of 'Bless the Lord,' and I could bring a lighter tone to Sonia's 'Turn Back, O Man' that was less vampy and more campy."

Schwartz was always eager to get ideal singers for the parts and made a case for Robin Lamont to play her own role, since she had sung on the hit single of "Day by Day," so she was cast in the film.

Greene chose Gilmer McCormick to play her role. She could display her lighthearted comedy and facial expressions on screen.

Katie Hanley felt most attuned to Robin's role because she had performed it so often in the past. In early 1972, she was cast in the original Broadway production of *Grease*, but one night she was to be asked to urgently fill in at *Godspell*, so she arranged for her understudy to take over her Broadway role. Back in *Godspell* she played "Peggy" and sang "By My Side." That happened to be the night Greene saw the show at the Promenade in New York. "David Greene told me that the minute he saw me he wanted me in the film," Hanley recalls. "It didn't mean he wanted me for Peggy's role, necessarily. Nobody could sing 'By My Side' like Peggy on stage. She was mesmerizing." But Peggy was diagnosed with tonsillitis and required surgery. Hanley continues, "She called me the day I was cast in the film and congratulated me. It was so typical of the spirit they created in that show."

As for the men, Jeffrey Mylett's impish looks and behavior were suited to film, and he was cast as "Jeffrey." According to Lansbury, the director liked Merrell Jackson for his "youthful looks and his voice, which had a quality that was particularly appropriate for the harmonies," and he was chosen over the mature-looking, vocal powerhouse Lamar Alford for the "Lamar" role. Boston company member, Jerry Sroka, was a master of facial expressions and voices, which would work well on film, so he was selected as "Herb." David Haskell had originated the John/Judas role and was tapped for the part for the movie as well.

The last stop on the casting tour was Toronto, Canada. That's where Greene noticed Victor Garber's star quality and knew he had found his Jesus. Stephen Nathan was naturally disappointed he wasn't chosen to be the film's Jesus, but recalls, "The simple truth is that David Greene wanted Victor and not me. While I had always been promised the role by Edgar and Joe (John-Michael and I had even been talking about a concept for how the film could be done, keeping the same tone and feeling as the show), David Greene had final say. It was a surprise to me at the time, but I knew Victor was an incredible talent and had done a wonderful job as Jesus in Toronto. I was very happy for him and I have continued to love his work…."

Once gathered, the actors faced the challenge of re-creating *Godspell* in a new medium. The emotional arcs they knew for each character were out of whack, in part because they had cast two Joannes (Joanne and Lynne) and two Robins (Robin and Katie). Katie Hanley felt quite challenged playing another part, but gradually adjusted to it. "I had performed Robin's role so I felt able to freely be myself on stage. In the film, when I was doing Peggy's clown, I didn't identify with it so I was a little lost. That's why David Greene gave me that red hat. He said, 'You looked kind of perplexed. I'm going to give you that red hat and when you're finally more comfortable, I'll say in the middle of a scene, Katie, throw off that hat.' So that happened and it was then on my shoulders the rest of the time."

Locations and Film Concept

Lansbury didn't believe that the intimacy of theater could be translated to the new medium, and therefore they needed a unique concept. "That's the challenge any film has when you're making a film out of a play," he says. "You have to find the language, metaphor or whatever to keep the idea." It didn't seem likely that having three cameras focused on stage actors would do the trick. "It would be very inadequate I think," continues Lansbury. "That would just give you a record of the play. I wouldn't have liked that, I must say."

Tebelak was excited about generating ideas for the film. He told his friend Howard Sponseller that he wanted to incorporate many different film styles, reflecting the stage show's variations with its theater games, charades, drama, and so on. In the movie, he wanted one of the parables to be done as an animated cartoon. Although the animation didn't happen, diverse settings would help create visual interest for viewers.

Stephen Schwartz recalls his dissatisfaction with the state of movie musicals at the time, such as *Paint Your Wagon* and *Finnian's Rainbow*. He had been particularly disenchanted with the 1970 film *On a Clear Day You Can See Forever*, which had starred Barbra Streisand and Yves Montand. "I most specifically remember Yves Montand being on top of the Pan Am building and singing 'Come Back to Me' and it seeming absolutely ridiculous." For *Godspell*, he very much wanted to overcome some of the challenges inherent in having people singing in natural settings.

At a meeting with Tebelak and Greene, he suggested that the world of *Godspell* had to somehow be made fantastical. "I thought it was important for the experience to be magical and not real," Schwartz comments. Tebelak had previously developed the notion of an abandoned playground with the cyclone fence boundary. It was Schwartz's idea to extend this into New York City and somehow create an empty city as a backdrop. If they could film it so that none of the millions of inhabitants and visitors were visible, he felt it would be strikingly different. "It wouldn't be a normal day-to-day world, and therefore, people could sing."

To do this they would need to isolate the cast in selected settings or make special arrangements to hold people back from the film area. At the same time, they had to capture the charm of the performances against unexpected backdrops.

They planned two indoor scenes. One would be for "Turn Back, O Man" in the Andrew Carnegie Mansion on 91st Street, which meant filming on an ornately carved wooden staircase and other settings there. The other would be for the Prodigal Son scene in the Cherry Lane Theatre, returning *Godspell* to its original Off-Broadway home. It was director Greene's idea to use old clips of movies as a backdrop, and those could be shown in the theater.

New York City's celebrated outdoor settings would serve for all the other scenes. The locations staff had many permits to arrange. Choreographer Sammy Bayes met with Greene and others when planning musical numbers and joined in the location search. So there was a synergy between place and dance concept. He recalls that an "…exciting part of my earliest time on the film was scouting the right locations, parts of the city that wouldn't just visually best serve our ideas, but even at times affect a change in our concept of a particular number."

Schwartz suggested that part of "All for the Best" be filmed in front of an electronic sign that flashed above Times Square advertising Bulova's Accutron watch. For the baptism scene, they decided on Central Park's historic Bethesda Fountain topped by an angel sculpture, and they would use several other Central Park locations. The Lincoln Center and Fordham University area seemed promising for a few scenes. They also chose Ward's Island at the east edge of Manhattan, a couple of bridges, several landmark buildings, Chelsea Pier, and even a tugboat.

David Greene insisted that everything be shot in sequence rather than by location. It involved more work, but meant that the ensemble's connection with each other and the material over time might subtly be captured.

Script and Score Changes

Greene spent several months working on a shooting script, sometimes meeting with Schwartz and Tebelak at the Lansbury/Beruh office to discuss ideas. For some reason, Greene changed the order of scenes. For example, he moved the Sheep and Goats parable to an early scene in the movie, whereas in the stage show it fits in the second act along with other apocalyptic material. He also deleted several other standard parables and expressions from the film. It meant that the film could never be used as a model for theater groups, but that wasn't his goal.

Together Greene, Tebelak, and Schwartz made some decisions about what musical numbers would be included. To open the film, they agreed to replace the theatrically rich "Prologue" with a cinematically rich opening that showed John the Baptist inspiring (by way of a blast on his shofar) the men and women who would form Jesus' merry troupe to drop their work-a-day life and head to Central Park's Bethesda Fountain for a baptism.

The director decided to include "Prepare Ye," "Save the People," and "Day by Day" in the order they are sung in the show, but he wanted to drop "Learn Your Lessons Well." Instead of singing it, the clowns would hum the tune during the junkyard scene.

Greene also felt that the high-energy theatricality of "We Beseech Thee" wouldn't translate well to the film medium. Instead, the music (without lyrics) could underscore the Prodigal Son scene. Schwartz went along with the decision, in part because it meant he was justified in writing a new song. He chose the title "Beautiful City" to suit their approach to the film.

Recording the Soundtrack

Before filming started, the musical numbers had to be recorded for use on the movie set while the actors lip-synched to them. Stephen Reinhardt remembers that Stephen Schwartz wanted the soundtrack to be great. "Now that *Godspell* was going to be a movie, it was going to be a really big kind of recording event, and so we did it at A & R Recording studios with one of the top engineers in the city at that time."

Schwartz, as producer of the album, was glad to work with Elliot Scheiner, who had become a skilled engineer at A & R Recording, a leading studio on West 48th Street. In the 1960s, artists like James Taylor, Aretha Franklin, and Bob Dylan had all recorded at A & R.

Rather than developing an orchestra-based movie score, Schwartz wanted to stick with his rock band approach, yet enhance several of the tracks, following the model of contemporary pop recordings. In addition to the usual *Godspell* band of Reinhardt, Cutler, La Bonte, and Shutter, he brought in musicians who could layer in strings, woodwinds, percussion, guitar, banjo, harp, and keyboards. Reinhardt says, "We rented a lot of great equipment, synthesizers and percussion instruments, and Steve Schwartz got to do a lot of the things with that score that he couldn't do with the show. For the stage show there wasn't room on the band platform for anybody else and it wasn't scored for anything else. But here he was going to have an opportunity to add guitar solos, to bring timpani into the studio, and put things in the score that would be a one-time only thing."

To ensure the best accompaniment under studio time pressures, Schwartz had Paul Shaffer flown in from the Toronto production because he and Reinhardt had been so impressed with his keyboard ability. It was Shaffer's first trip to New York City, a place where he'd end up a celebrity performer for David Letterman and other shows. Shaffer recalls about *Godspell*, "He brought me in for a couple of things specifically. One was what I was doing with 'Bless the Lord.' I was kind of funking it up even more, and he liked that." Shaffer had been playing creatively with the score for a while. "I made up my own stuff based on what they were doing on the red [original cast] album. I was doing it in Toronto, and when Stephen Schwartz came to look at our show, he would hear everything, so he knew exactly what I was doing on each song."

One of the unusual instruments that Shaffer played on the "All for the Best" track was the tacked piano – a piano modified so that metal tacks hit the strings to make a clinky sound. Shaffer explains, "It is honky-tonk at its essence and it is silent movie-esque. At that time it was standard in a lot of studios that they would have a tacked piano."

Schwartz knew that Shaffer could play a Hammond B3 organ and invited him to improvise. "I happened to love that instrument," Shaffer states. "He just said play a solo here," and it ran while the end credits rolled.

"Beautiful City" was new for everyone. Victor Garber told one interviewer, "I was very excited about 'Beautiful City,' but recording the soundtrack was the most fun for me anyway. I was used to singing in a studio, and I felt comfortable there. And Stephen was so sure of what he wanted, and so smart."

Although most of the singing was performed by the cast, several other singers were brought in for vocal sweetening. Ben Vereen sings about eight seconds of "All Good Gifts," and Howard Sponseller recorded some notes that were added to support David Haskell's vocals for "Prepare Ye the Way of the Lord."

Costumes

Another part of the preparation was costume design. The producers hired Sherrie Sucher to spin off of Susan Tsu's designs. If Schwartz had his choice, he would have changed the costuming and made them more clownlike and less hippie looking. He explained later, "Because the show was originally produced in the hippie era, and because the director of the *Godspell* movie somewhat misinterpreted the characters as hippie-esque, that misunderstanding has come to haunt stage productions of the show a bit [because some directors have taken visual cues from the film]. The characters…were supposed to be putting on 'clown' garb to follow the example of the Jesus character as was conceived by *Godspell*'s originator, John-Michael Tebelak, according to the 'Christ as clown' theory…."

A few of the design themes from Tsu were closely replicated in the film, such as the Jesus and Judas costumes, Jeffrey's bowler hat with coon tail, and Gilmer's dress.

Filming *Godspell* in NYC

Shooting began in August 1972. Tebelak liked to say they would be filming for 40 days and 40 nights. Much would depend on the weather.

The first few days served as a belated screen test. Apparently, an actor could have been replaced at that point, but no one was. They all adapted quickly to being on camera.

They began at the Bethesda Fountain in Central Park where the cast splashed joyfully in the water. "I will never forget when we were shooting at the sacred fountain," says Katie Hanley. "David Greene asked, 'Who would dive in head first?' There was a pause, so I offered. He said, 'Excellent, but you have to do it in one take because we have only one costume for you.' Done!"

In this scene, as in all the others, the cast sang along to their own soundtrack performances, which they could hear as they were filmed. The city was too noisy to record live singing or speaking, so the final audio for the movie would be supplied by the soundtrack and by their post-filming sessions in a looping studio.

The actors didn't have a copy of the shooting script, and were simply told which parable or scene they would be doing the next day. They were all so experienced with the musical that they didn't need much rehearsal. They would show up in the morning ready to improvise, explore the possibilities in the location, and then start the shoot. "They brought us to the set and said, 'Okay kids, you have half an hour to come up with stuff,'" recalls Lamont. "We were all used to coming up with bits."

She remembers setting her clock radio for 4:30 or 5:00 in the morning to get to the set on time. As if it was a bonus for her summer work, "Day by Day" would sometimes come on the radio and she'd hear herself singing. Then she'd hop on the subway for the trip from Brooklyn to Manhattan.

"I loved being on the movie set," says Lamont. "I loved the sense of this huge group coming together, and the crew was so good to us! They were so much fun to be with. Many of them had worked on *The Exorcist*, and they were stunned over all the things that used to go wrong on and off their set. They were so happy to work on *Godspell* where things would always seem to go right."

Jerry Sroka was grateful that David Greene created a working space for the actors, helping them feel comfortable performing even with the hubbub around them as the crew set up shots. "He created an environment that was safe to try anything," Sroka comments. The actors almost made a game of getting their director to laugh. "He would just fall out of his chair laughing at what we did," says Sroka. "If David was happy, I was okay."

As exciting as the experience was, there was a great deal of focused work to be accomplished, especially as the actors were not following the same movements as they would on a small stage. The dance movement was a combination of direction from Greene, choreography by Sammy Bayes inspired by the stage show, and comments from Joanne Jonas. "I was asked to be the assistant choreographer to bring the innocence of the stage movement to the film and help communicate to the actors some of the nuances Sammy was going for," says Jonas. Some moments were easier than others, especially working with actors who were, for the most part, not trained dancers. "I remember working on the reflection pond scene at Lincoln Center during 'All for the Best'—how challenging it was for the actors to do the side by side movements and the about-face turns leading to David's turn and falling into the pond, then scene-switch to him on a float in a pool high atop a building." They decided to use most of the rest of the moves that had been perfected for the stage show for that particular song so the actors would feel more at ease in the many varied locations planned for that piece.

The most challenging scene for many of them was on top of the World Trade Center, where they finished "All for the Best." The tower they were on was unfinished and there were no safety walls. They were first brought to a level that would house the Windows on the World restaurant where they would put on makeup, and then brought to the open roof.

McCormick shares her experience on the tower: "That thing was swaying. It was terrifying. And they said it's exactly what it's supposed to do. But you're standing up there and you'd be swaying and the wind is blowing 2000 miles an hour. Finally, when the dawn came up, they said it's ready to go. They showed us a steel ladder that was probably 17 to 18 rungs that went up to the final roof. We looked up and there was a hole in the ceiling (top of ladder) and I said no way am I climbing this ladder. Lynne said 'come on.' She got behind me and literally pushed me up this ladder. I almost sent a double. We got up to the top of that thing and I just froze. The tears started coming, I was so frightened. Lynne just took me by the hand and led me to the edge of that. (It was one edge but probably you could have fallen to the next ledge and lived as there was another ledge down there.) We stood and put our arms out and the wind just held you. Pretty soon we were just giggling and giggling and I was able to do it."

She remembers that an even riskier job seemed to be that of the cinematographer in the helicopter, which was hovering and zooming out on the scene. "The cinematographer had a belt on and was hanging literally out of the helicopter with this seventy-pound camera." McCormick adds, "I could not wait to get down off that place! I could not wait. It was so scary. But I'm glad I have the memory."

Lynne Thigpen actually enjoyed the moment. "It hadn't been opened yet. It was just a new building. There were all these people in clown costumes standing on the top, dancing around and carrying on. Of course, we couldn't resist facing the Empire State Building and waving in our clown outfits. There were a couple of people who didn't like heights. I like heights so it was really amazing. We got there very, very early in the morning, before sunrise, so the sun was coming up. You could see the East River and the tributaries and watch everything go gold. It was quite extraordinary."

Another extraordinary moment came toward the end of the shooting process in September. The air was cooler by then. Robin Lamont reports, "I remember one specific moment from the movie that the crew found very odd and attributed it to being *Godspell* and sort of good vibes. Wards Island was very cold on the days we were shooting the Crucifixion scene. Every time David would yell 'cut,' the crew would be running out there with our coats because it was 40 degrees, and they'd cover us with coats and give us hot tea. It was difficult to shoot because it was cold. They didn't want to have to do very many takes. But I remember that they were hoping there would be a breeze. They did not have a fan for when Victor was singing 'Oh God, I'm dying.' Still, the red ribbons on his wrist would kind of flutter in the breeze. On the last take of 'Oh God, I'm dying' the breeze came up as he was singing and fluttered the ribbons. And then when he sang, 'Oh God, I'm dead,' the breeze died down and you see the ribbons just fall. Every time they took it, it did the same thing. I remember the crew being very struck by that—very amazed."

McCormick confirms that the ribbons blew in the wind during most of the scene and then "at the very end we hold the note 'dead' and the ribbons died. It was almost as if someone said, 'Turn the fan off.'"

Editing, Opening, and Reviews

It wasn't until the movie was edited and released that Schwartz realized that the movie on screen wasn't the one he had in his head. "For me, the model was [the Beatles film] *A Hard Day's Night*. I thought the movie was going to look like that slightly anti-establishment, wild, inventive filmmaking." But at the time, he was going along with Greene's plan and the group's decisions, hoping for the best when the scenes were all edited together.

At some point during the summer, Tebelak decided that his creation was being co-opted (says his sister, Trudy), and he walked away from it. During the shoot, the cast had relied on their own in-the-moment improvisations anyway, without new input from him. But he was still involved part time, especially in the Act II scene with the Pharisee monster, for which he supplied the voice.

In 1973, the soon-to-be-released *Godspell* movie opened the Cannes Film Festival. Victor Garber, David Haskell, and Robin Lamont flew to the French Rivera to represent the movie, along with the producers and writers. Lamont recalls the exhilarating experience of attending the screening: "I'm getting out of a limousine and they're taking my picture like I'm Ingrid Bergman. Afterward, there was dinner and I was seated next to the minister of culture of France. It was stunning. It was a highlight of my life."

Columbia Pictures scheduled other openings, including one in Los Angeles and one at the New York Film Festival. In

Lansbury's recollection, "It was well received," but it didn't catch on at the box office either domestically or internationally. Reviews were mixed, and it wasn't nearly as popular as they had hoped.

Later, when the *Godspell* movie adaptation was released on video, DVD, and screened on television, it ended up reaching a wide audience. Lansbury remarks, "It's amazing that it didn't do better as film; in retrospect, with ancillary rights or whatever, it has done very well." The actors report still receiving fan mail regularly from people who have watched the movie over and over.

Overall, Lansbury is pleased with the results, even though he heard complaints from people who loved *Godspell* on stage. "There are those who think he should have stuck closer to the theatrical version, but David and John-Michael, and Stephen Schwartz to a certain extent, worked together to create a concept. It was an interesting concept, and I think very much a filmic version of the theater production. It was very much in the language of film."

"For me there were two major flaws of the film," concludes Stephen Schwartz. "One is a philosophical flaw and one is technical. The philosophical flaw is that David Greene as an Englishman didn't really understand John-Michael's revolutionary concept or who these kids were. To me the movie just looked like happy flower children skipping around, and that's obviously not what the show is. I also feel like, frankly, they didn't get enough coverage. They didn't shoot enough footage so they could edit together something that looked like *A Hard Day's Night*, with its quick cuts and sense of anarchy. And that's a budgetary thing. I think it was under budgeted—not that they needed a whole lot more, but they needed more days of shooting to get enough coverage to really edit it together in a way that was cinematically exciting."

As it happens, the concept of using an empty New York City as a backdrop meant that cinematographer Richard Heimann preserved some of the city's heritage on film. The "All for the Best" scene at the World Trade Center serves as a visually stunning memento for the towers that were felled on September 11, 2001. Armchair travelers who like seeing New York on film can enjoy so much of what is beautiful in the city.

Film commentator Andrew Martin characterizes the movie as successful in the long run. "Turner Classic Movies shows it every Easter morning. It retains a cult following for a lot of different reasons. I think Victor Garber may have something to do with that. I think children tend to really like the movie because it's a relatable story; it doesn't feel like you have to sit through Bible class – it's just a fun, fun thing. Also there's a time capsule aspect to it because it's very early 1970s. It's an effective film and it holds up."

The soundtrack album scored well after its 1973 release, quickly reaching the Billboard pop charts.

The state of *Godspell* in the movie adaptation

In a complete pendulum swing from the rough and somewhat in-your-face production of *The Godspell* at Carnegie Mellon University, *Godspell* as a movie was now pretty and polite. Roger Ebert, in his review, described the impression it makes with its Manhattan setting: "Against this wilderness of steel and concrete, the characters come on like kids at a junior high reunion, clothed in comic book colors and bright tattered rags." *The New York Times* reviewer Vincent Canby described a flower-child escapism quality, which to him seemed oddly conjoined with some sophisticated show business song-and-dance material. He concluded, "I like its music, its drive and its determination, even when it's pretending to a kind of innocence and naiveté that I never for a second believe."

When some of the darker and more adult material from *Godspell* was cut, the naïve quality became more predominate. The playful sexual interplay between the Sonia character and the Herb character on stage was missing from the film. The movie adaptation also trimmed some of the darker material from the Bible that gave the show a more varied tone, such as John the Baptist's apocalyptic speech centering on the condemnation of the Pharisees, and most of the warnings or prophesies. Schwartz trimmed a verse from the angry "Alas for You" song.

Some commentators believe that the storytelling was compromised by the organization and omissions, such as the missing musical numbers and the set up for several of the songs. Joanne sings "Turn Back, O Man" in the first half of the movie whereas in the stage production the song is suitably placed as the Act II opener, where it helps signal the audience that a major shift in mood is going to take place. ("Turn back" means "stop doing what you're doing"—something else needs to happen.) "Bless the Lord" is normally set up by having the Joanne clown lead the parable of the rich man who hordes crops and belongings, and that parable was cut from the film.

The transition into "By My Side" in the play is the story of the woman caught in adultery whom Jesus saves from being stoned to death. In the movie, that adultery story was cut. The movie's Peggy clown, Katie Hanley, doesn't sing "By My Side" out of new devotion, but rather to comfort Jesus who is about to face his biggest challenge. Interestingly enough, the poetic song adapts to the new context without any lyric changes.

Differences inherent in the mediums of stage and film are emphasized further with a stage show that invites the audience into its world in a more interactive way. Herb Braha comments, "The movie seemed to say, 'we will entertain you,' and so the audience sat back and waited to be entertained." He felt that was the movie's downfall.

For musical numbers that involved closer contact with audiences in a live production, the divergence is most profound. During "Day by Day," stage audiences clap and sing along with the actors as they parade up and down the aisle near them, but movie audiences simply watch. Movie actors can't invite audiences to join the cast on stage during intermission after "Light of the World." Sonia can't saunter down the movie theater aisles during "Turn Back, O Man," nor can Jesus be carried down the aisle during the "Finale."

What the movie trades in content, it contributes in visuals, even ones that echo other films. For example, Schwartz contributed the idea for a scene in "All Good Gifts." He explains, "The 'choreography' of that section was patterned after the last shot of Bergman's *The Seventh Seal*, with the traveling troupe of players dancing along the hillside in silhouette."

Knowingly or unknowingly, Greene's use of silent film clips for the Prodigal Son parable created an homage to some of the silent film comic actors who had inspired *Godspell*'s clowning in the first place.

"The screen wants to narrow the focus, and the stage wants to expand the focus. Part of the success and charm of 'Godspell' was its expansiveness."

—Joanne Jonas

The Godspell Movie

ABOVE: Victor Garber and cinematographer Richard Heimann take a break.
BELOW: Robin Lamont and Katie Hanley on the film set.

The Godspell Experience

Godspell movie group: Front row from left: John-Michael Tebelak, David Greene, Edgar Lansbury, Katie Hanley, Lynne Thigpen. Middle row, from left: Merrell Jackson, Joanne Jonas, Jerry Sroka, Victor Garber. Back row from left: David Haskell, Gilmer McCormick, Robin Lamont, Jeffrey Mylett.

CHAPTER 36

2011 Broadway Revival

At the end of May 2011, *Variety* announced that the first Broadway revival of *Godspell* would be spearheaded by Ken Davenport, and that he had booked a coveted venue for the project. The Circle in the Square Theater, with its theater in-the-round design, has about 700 seats and is one of the smaller Broadway houses. Davenport felt it was ideal for a more intimate experience with the musical, and when another show closed there, he nabbed the space. A pleasing consequence for Stephen Schwartz was that two of his musicals would be running in the same building and sharing the same marquee on 50th Street: both his blockbuster musical *Wicked* and the revival of *Godspell*. Fans started calling the area in front of the theater doors "Schwartz Alley."

Davenport aimed for a November 7, 2011 opening, which meant that all the production details needed to settle in quickly. It helped that the creative team was already in place. The revival had initially been inspired by a well received 2006 production at the Paper Mill Playhouse in New Jersey, and most of the creative team from that production would transfer over: Daniel ("Danny") Goldstein (direction), Christopher Gattelli (choreography), David Korins (scenic design), and Miranda Hoffman (costumes).

A revival aimed for 2008 had fallen through for financial reasons, but this one was made possible due to Davenport's determination and his innovative notion to crowd source some of the funding. Through his daily blog, "The Producer's Perspective," Davenport had been regularly reaching thousands of theater enthusiasts. He eventually gathered over 700 people to join

"The People of *Godspell*" effort, each contributing $1,000 or more, to make up half of the capital needed to produce this Broadway show.

Davenport believed the show was beloved enough to draw a crowd. But rather than revive a version that might inspire nostalgia, he and Goldstein wanted to innovate. They listened to comments from Peggy Gordon and others, but more or less went in their own direction.

New Cast; New Sound

Goldstein and company took a risk by not casting movie or music celebrities to attract ticket buyers. Hunter Parrish, whom Goldstein chose to play Jesus, had gained some renown for his lead role in the TV show *Weeds* and had a Broadway credit for *Spring Awakening*. Anna Maria Perez dé Tagle was known by younger audiences for her role in *Hannah Montana*. All the others were members of the Actors' Equity union who had Broadway, regional theater, or tour credits. Schwartz commented in the summer 2011 issue of The Schwartz Scene newsletter for fans, "Though some people know our Jesus, Hunter Parrish, there are no major stars in the show—we have instead gone with the very best people we could find. I don't know if that will make marketing the show more difficult in today's highly star-driven climate for Broadway revivals, but ultimately the production team felt that *Godspell* has always been a show where stars of the future are discovered…and that it was better to stay true to the essence and spirit of the show."

In addition to Parrish and Perez de Tagle, the cast included Wallace Smith (John/Judas), Uzo Aduba, Nick Blaemire, Celisse Henderson, Morgan James, Telly Leung, Lindsay Mendez, and George Salazar, along with understudies Julia Mattison, Joaquina Kalukango, Eric Michael Krop, and Corey Mach.

Right away, Goldstein lobbied for new orchestrations. He believed that using older orchestrations was unthinkable for a revival. "It would be like borrowing someone else's wedding dress. You wouldn't do it." As part of envisioning the show afresh, he wanted to have input on the overall tone. "I had my own ideas of what the music should sound like and what the energy of it is. I wanted the music to sound like it was written yesterday without it sounding of today. I wanted it to sound timeless."

Schwartz made a short list of recommended arrangers, and Michael Holland, a singer-songwriter whose CDs Schwartz had enjoyed, got the job. Holland was fortunate to have a vocally skilled cast interpret his work, as they could take on any harmonic or rhythmic challenges put to them. They worked under the direction of Charlie Alterman, an experienced Broadway music director who also guided the cast recording session.

Working in the Space

Goldstein's choice for a scenic concept was an old leaky theater, with a drip from the ceiling that would land in a tank to be used for the baptism. "A theater is a world of potential energy," says Goldstein, "and frankly, *Godspell* is a play that, if nothing else, celebrates what theater and only theater can do."

Goldstein's idea for the "Prologue" to be sung unaccompanied was related to the scenic design. "I thought it would be really great in this circumstance if we're coming into an empty theater and see no instruments and no people playing instruments. And somehow they sneak in there and start to play their instruments." That meant he didn't even want a traditional orchestra pit or place for the band, but only a piano near the stage. Three guitarists would be distributed around the seating area, and the drummer would have his own box toward the back.

(The expectation was that audience members in those areas would enjoy sitting near the working musicians.)

The rehearsal process for the show mimicked the original production, with actors playing theater games and finding their own improvisations based on experiences. "In rehearsal we didn't really use the script so much as used the text from the Bible for the parables so that we could feel free to create where we wanted to," Goldstein asserts.

The result was a show full to the brim with new energy and new jokey cultural references, and a cast group that had a blast being creative. "It's not like work for us," says Anna Maria Perez dé Tagle about the playful process. They all became friends during the process.

Davenport had come up with the idea of letting actors actually bounce during the bouncy song, "We Beseech Thee." This meant having little trampolines installed on the stage under trapdoors. During the show, the actors opened the doors just before hopping onto the trampolines that boosted them several feet above the stage, leaping with joy quite literally.

Like the original group, the revival cast contributed whatever talents they had, whether it was playing an instrument or doing impressions. Telly Leung created a scene-stealing moment during which he sandwiched in as many as ten impressions in a row, from Katherine Hepburn to Jimmy Stewart.

Response

The show opened as Davenport had planned, on November 7, 2011. Reviews were mixed, but audiences were pleased enough to regularly give the actors standing ovations.

The varying impressions of the revival itself represent different views of what *Godspell* actually is. Reviewers were rating it as entertainment, and many of them felt it went too far.

It's something easy to do with comic material, especially when humor mocks someone (in this case Donald Trump and his TV show). Many of them criticized the zeal to connect to a modern audience, which ultimately fragmented the whole effect of the show.

The New York Times critic Charles Isherwood called the production "relentlessly perky" because it rarely stopped bouncing and bounding around. While some audiences liked the energy, it reminded Isherwood of "being trapped in a summer camp rec room with a bunch of kids who have been a little too reckless with the Red Bull." *New York Magazine* writer Scott Brown suggested, similarly, "To fully appreciate the show's rapid-fire eagerness to connect, it helps to have the mental metabolism of a properly medicated *Nickelodeon* viewer." Another reviewer recommended it primarily for the under 30 crowd, especially those with attention deficit disorder.

Writing for *Variety*, Steven Suskin suggested there was a problem in bringing an anachronistic telling of the age-old gospel up to date, such as with jokes about Lindsay Lohan or about Steve Jobs using an iPad in Heaven. *Godspell* already straddles Jesus' time and the 1970s style of theater. With yet another layer, the show drifted aimlessly between periods.

The show was not without its critical praise. Terry Teachout of the *Wall Street Journal* praised Goldstein for blowing the dust off *Godspell*, "…and the result is not a stale exercise in boomer nostalgia à la '*Hair*' but a fizzy, family-friendly show that deserves to run…well, forever."

Some long-term *Godspell* fans missed traditional material that had been cut from the show, such as the humming circle and "God speech" opening, as well an instrumental accompaniment to the "Prologue."

Schwartz and others who are especially appreciative of the joy value of the show, along with its examples of compassion and community creation, believed that the revival succeeded artistically. Many theatergoers appreciated the effort made by the actors to reach out to the audience. In several scenes, an audience member sitting close by would be chosen to join the actors on stage. One would create a drawing for a Pictionary game (a substitute for the show's usual charades). Another would play Lazarus during the Abraham/Lazarus scene, and would be asked to read a line off a card and then lie down as if dead. These scenes went on for about five minutes longer than they would if an actor played them, and gave the show an air of a personal party.

Unfortunately for investors and the performers, the party didn't last anywhere near as long as hoped. Toward the end, Corbin Bleu of *High School Musical* fame stepped in as Jesus but his name and performance didn't save the show. Revivals often close within about a year, especially if, like this one, they are not honored at the annual Tony Awards. The revival of *Godspell* received no nominations by any of the awarding entities. It closed on June 24, 2012, after 264 performances without recouping the investment.

Would a vintage reproduction of the show have run longer? No one knows, especially since, by the time the revival opened, *Godspell* had been performed in almost every corner of the world during the previous four decades. Critic Peter Filichia comments about the revival performances: "Some may complain that everyone's a little too bright and eager, but the Story-Theater-ish *Godspell* has always invited such excesses."

Only two of the original *Godspell* cast members actually attended the revival, although most of them heard reports and were disappointed to learn that it didn't more closely follow the script they helped create.

Peggy Gordon notes, "The main purpose of doing a revival is to revive what made the show iconic to begin with." She felt the revival missed the mark in many ways, from not using clown makeup to not following the character arcs that her cast developed. For example, at the Circle in the Square, an actor narrated the seed parable as a comedy routine. In Gordon's view, this didn't support the show. "John-Michael insisted we have a discernible growth process throughout the parable, showing the audience what we learned as a result of the experience; using the parables merely for pop or politically topical one-liners defeats that purpose."

She was also disappointed in the loss of childlike innocence. This, she believed, was due to "the standup comic-style cynical contemporary topical jokes (including critical jokes about famous people) that were not in the nature of the timeless show John-Michael conceived."

Stephen Schwartz was satisfied with the revival and glad that it ran over eight months on Broadway (none of his mid career flops lasted that long). Early in the run, he praised the effort, saying, "I am extremely happy with this production, the creative and highly energetic staging by director Danny Goldstein and choreographer Chris Gattelli, and the extraordinarily talented cast who just sing their faces off. One of the fun things for me is that every time I have seen it, there have been a couple of new and current jokes thrown in, so there is always something new for me to laugh at in what is already a pretty hilarious production."

Although ticket sales were disappointing, the actors were pleased with the feedback they received, especially from younger audiences. Many of these theatergoers would wait in the "rush" line, hoping to buy one of a limited number of discounted tickets that placed them next to the stage on pillows rather than in chairs. Some returned frequently, including one young man who saw the show more than 100 times. "We were taken aback by it because they would laugh with us and they would sob with us," recalls George Salazar. "They would come up to us after the show and talk about how much the show meant to them. A lot of these kids were outcasts in some way, and they found a community of their own through seeing our show and it made them feel that they were a part of something really special."

Ken Davenport (by the piano, wearing a cap) welcomes the entire Broadway revival company of *Godspell* on their first day of rehearsal. Schwartz's assistant, Michael Cole, was also invited to the traditional "meet and greet" session. Cole reports that it was held in a large, bright rehearsal room on the 10th floor of Ballet Hispanico on West 89th Street. The floor was a patchwork of masking tape in various colors denoting the location of set pieces, trap doors, the piano, and the edge of the stage. This room would serve as the rehearsal space for the show.

2011 Broadway Revival

ABOVE: Director Danny Goldstein and composer Stephen Schwartz at the first day of rehearsals. BELOW: The Broadway revival cast of *Godspell*. Front row, from left: Wallace Smith, Lindsay Mendez, Uzo Aduba. Second row, from left: Anna Maria Perez dé Tagle, Nick Blaemire, Telly Leung. Back row, from left: Celisse Henderson, George Salazar, Hunter Parrish, Morgan James. (Photo by Jeremy Daniel)

The Godspell Experience

The revival cast ends Act I with a bang. Circle in the Square Theatre, 2011. (Photo by Jeremy Daniel)

> *"At the end of the show there was a never a moment that people were not on their feet giving a standing ovation. They took something away from it."*
> **–Wallace Smith (revival cast member)**

A note for groups licensing the 2012 revival version of the script from MTI: Except for Jesus and John the Baptist/Judas, the character names have been changed to the Broadway revival actor names. In terms of the songs they sing and some of their dialogue lines, the newly named clowns are roughly equivalent to the following original characters: Nick is Jeffrey, Telly is Lamar, George is Herb, Anna Maria is Robin, Celisse is Gilmer, Lindsay is Joanne, Morgan is Sonia, and Uzo is Peggy.

Epilogue

Reflections on *Godspell* as a Transformative Musical

John-Michael Tebelak's hope was that *Godspell* would make a difference in people's lives. Peggy Gordon remembers him saying words to the effect of, "I want this to be two hours that the audience gets so drenched and embraced by love and joy that they walk out of here transformed, on whatever level. It doesn't necessarily have to be religiously, but on some level they walk out of here transformed."

His hope has been realized time and time again. A *Godspell* audience member was once heard saying after the show, "I was going to sue a woman over a parking traffic accident we had but now I'm not going to." It's a small thing, but suggestive of a phenomenon: this musical can help people change their emotional priorities and adopt a new outlook on their lives.

No doubt attending other musicals and plays also reaps positive rewards. With *Godspell*, the show's creators looked at what could be the most powerful approach, and layered that in.

For one thing, it's a show with inspirational content about human behavior and emotion. As actor Bob Garrett notes, "The point of this play is that everybody takes Jesus' teachings and infuses them in their hearts." It's an effortless process.

For another, they knew that in our jaded society, innocence has power. Peggy Gordon suggests that the childlike innocence of clowns impacts the audience in a reciprocal way. A childlike performance moves them into a more profound state of vulnerable receptivity. That is, when they set aside their adult mindset and become more like innocent children themselves, they might be more readily transformed or uplifted by the content of the show. In her words, they might receive "spiritual sustenance that only their vulnerable receptivity would allow them to experience."

For older performers and audiences, watching or being involved in childlike play was at the foundation of the show's development, and continues to inspire people involved with the show.

Stephen Nathan suggests, "*Godspell* was really all based on play, the innocence of children who see the world uncorrupted—that is how the whole piece evolved. Through improvisations we found what worked and what didn't work. Ultimately, in the rehearsal process, we solidified those moments that seemed alive and true, and suited the structure of the piece. It was a very transformative process."

When performers joyfully create and support each other's efforts during rehearsals, the benefit of their positive experience is palpable. Robin Lamont's sister, Thrae Harris, noticed the cast members' love and openness: "There's something happening between each of them that moves into the audience.... I had gone to *Camelot* and *The King and I* but *Godspell* was intimate and amazingly exciting."

Everyone interviewed for this book testified to the transformative and uplifting power of either performing in the show or watching it. For this Epilogue, three people provide details of that experience.

Reflections from Don Scardino

After about a year of playing Jesus in Toronto, Scardino stepped into the part in New York, both Off Broadway and on Broadway—in all, over 1,000 performances. Afterward, he continued performing in other shows and started directing. He directed one of the Off-Broadway revivals of *Godspell*, the popular television show *30 Rock*, as well as other shows and films.

For Scardino, playing Jesus wasn't about his preconceptions about the man, but rather about the direct experience he had every night during the show. His point of view is a spiritual one.

Scardino: The show is blessed by the spirit of Christ. The spirit descends upon the show, takes over, and leads everybody through it. And it never didn't work. We could be tired. At one point they changed the schedule for two shows on Friday night, two on Saturday and one on Sunday, and it was like five performances of *Godspell* in three days, and you know physically it's really hard. Saturday night, for the second show you just feel like 'I can't do it,' but you'd go out there and the audience is all like, 'we're at *Godspell*!' and the show would pick you right up. The audience's energy and everything would pick you right up. There is no single performing experience I've ever had like it. Ever.

I got letters from people who had quit drugs (including heroin), or gone back to their Bible, or patched up relationships with their mother or father after seeing *Godspell*. They would say it's the power of the show and you playing Jesus, and I knew it had nothing to do with me. I would always write back and say it is the show. The show is divinely inspired.

It came at a time when people needed to hear those words. Sometimes the whole stage would be filled with light. People left transformed; they left changed. It not only did what theatre should do, which is transform you so you're different when you come out, but it also did what church should do. It did what the Bible should do–reach people on a soul level, on a heart level that was transformative.

A Transformation Story from Michael Cole, Assistant to Stephen Schwartz

Having spent a large part of my adolescence on a small family farm raising sheep and pigs and milking the goats twice a day, I had never heard the name Stephen Schwartz nor was I aware of this show called *Godspell*. I was living in a tiny town in rural Oregon, population 1,515. I was headed down the same path as my older brother, winning a small collection of ribbons and trophies at the county and state fairs, but never quite equaling his achievements. The day I didn't get elected as an officer of the Cascade Future Farmers of America Chapter (like my brother) was the day I decided to audition for the Cascadians, our school's elite singing group. It was something my brother would never do. It was also something that I was terrified of, but the disappointment over my failed campaign inspired my determination to do it. Being accepted into this group gave me confidence and was a first step on my own new and exciting path.

In 1982, my senior year, our choir went to see a local college production of *Godspell* because it was announced our school was going to mount the show. I went along because Mr. James, my choir director, told me there might be a part in it for me. From "My name is known, God and King" all the way through to the final curtain call I was transported—swept up by the music and the energy and the "sexiness." There was something very seductive about it in terms of how it lured me into a world of sets and costumes and lights and applause. And glorious singing—the music flowed to the core of my being. The sound of it was thrilling.

I sat on the school bus during the ride home that evening, listening to everyone talk about what roles they wanted to play and what songs they wanted to sing. I felt uncomfortable announcing my role of choice, so I kept it to myself. Inwardly, I was giddy with excitement, dreaming of portraying Jesus. I don't remember the moment when I learned I had been cast, but I do remember somehow knowing all along that the part was mine.

One of the most vivid memories of my experience with *Godspell* is actually not a pleasant one. As I was leaving my house on opening night, my father said, "I can't wait 'til *Godspell* is over so you can get some work done around here." Needless to say, his lack of support had a huge impact on me. I got to the theater and was very emotional. Mr. James consoled me and said all the right things – he provided the support I didn't get from my father. I'll never forget that.

It was my father's turn to cry the night he came to see *Godspell*. I'm sure the message of the show got to him, but I also imagine he was touched by the passion he saw in my performance. To this day, my parents compare every role I play to that of Jesus in *Godspell*. Even at what I feel is my best, they still say, "You were good in this, but it wasn't *Godspell!*" The truth is, I had no idea what I was doing. The fact that my parents and others responded favorably was probably because they were seeing in my performance the raw emotion of me reveling in my new passion. I was lucky enough to discover musical theater by being part of a production of *Godspell* where the message of the show is the formation of community. I loved being part of that community every night, and *Godspell*'s message reinforced my desire to seek out other opportunities in musical theater.

I have few other specific memories of that production of *Godspell*. However, I do recall coming to the realization that I had to be prepared every night: I couldn't merely show up and do the show. I had to concentrate. I had to warm up. I had to place my props and stuff my pockets with changing scarves and magic canes and flowers….

Another fond memory I have is of the photo shoot where the cast spent an afternoon in downtown Salem, Oregon, posing with or mimicking statuary and architecture. The pictures were used in a slide show presentation that accompanied the concert choir singing the song "Beautiful City" each night before the show began. We felt like we were in our own *Godspell* movie, running from building to building and statue to statue, all dressed up in our colorful costumes. It was a special moment in the formation of our community.

Shortly after my arrival in New York City in 1993, I met Stephen Schwartz, who shared a music studio and office with a new friend of mine. I remember trying to act all cool and matter-of-fact—like this kind of thing happened every day. Inwardly, I was turning cartwheels! There was no need for me to act cool because Stephen is so unassuming and down to earth.

One day Stephen mentioned to me that he wasn't happy with the cleaning service he was using, so I offered to do it for him and began cleaning his studio once a week. He asked me if I could type a letter for him, which I did, and I slowly took on more and more responsibility until I had a full-time position as his personal assistant. Now I count Stephen as one of my best friends and can always depend on him for support and advice.

One of my favorite assignments of recent years was to create the director's script of *Godspell*, a new script with notes about staging transitions, directorial intentions and the like. Because Stephen had seen many productions where he felt the director missed the point of *Godspell*, he wanted to create a script that would allow directors access to a record of John-Michael Tebelek's original intentions of the show. Stephen asked me to watch the recording of the Off-Broadway production so I could remind him of staging bits that he had forgotten (but believe me, he hadn't forgotten much, having directed so many productions around the world!). I sat in a cubicle in the New York City Performing Arts Library laughing and crying and taking notes. I was able to offer suggestions of things Stephen might want to include or remove from the script. I particularly liked that assignment because I got to revisit *Godspell*, knowing my efforts would help preserve the integrity of the show for years to come.

Reflections from Stephen Reinhardt

Stephen Reinhardt writes a concluding remark about the whole *Godspell* journey: The Woodstock festival of 1969 was a "Happening" — something that occurs when a creative work and its audience arrive on the scene in conscious harmony. *Godspell* was such. For Woodstock, no one who organized it or performed there realized the defining role they were playing; nor did we with *Godspell*. To this day, I meet people who, discovering Gilmer's and my role in its creation, go wide-eyed, for either they had a life-changing experience as an audience member, or they performed in it. This Happening will outlive us. It will go on transforming the ordinary into the extraordinary, the mundane into the meaningful, for generations to come.

The Godspell Experience

LEFT: Michael Cole in the role of Jesus in his high school production of *Godspell*. BELOW: Cole "hard at work" in Stephen Schwartz's office/studio in Manhattan.

Epilogue

Don Scardino as a joyous Jesus in *Godspell*, with the *Godspell* company at the Promenade Theatre.

Appendix A

Interview by Thomas A. Barker, originally published in *Dramatics Magazine*, January, 1975. Copyright 1975 by *Dramatics Magazine*. Reprinted by permission. Dramatics is published by the Educational Theatre Association, online at www.schooltheatre.org.

Interview with John-Michael Tebelak and Stephen Schwartz; a candid conversation with the visionary creators of 'Godspell'

In the mid-1960's, a 'young Honor Thespian of Troupe 612 at Berea High School in Berea, Ohio, plastered a putty nose in place to play the title role in Rostand's CYRANO CE BERGERAC, while across the country at Garden City Park, Long Island's Mineola High School another Honor Thespian of Dan Wargo's Troupe 276 eyebrow penciled a moustache on his upper lip to play Anne's father in DIARY OF ANNE FRANK.

Short years later, these two men met as undergraduates on the campus of Carnegie Mellon University. But it wasn't until mid-May in 1971, in the lobby of New York's off Broadway theatre—the Promenade, that John-Michael Tebelak and Stephen Schwartz re-met to form an artistic union that would give the theatre-going world GODSPELL, the show that this month, passed THE BLACKS to become the fifth longest running play off-Broadway.

Despite negative reviews (most notably from *The New York Times*' Clive Barnes,) the audiences at the Promenade quietly grew large, the ticket became 'hot," and soon half-a-dozen American cities had resident companies. Two companies were touring the country (one in England,) the show was translated into nearly a dozen foreign languages, racked up four Drama Desk Awards, and a Grammy.

This month, after nearly a four-year wait, performance rights to GODSPELL have become readily available to non-professional production companies. (Some metropolitan areas in the Northeast still must wait a bit for performance permission.) Music Maximus (1650

The Godspell Experience

Broadway, New York, 10038) who is "agenting" the show reports their Switchboard jammed for several days, following a mass mailing announcing the availability of rights to high schools across the country.

Meanwhile, at the Promenade, at 7:26 each night a sold-out crowd hears ten voices from backstage chanting the "GODSPELL Motto," as they prepare to take the stage: "Keep the corners of your mouth turned up. Speak, in a low, persuasive tone. Listen, be teachable. Laugh at good stories, and learn to tell them . . . for as long as you are green, brother, you can grow." As last year ended, DRAMATICS Editor Thomas A. Barker talked with both John Michael Tebelak who wrote the script and "conceived" the production and with Stephen Schwartz who added music and lyrics, at their homes in New York and Connecticut.

BARKER: Stephen, you're the married member of the team. Do you have children?

SCHWARTZ: Yes, I have one son, ten months old.

BARKER: It's early to tell if he'll compose, but does he sing?

SCHWARTZ: Yes, he sings. Not particularly well, but he sings rather constantly.

BARKER: John-Michael, even though you are unmarried, you have a family of three. Are they pre-GODSPELL or post-GODSPELL acquisitions?

TEBELAK: I think I've gotten one every year since GODSPELL opened. No, I've missed one. I have a nice mongrel from the "Bide-A-Wee" home in New York. I have an old English sheep dog from right around my area here and a chow from New Haven. I really don't have a very good pencil sharpener. I keep them for that excuse.

BARKER: John-Michael, by now most of the world knows you wrote and directed GODSPELL, but your billing always boasts, "Conceived by..." Is writing a conception?

TEBELAK: You really can't put your finger on how you write something. I remember hearing of one playwright—I think he was in his mid-40's before his first play was done—and someone asked, "How long did it take you to write your play?" He said, "Well, 39 years to live, and I think, maybe three days to put it down on paper."

BARKER: Is that the GODSPELL legend?

TEBELAK: I think I kind of agree with him. It may take a short time to really put it down on the paper, but that's not the important part. Plays are to be spoken—they are to be lived more than read.

BARKER: Trace for us the history of the show from pre-pencil and paper to last night's performance at the Promenade.

TEBELAK: I had been a student at Carnegie-Mellon University in the drama department—a directing major. Most of my work had been done with mythology—something I feel is a part of theatre. But the Greek myths seemed to have no relation to my casts or audiences. The Greek mythology is so different—so distant to our way of thinking— that it was difficult for a cast to portray the feelings, the emotions, or even the power of certain characters.

BARKER: Does what you're speaking of involve the Greek mythological gods?

TEBELAK: Yes. Our concept of Zeus is not the same as the Greek's concept would have been. We think of Zeus as a "father-image." He was really not—he was much more a human image. The Judeo-Christian ideas of Zeus are "god-the-father" images. Because of that conflict, I began looking for a mythology that seemed a bit closer to me, closer to a cast, closer to the audience. The Judeo-Christian mythology was the obvious choice. I read miracle plays, cycle plays, passion plays, but nothing really excited me. They all seemed to be very heavy— downtrodden. Finally, I turned toward the Gospels and sat one afternoon and read the whole thing through. Afterwards, I became terribly excited because I found what I wanted to portray on stage.

BARKER: Which was...

TEBELAK: Joy! I found a great joy, a simplicity—some rather comforting words in the Gospel itself—in these four books. I began immediately to adapt it. I decided to go to Easter sunrise service to experience, again, the story that I had gotten from the Gospel. As I went, it began to snow which is rather strange for Easter. When I went into the cathedral, everyone there was sitting, grumbling about the snow, and the fact that they had already changed their tires. They weren't going to be able to take pictures that afternoon. Snow was upsetting their plans. As the service began, I thought it might be a little different. Instead, an old priest came out and mumbled into a microphone, and people mumbled things back, and then everyone got up and left. Instead of "healing" the burden, or resurrecting the Christ, it seems those people had pushed Him back into the tomb. They had refused to let Him come out that day. As I was leaving the church, a policeman who had been sitting two pews ahead of me during the service, stopped me and wanted to know if he could search me. Apparently he had thought I was ducking into the church to escape the snowstorm. At that moment—I think because of the absurd situation—it angered me so much that I went home and realized what I wanted to do with the Gospels: I wanted to make it the simple, joyful message that I felt the first time I read them and recreate the sense of community, which I did not share when I went to that service. I went to my teachers at Carnegie and asked if I could work at my own special project for my masters' degree, and they agreed. That following fall, in October, we began rehearsals at Carnegie.

BARKER: At this point, did the show have music?

TEBELAK: Yes, it had a rock score that was assembled by myself and my roommates—all medical students. It was an all-doctor band. Basically, because it was a pure rock score, it really didn't have the dimension of different sounds. It wasn't eclectic enough. Part of the GODSPELL concept is to be eclectic and gather from all sources. We had many of the same words, though. Some are based on old hymns. "Day By Day" was written by Sir Richard of Chitchester in the late 14th Century. "Turn Back, O Man" was a rather popular Victorian hymn. Obviously "We plow the fields and scatter…" is a traditional sort of hymn.

BARKER: Let's trace back to Carnegie again. You're about to open.

TEBELAK: Yes. It was December, and we decided that GODSPELL would be our Christmas gift to the theatre department. It went over quite well for the four performances we did. We thought at that point we'd never see or hear of it again.

BARKER: At this moment, in the conception of GODSPELL, where was JESUS CHRIST, SUPERSTAR?

TEBELAK: SUPERSTAR was written first.

BARKER: Stephen, before you added your music and lyrics to John-Michael's script, did you listen to SUPERSTAR?

SCHWARTZ: The album was released in, I believe, December, 1970. I had a copy of the album, but had not listened to it. I was asked to do GODSPELL and consequently I did not listen to it until I finished GODSPELL

BARKER: Was that purposeful?

SCHWARTZ: Once I knew I was going to do GODSPELL, yes, it was on purpose. I didn't want to be affected either by subconsciously imitating it or consciously striving not to imitate it. I just wanted not to know about it at all.

TEBELAK: SUPERSTAR came out as a recording just the summer I was writing GODSPELL. I had not heard it because I was so busy directing and writing. It wasn't until I moved to New York that I actually heard it. In fact I know the exact date: May 20th, just three days after the show opened in New York.

BARKER: Have you spoken to SUPERSTAR creators, Webber and Rice? Your creations draw several parallel lines.

TEBELAK: About two weeks after we had opened, Lloyd Webber and Tim Rice came down to see our show. They had heard we were playing a pirated version of their show. They came in very tersely, with looks like "We're not going to enjoy this.' Afterwards, we met with them and they had enjoyed it a great deal and were happy we were so totally different. It was fun then, to sit and compare notes.

The Godspell Experience

BARKER: I've sidetracked the discussion. When we left the development of GODSPELL, John-Michael, you had just closed at Carnegie. What came next?

TEBELAK: After we closed in Pittsburgh we thought we'd never see or hear of GODSPELL again. I went to New York for rest, and in my travels, I met with Ellen Stewart who founded La Mama Theatre and I mentioned my play. She thought it sounded interesting, but unfortunately she wasn't then able to do anything for about a year. Two days later she called and asked "How soon can you be here?" I very quickly said, "Six weeks," and she said, "Fine!" She had had a cancellation. We started rehearsals the following week and five weeks later, we opened at La Mama with the workshop production we had done at Carnegie. At La Mama, producers Edgar Lansbury, Stuart Duncan and Joseph Beruh came and saw the show. Afterwards we met and started negotiations for an off-Broadway production. They asked if I would like to change the show in any way, and my first reaction was: music. I wanted something a little more eclectic than pure rock. They said, "Fine, we'll send down a young composer we have heard a score from."

BARKER: It sounds like you're leading up to something.

TEBELAK: The night he was supposed to come, I was waiting in the lobby. I thought someone would introduce themselves to me, but instead there were mostly old friends from school, and while I was talking with them, one of the old friends happened to be...

BARKER: Stephen Schwartz!

TEBELAK: Right. I said, "How did you enjoy it?" And he said, "Fine, I can't wait to get back to Edgar and Joe," and I realized that this was the "young composer." Five weeks later we had a complete score for the show. We went into rehearsals at the Cherry Lane Theatre and after four weeks we opened, on May 17th—which was also my graduation. I had not returned to school, obviously, from the time I had left at Christmas, and I was a little afraid of what the school would think about my—in a sense—running away. My professor in directing had given me $100 to get a truck so I could move all of my things to New

York with our sets and costumes. Opening night, the department sent me a telegram that said, "No matter what the critics say, you've passed with us," and then announced that I would graduate.

BARKER: From the Cherry Lane, you moved to the Promenade. When?

TEBELAK We opened in May and moved in August.

BARKER: Stephen, since GODSPELL, you've written—with a flourish, and not without acclaim, PIPPIN and THE MAGIC SHOW, both with a rock flavor. What sort of affect do you think you've had on rock music, in general, and it on you?

SCHWARTZ: Well, I would say that my affect on the current rock scene, up to this point, has been virtually nil. The affect of rock music on me, I think, is quite large, as one can see from my writing. The kind of music that I listen to, say, 75 percent of the time, is bound to have an affect sooner or later. With GODSPELL, where the score had to be concocted very, very quickly, I often thought that this should have a "James Taylor feel" or such-and-such should have whatever kind of feel. I think that's implicit in the music. I believe that I've developed enough of a style so that no matter where my influences come from the, the music is identifiable as my own.

BARKER: You have. Who's your favorite rock artist?

SCHWARTZ: I think that the person I have really admired most for years—for two, three, four years is Joni Mitchell. She's unquestionably the finest songwriter in America today—bar none. I think Paul Simon is also a great songwriter.

BARKER: John-Michael, want to play the favorites game?

TEBELAK: Oh, I think Loggins and Messina have come out with some very exciting records. I like Gladys Knight and the Pips. I listen, quite often, to Aretha Franklin.

BARKER: Let's talk about theatre artists for a moment. Stephen, some are calling Stephen Sondheim the musical Neil Simon.

The Godspell Experience

SCHWARTZ: Well, I think that's both over-praising Steve and belittling him at the same time. He's not nearly as successful Neil Simon, and at the same time, I think what he's doing is probably of finer quality.

TEBELAK: Oh, Simon's a genius. Someone once said, "If Shakespeare were alive today he'd be writing for Desilu." There nothing wrong with that—writing for the masses.

BARKER: GODSPELL will soon be available to masses of non-professionals. What sort of advice can both of you offer a cast and director about to begin work on your very delicate show?

SCHWARTZ: I could go on forever, of course, but let me say the three things that I think are most important: First, the creation of a family feeling between all the cast members is vital. It's very important that the audience feels the connection between the cast members on stage. If everybody is out there doing his individual "shtik" then the whole fabric of the show will disintegrate. It is very hard to create that kind of family feeling. Off-stage exercises and theatrical games—I would recommend that very highly. The second thing to bear no mind, and this is advice to the director, that the story of GODSPELL is almost entirely subtextual, and therefore it's very important for him to know what kind of development he wants to see and be able to put it on stage. By that, I mean that really what happens in GODSPELL is that ten separate individuals come together and then turn to the audience and attempt to get them to also become a unit—with them. This happens very slowly. I think that if everyone's out there just making jokes, doing "shtiks," and has no overview of the show—it will fall apart. The third thing I would advise is that the director exercise as much taste as he possibly can. With a show like GODSPELL, it is very easy to go for cheap gags—what I call television humor."

TEBELAK: The basic structure must be adhered to, and there are certain qualities that must be maintained. The honesty of each performer—trying to find a clown within himself, as opposed to adding a clown character on top of what is inherently funny about that individual. Trust is one of the most important elements in the show. As long as the cast has that image of trust, and friendship, and working ability, and ensemble among themselves, I don't think that there could be a bad GODSPELL. The important thing to do is to enjoy the experience—enjoy each other. I secretly wrote a part for myself, but I've never been able to perform it.

BARKER: Which part is yours?

TEBELAK: If you notice, there's one character who usually wears overalls. I'm kind of known for wearing my overalls.

BARKER: John-Michael, while you're giving away secrets, what's the secret of GODSPELL's universality? You've translated the show for companies in Australia, England, France, Holland, Norway, Germany, South Africa... How can you take a line that is typically and topically American—say a catch phrase from a television commercial—and get a South African and a housewife in Sidney together to laugh at it. Or going even one step farther, how do you get a Bostonian and a Denverite to chuckle at the same line?

TEBELAK: That's part of the fun. When people read our script, I think it scares them a little. It doesn't look like a very funny show or even a very amusing show. It's basically just the text of the Bible. And in workshops and in rehearsals with the cast you can begin to develop the show. Because of this, in almost every country we have gone to, the cast—in a sense—translates the show. Not only in other countries, but also in America. We "localize" it for each particular city - each part of the country. And the cast basically does that work.

BARKER: You're not giving a carte blanche to anyone who wants to rewrite GODSPELL are you?

TEBELAK: No, I don't think so. The important thing is to keep the basic structure, which is terribly important, but the improvisation that goes around the basic structure can be changed—should be changed—for each particular company. It's very much like a pianist playing Bach. He really can't do very good Bach improvisation until he has Bach down.

BARKER: How does the show play in England? It seems British humor is a completely different color from America's.

TEBELAK: This is an example of how a cast can translate a show. We were running previews in England and I was so worried that we hadn't become "British" enough. As I was leaving the theatre one night, two gentlemen from England were talking. One said, "It's a teddibly delightful show, but I don't see how they're ever going to take it in the United States...it's so teddibly British!"

BARKER: Critics were mixed when the show opened in New York. Barnes (New York Times) was negative. Stephen, what do you think of the critics?

SCHWARTZ: I know I—and I have a great deal more musical training and probably a better ear—I have no way to evaluate a score upon first hearing it. So how they can do it is utterly beyond me. Because of this, critics tend to like scores which are accessible, and in the end turn out to be rather dull, and find scores that make more demands on them...for those they use phrases like, "There's nothing whistle-able," or they call it "unmemorable," because they aren't able to leave after one hearing having memorized the score. Critics obviously are necessary to get people into the theatre and so one has to "get by" the critics.

BARKER: John-Michael, where are those kids who came to New York with you from Carnegie? Did most of them go back to Pittsburgh and graduate?

TEBELAK: Most of them have gone on to other jobs. Eight of the original Cherry Lane cast were from Carnegie; three were students at the time.

BARKER: Where are they now?

TEBELAK: David Haskell is in California now working in television; Robin Lamont is doing GREASE, and of course Sonia Manzano is on *"Sesame Street."* Lots of times they come back to New York and do the show for a while. Right now we have Gilmer McCormick from the original company back in New York.

BARKER: GODSPELL must be magnetic.

TEBELAK: Often their agents or people around them say, "Why are you going back?" "Well, it's enjoyable," they say. Most of them, as soon as they get back, say to me, "Oh, you must come down. It's a totally different show, and I'm doing all of these new things!" I remember one particular party in England, where the company had been on tour for a year and a half. On stage you would hear an actor say, "Oh, my goodness, not 'Day By Day' again!" Then one night, we had about six new members going into the show. Half of the cast was leaving. Instead of having a party to really forget GODSPELL, everyone sat down and sang the entire score.

BARKER: Both of you were active in Thespian Troupes in your high schools. What did that experience mean to you. Does it affect your work today?

TEBELAK: I was already working in the professional theatre when I was in high school, so it wasn't really until my last year and a half in high school that I was finally in shows at school myself. I got to do "Cyrano," which excited me. I was an Honor Thespian, but I think the important thing is the sense of recognition in one's own school. It's like a sports sweater – it gives responsibility to the school's progress. I think I was very fortunate in having an instructor in high school who gave great deal of freedom. And because of that we were able to try things—which you aren't always able to do in similar situations.

BARKER: Stephen?

SCHWARTZ: I saw a letter you wrote to Shirley (Bernstein, Schwartz's agent) that said I was one of your most distinguished alumnae. What astonishes me - and I mentioned this to my wife last night- is that I just assumed that anybody who was interested in the theatre when in high school was a Thespian. That's where the experience was. I don't know how the system works in other schools, but I know under (Dan) Wargo (who is still Sponsor of Schwartz' old Troupe at Mineola High School in New Hyde Park, Long Island,) students were given enormous amounts of freedom and permitted—really permitted—to make their own mistakes and also to have their own successes. I don't know how old the Thespian Society is.

BARKER: We began in 1929.

SCHWARTZ: ...then I really don't understand how I can be one of your most distinguished alumnae, since I figure that anyone who has gone through high school and wound up in the theatre would have been involved in the Thespian Society.

BARKER: Stephen, what advice do you have for someone contemplating a career in professional theatre. What should he do?

SCHWARTZ: Well, I think that any student who is reading your magazine is already doing the right thing. He must be actively working as much as possible at what he wants to do and while in high school the best way is to be involved in whatever extracurricular theatre there is. I really believe that if somebody is talented—that if they are really to succeed in show business today—they need a great deal of determination and talent. I deliberately put determination first, because you have to resign yourself to really wading through a lot of crap—to put it more mildly than I usually do. Sooner or later, if one is really determined, they'll make it. And I think it's rather easier than people generally think.

BARKER: John-Michael, any parting words?

TEBELAK: Tell everyone who is going to do GODSPELL to have fun.

SCHWARTZ: Your readers should realize that it is in their power to change the theatre in whatever way they want. In a few years it is going to be up to them and I think that's something for them to be excited about.

Appendix B
Credits for Productions

The following credits sections are based on the author's analysis of credits and of the songs that were included in each production.

Credits for *the Godspell* at CMU

The Godspell at Carnegie Mellon University 1970
Cast: Andrew Rohrer (Jesus), David Haskell (John the Baptist/Judas); Randy Danson, Martha Jacobs, Stanley King, Robin Lamont, Sonia Manzano, Robert Miller (Bob Ari), Mary Mazziotti, James Stevens

Conceived and Directed by John-Michael Tebelak
Composer: Duane Bolick
Lyricists: writers of traditional hymns from the Episcopal Hymnal of 1940; writers of a psalm and the Gospels of the New Testament
Band: Duane Bolick, Captain Horton, unnamed friend
Costumes: Susan Tsu
Lighting: Lowell Achziger

Songs:
Prepare Ye the Way of the Lord
Save the People
Day by Day
Bless the Lord
All Good Gifts
Sermon on the Mount
Turn Back, O Man
On The Willows

The Godspell Experience

Oh God, I'm Busted…
Prepare Ye the Way of the Lord (reprise)

Credits for *the Godspell* at Café La MaMa

Cast: Stephen Nathan (Jesus), David Haskell (John the Baptist/Judas); Herb Braha, Jimmy Canada, Prudence Holmes, Peggy Gordon, Robin Lamont, Sonia Manzano, Gilmer McCormick, Jeffrey Mylett
Conceived and Directed by John-Michael Tebelak
Composers
- Duane Bolick (all songs except for two),
- Peggy Gordon (music, "By My Side),
- Jeffrey Mylett (music, "The Raven and the Swan")

Lyricists
- Writers of traditional hymns from the Episcopal Hymnal of 1940, psalm lyrics, or Bible passages
- Jay Hamburger (lyrics for "By My Side")
- Jeffrey Mylett (lyrics for "The Raven and the Swan")

Songs (as before)
- Prepare Ye the Way of the Lord
- Save the People
- Day by Day
- Bless the Lord
- All Good Gifts
- Sermon on the Mount
- Turn Back, O Man
- On the Willows
- Oh God, I'm Busted…
- Prepare Ye the Way of the Lord (reprise)

New Songs Added for La MaMa

- "By My Side," "The Raven and the Swan"

Band: Richard Quinn, keyboard; Doug Quinn, guitar; Marty Quinn, drums

Costumes: Susan Tsu
Lighting: Lowell Achziger
Stage Manager: Nina Faso

Credits for *Godspell* a the Cherry Lane Theatre

Cast: Stephen Nathan (Jesus), David Haskell (John the Baptist/Judas), Lamar Alford, Herb Braha, Peggy Gordon, Joanne Jonas, Robin Lamont, Sonia Manzano, Gilmer McCormick, Jeffrey Mylett
Conceived and directed by John-Michael Tebelak
Music and new lyrics by Stephen Schwartz except for "By My Side"*
*"By My Side" Peggy Gordon, music; Jay Hamburger, lyrics

Songs:
1. Tower of Babble ("Prologue")
2. Prepare Ye
3. Save the People
4. Day by Day
5. Learn Your Lessons Well
6. Bless the Lord
7. All Good Gifts
8. Light of the World
9. Turn Back, O Man
10. Alas for You
11. By My Side
12. We Beseech Thee
13. On the Willows

14. Finale

Band:
- Keyboards: Steve Reinhardt
- Acoustic and lead guitar, bass: Jesse Cutler
- Rhythm guitar and bass: Richard La Bonte
- Drums, percussion: Ricky Shutter
- Additional keyboards: Lamar on "Learn Your Lessons Well," (Live only)
- Stephen Schwartz on "Day by Day" (cast album only)
- Additional guitar on "By My Side" Peggy Gordon, Gilmer McCormick, and Jeffrey Mylett
- Ukulele: Stephen Nathan for "All for the Best"
- Shofar: David Haskell on "Prepare Ye"
- Recorder: Jeffrey Mylett on "All Good Gifts"
- Concertina: Jeffrey Mylett on the Good Samaritan parable (not recorded)

Producers: Edgar Lansbury/Stuart Duncan/Joseph Beruh
Lighting: Lowell B. Achziger
Costumes: Susan Tsu
Production Stage Manager: Nina Faso
Associate Producer: Charles Haid
Music Director: Stephen Reinhardt
General Press Representative: Gifford/Wallace
Musical Arrangements and Direction: Stephen Schwartz

Notes

The Godspell Experience is based primarily on the author's original research in the form of interviews with over 50 people. The vast majority of quoted comments came from these interviews and personal correspondence conducted between 2000 and 2014.

The notes that follow only include the limited number of published sources that served as a reference. All other quotations are from interviews or correspondence with the following people:

Original cast members: Herb Braha, Peggy Gordon, Joanne Jonas, Robin Lamont, Sonia Manzano, Gilmer McCormick, Stephen Nathan, and the original stage manager, Nina Faso.

Movie cast members (in addition to Jonas, Lamont, and McCormick): Katie Hanley and Jerry Sroka, as well as Lynne Thigpen before she passed away.

Carnegie Mellon University and La MaMa cast members: Bob Ari (formerly Robert Miller), Prudence Holmes, Mary Maziotti, and Andy Rohrer

Stephen Schwartz and Trudy Tebelak Williams (John-Michael Tebelak's sister)

Additional cast members from later productions, friends, and others connected with the show: Colette Bablon, Mary Rose Betten, Jesse Cutler, Ken Davenport, Bob Garrett, Daniel Goldstein, Gary Gunas, Jay Hamburger, Alexandrea Haskell, Heather Hutchison, Leon Katz, Rex Knowles, Paul Kreppel, Jeanne Lange, Sherry Landrom, Edgar Lansbury, David Lewis, Andrew Martin, Carla Meyer, Nan Pearlman, Reet Peel, Tom Peters, Bill Phillips, Dean Pitchford, Stephen Reinhardt, George Salazar, Don Scardino, Sheila Schwartz, Elliot Scheiner, Paul Shaffer, Rick Shutter, Marley Sims, Wallace Smith, David Spangler, Howard Sponseller, Jerry Sroka, Bill Thomas, Susan Tsu, and Valerie Williams

CHAPTER 1: The Lights Go Up

"cheerful ebullient Passion…" Lee Mishkin, "The *'Godspell'* According to Schwartz,' *Morning Telegraph,* May 19, 1971.

"jubilation in their…" Edward Hipp, "'*Godspell,*' and More," *Newark Evening News,* May 18, 1971.

"Innocence reigned like…" Clive Barnes, "The Theater: *'Godspell'*; Musical About Jesus Is at Cherry Lane," New York: *The New York Times,* May 18, 1971.

"I remember hearing…" John-Michael Tebelak in Thomas A. Barker interview, *Dramatics Magazine,* January, 1975 reprinted here as Appendix A.

CHAPTER 2: Tebelak and Schwartz: Theatrical Childhoods

"I used to go…" Stephen Schwartz interviewed by Michael Kerker at the Kennedy Center, May 1 2006.

CHAPTER 3: An Eclectic Talent Gathering at CMU in the 1960s

"In terms of liberation…" Stephen Schwartz in an interview in Jem Aswad, "It's An Art: Reflections on a Life in Song." (No longer available)

CHAPTER 5: The College *Godspell*

Regarding spiritual inclinations of her family, Trudy Tebelak Williams also comments: "When my parents got married, my mother told my father, 'I won't go to a church where I cannot understand what anyone is saying, so we're going to have to compromise.' They chose the Episcopal Church. The trappings appealed to my father. Their local church had many college professors as members, and my mom enjoyed the social part of it."

"The Greek myths seemed…" Tebelak, John-Michael in Thomas A. Barker interview, *Dramatics Magazine,* January, 1975 reprinted here as Appendix A.

"Afterward, I became…" ibid.

"An old priest came…" ibid.

"our jaded modern consciousness..." Harvey Cox, *The Feast of Fools: A Theological Essay on Festivity and Fantasy*. Cambridge, MA: Harvard University Press, 1969, page 139.

"I held a rehearsal..." John-Michael Tebelak in Edwin Miller, "Singing about Jesus, sighing over Shangri-La," *Seventeen Magazine*, April 1973.

CHAPTER 6: Experiments in New York City

"She thought it sounded..." John-Michael Tebelak in Thomas A. Barker interview, *Dramatics Magazine*, January, 1975 reprinted here as Appendix A.

CHAPTER 7: Enter Lansbury, Beruh, and Schwartz

"I wanted something a..." ibid

CHAPTER 9: Mishaps, Miracles, and a Completed New Musical

"No matter what critics..." John-Michael Tebelak in Thomas A. Barker interview, *Dramatics Magazine*, January, 1975 reprinted here as Appendix A.

"Four trestles, four boards..." *Oxford Dictionary of Quotations by Subject*, edited by Susan Ratcliff. New York: Oxford University Press, Inc., 2010.

CHAPTER 10: Long Live *Godspell*

"We literally did..." Peggy Gordon interviewed in Andrew Martin, "The Original Women of *Godspell* Are Still Almighty." Blog Posted: August 2, 2011. http://themartinreport.wordpress.com/2011/08/02/the-original-women-of-godspell-are-still-all-mighty

Part II Introduction

"A production can often..." Peter Filichia, *Let's Put On A Musical*, revised second edition. New York: Back Stage Books, 2007, page 39.

"a group of disparate..." Stephen Schwartz in Author's Note to the Director" published in Script Notes and Revisions by Stephen Schwartz 1999 (in the script) and on his discussion forum at www.stephenschwartz.com

CHAPTER 11. Why Send in the Clown Characters?

"I wanted to show…" John-Michael Tebelak in a *Godspell* souvenir book.

"Clowns can ease tense…" David Haskell in *Scholastic SCOPE,* February 26, 1973, page 3.

CHAPTER 12: What Holds *Godspell* Together?

"It is easy for…" Stephen Schwartz in Author's Note to the Director" published in Script Notes and Revisions by Stephen Schwartz 1999 (in the script) and on his discussion forum at www.stephenschwartz.com

"Above all, the first act…" ibid.

"era of increasingly shrill..." Ken Davenport, "81 Days 'til *Godspell*: Washington reminds me why *Godspell* why now." July 24, 2011, a special day by day report on *Godspell* as part of Davenport's daily blog *The Producer's Perspective.* www.TheProducersPerspective.com

CHAPTER 15: Q & A: Is *Godspell*'s Comic Tone Spiritually Appropriate? And Other Concerns

"*Feast of Fools* says…" John-Michael Tebalak in Edwin Miller, *Seventeen Magazine,* April 1973, "Singing about Jesus, sighing over Shangri-La."

"Why are we naturally…" James Martin, SJ, *Between Heaven and Mirth: Why Joy, Humor, and Laughter are at the Heart of the Spiritual Life*, page 29.

"Each audience member can…" Stephen Schwartz, Discussion forum archives at www.StephenSchwartz.com. *Godspell* Notes for Performers.

"I didn't want to be…" Stephen Schwartz in Thomas A. Barker interview, *Dramatics Magazine,* January, 1975 reprinted here as Appendix A.

"About two weeks after…" John-Michael Tebelak in Thomas A. Barker interview, *Dramatics Magazine,* January, 1975 reprinted here as Appendix A.

"And when the Christ…" Prideaux, Tom, *Life Magazine,* August 4, 1972.

"Over the years, there..." Stephen Schwartz, Discussion forum archives at www.StephenSchwartz.com. *Godspell* Notes for Directors and Musicians.

"While a creative director..." ibid

CHAPTER 16: Notes on the Score, Recordings, and Lyrics

"It's been said that a character..." Stephen Schwartz, Discussion forum archives at www.StephenSchwartz.com. Advice for Songwriters.

CHAPTER 17: *Godspell*'s "Prologue" and the War of Words

"Since the show is..." Stephen Schwartz, Discussion forum archives at www.StephenSchwartz.com. *Godspell* Notes for Directors and Musicians.

CHAPTER 24: "All Good Gifts" – *Godspell*'s Thanksgiving

"Those who have looked..." and "Virtually all the Episcopal..." ibid.

CHAPTER 30. "On The Willows" – The Ballad of Psalm 137

"The adaptation of the..." Stephen Schwartz, Discussion forum archives at www.StephenSchwartz.com. *Godspell* Songs.

CHAPTER 33: *Godspell* Worldwide: The Stories Continue

"We had a full house...." David Essex, *Over the Moon*, London: Virgin Books, 2012, page 104.

"In contrast to the Englishness...." Ian Bradley, *You've Got to Have a Dream: The Message of the Musical*. Louisville, KY: Westminster John Knox Press, 2004, page 133.

"like a demented child...." Martin Short, *I Must Say: My Life As a Humble Comedy Legend*. New York: Harper, 2014, page 75.

CHAPTER 35: The *Godspell* Movie

"I was very excited..." Victor Garber in Andrew Martin, *All for the Best: How Godspell Transferred from Stage to Screen*, Albany, GA: BearManor Media, 2012, page 53.

"Against this wilderness of..." Roger Ebert, "*Godspell*," found on www.rogerebert.com/reviews/godspell-1973.

"I like its music…" Vincent Canby, "The Gospel According to *'Godspell'* Comes to Screen," *The New York Times*, March 22, 1973.

CHAPTER 36: The 2011 Broadway Revival

Revival claim to Circle in the Square: Gordon Cox, "*'Godspell'* nabs Broadway venue." *Variety*, May 27, 2011.

"It's not like work…" Anna Maria Perez de Tagle in Mark Kennedy, "Broadway's *'Godspell'* is heaven-sent for its cast." This AP article was published in various publications on or around November 5, 2011.

"…relentlessly perky…." Charles Isherwood. "A Vision of Spirituality Returns to Broadway." *The New York Times*, November 7, 2011.

"To fully appreciate the…." Scott Brown. "Theater Review: Is *Godspell* Worthy?" *New Yorker Magazine*, November 7, 2011.

Variety reference: Steven Suskin. *Godspell*, November 7, 2011.

"…and the result is…" Terry Teachout, That Wild and Crazy Messiah, *Wall Street Journal* , November 11, 2011.

Bibliography and Resources for Further Information

WEBSITES

Licensing

www.theatre-maximus.com/

www.mtishows.com

www.broadwayjr.com for *Godspell Jr.*

www.samuelfrench-london.co.uk

For more resources about *Godspell* see

www.The*Godspell*Experience.com

www.*Godspell*.com

www.StephenSchwartz.com Forum Archives

www.MusicalSchwartz.com

Updates on Stephen Schwartz's work

www.TheSchwartzScene.com

UK concert tour

www.godspellinconcert.com

BOOK BY THE AUTHOR

de Giere, Carol. *Defying Gravity: The Creative Career of Stephen Schwartz, from Godspell to Wicked*. New York: Applause Theatre and Cinema Books, 2008.

OTHER BOOKS

Bradley, Ian. *You've Got to Have a Dream: The Message of the Musical*. Louisville, KY: Westminster John Knox Press, 2004.

Brooks, Peter. *The Empty Space*. London: Penguin, 1968.

Cox, Harvey. *The Feast of Fools: A Theological Essay on Festivity and Fantasy.* Cambridge, MA: Harvard University Press, 1969.

Cutler, Jesse. *Starlust: the Price of Fame.* New York: Morgan James Publishing, 2008.

Essex, David. *Over the Moon,* London: Virgin Books, 2012

Filichia, Peter. *Let's Put On A Musical,* revised second edition. New York: Back Stage Books, 2007.

Flinn, Denny Martin. *Little Musicals for Little Theatres: A Reference Guide for Musicals That Don't Need Chandeliers or Helicopters to Succeed.* New York: Limelight Editions, 2005.

Jasper, Tony. *Jesus in a Pop Culture.* Great Britain: Fontana Books, 1975.

Jones, John Bush. *Our Musicals, Ourselves: A Social History of the American Musical Theater.* Lebanon, NH: Brandeis University Press, 2004.

Kasha, Al and Joel Hirschhorn. *Notes on Broadway: Intimate Conversations with Broadway's Greatest Songwriters.* New York: Simon and Schuster, 1987.

Laird, Paul. *The Musical Theatre of Stephen Schwartz: From Godspell to Wicked and Beyond.* Lanham, Maryland: Rowman & Littlefield, 2014.

Martin, Andrew. *All For the Best: How Godspell Transferred from Stage to Screen.* Albany, GA: BearManor Media, 2012.

Martin, James, SJ, *Between Heaven and Mirth: Why Joy, Humor, and Laughter are at the Heart of the Spiritual Life.* New York: HarperCollins, 2012.

Miller, Scott. *From Assassins to West Side Story: The Director's Guide to Musical Theatre.* Portsmouth, NH: Heinemann Drama, 1996.

Shaffer, Paul. *We'll Be Here for the Rest of Our Lives.* With David Ritz. New York: Anchor Books, 2009.

Short, Martin. *I Must Say: My Life As a Humble Comedy Legend.* New York: Harper, 2014.

Tatum, W. Barnes. *Jesus at the Movies: A Guide to the First Hundred Years*, Revised and Expanded. Santa Rosa, CA: Polebridge Press, 2004.

ARTICLES

Barker, Thomas A. "Dramatics Interview, John-Michael Tebelak and Stephen Schwartz: a candid conversation with the visionary creators of *'Godspell,'*" *Dramatics Magazine*, January, 1975.

Barnes, Clive. "The Theater: *'Godspell'*; Musical About Jesus Is at Cherry Lane." New York: *The New York Times*, May 18, 1971.

Barton, Joseph, S.J. "*The Godspell* Story," *America Magazine*, December 11, 1971.

Brown, Scott. Theater Review: Is *Godspell* Worthy? *New Yorker Magazine*, November 7, 2011.

Cox, Gordon. "'*Godspell*' nabs Broadway venue." *Variety*, May 27, 2011.

Hipp, Edward Sothern. "'*Godspell*,' and More." Newark Evening News, May 18, 1971.

Isherwood, Charles. "A Vision of Spirituality Returns to Broadway." *The New York Times*, November 7, 2011.

Mishkin, Lee. "The *'Godspell'* According to Schwartz.' New York, *Morning Telegraph*, May 19, 1971.

Miller, Edwin. "Singing about Jesus, sighing over Shangri-La," *Seventeen Magazine*, 1973.

Suskin, Steven, "*Godspell*," *Variety*, November 7, 2011

Teachout, Terry, "That Wild and Crazy Messiah," *Wall Street Journal*, November 11, 2011.

Acknowledgments

Thank you! Many wonderful people contributed their insights, stories, photos, and feedback in order to make this book possible.

I'm especially grateful to Trudy Tebelak Williams who provided information on her brother, John-Michael Tebelak, as well as rare photographs of family members and materials from John-Michael's papers.

I thank Stephen Schwartz for not only giving his time for interviews and manuscript review, but also for writing the colorful Foreword.

I very much thank all the original cast members, movie cast members, and many others that I interviewed or with whom I corresponded: Bob Ari, Colette Bablon, Herb Braha, Mary Rose Betten, Jesse Cutler, Ken Davenport, Nina Faso, Bob Garrett, Daniel Goldstein, Peggy Gordon, Gary Gunas, Jay Hamburger, Prudence Holmes, Katie Hanley, Heather Hutchison, Leon Katz, Rex Knowles, Paul Kreppel, Joanne Jonas, Jeanne Lange, Sherry Landrom, Robin Lamont, Edgar Lansbury, David Lewis, Sonia Manzano, Andrew Martin, Mary Maziotti, Gilmer McCormick, Carla Meyer, Stephen Nathan, Nan Pearlman, Reet Peel, Bill Phillips, Dean Pitchford, Stephen Reinhardt, Andy Rohrer, George Salazar, Don Scardino, Sheila Schwartz, Elliot Scheiner, Paul Shaffer, Rick Shutter, Marley Sims, Wallace Smith, David Spangler, Howard Sponseller, Jerry Sroka, Bill Thomas, Lynne Thigpen, Susan Tsu, and Valerie Williams

A special thanks to director Tom Peters for his *Godspell* expertise, to my friend Andrew Ribaudo who provided many of the Biblical references, and to other dear friends who devoted hours to providing feedback on manuscript drafts. I thank Eric Brown, Scott Cain, Ashley Griffith, Tony Gonzalez, Marianne Holdzkom, Heather Hutchinson, Morgan Lavere, Bettie Lavin, Susan Mazur, Tara Mazur, Shawn McCarthy, Jim Phillips, Michael Spresser, Bob Vieira, and others.

I will always be grateful to Michael Cole for sustaining my connection to Stephen Schwartz's world, and for his special contribution to this book.

Acknowledgments

For additional professional support I thank Nancy Rose, Charmaine Ferenczi, and Angela Vieira.

For photographs and illustrations, I thank everyone listed on the Photograph Credits page, as well as Cindy Simell Devoe and the staff of the New York Public Library Permissions and Reproductions Services department.

For contributing their time and special talents, I thank my editor Linda Massie, and the designers Jerry Dorris (cover) and V. Paul Smith Jr. (inside design).

This book could not have been written without the constant support of Terry de Giere, my patient husband, who also lent his photo processing expertise to the project and endured my flurry of activity.

The Godspell Experience

Lyrics Permissions

Alas For You
Finale
from the Musical GODSPELL
Music and Lyrics by Stephen Schwartz
Copyright (c) 1972 by Range Road Music, Inc., Quartet Music, Inc. and S & J Legacy Productions LLC
Copyright Renewed
Publishing and allied rights administered by Range Road Music, Inc. c/o Carlin America, Inc. and Quartet Music c/o BUG Music, Inc., A BMG Chrysalis Company
International Copyright Secured   All Rights Reserved
Used by Permission
Reprinted by permission of Hal Leonard Corporation and Range Road Music, Inc.

Save The People
Turn Back, O Man
On The Willows
We Beseech Thee
O Bless The Lord, My Soul
from the Musical GODSPELL
Music and New Lyrics by Stephen Schwartz
Copyright (c) 1971 by Range Road Music, Inc., Quartet Music and S & J Legacy Productions LLC
Copyright Renewed
Publishing and allied rights administered by Range Road Music, Inc. c/o Carlin America, Inc. and Quartet Music c/o BUG Music, Inc., A BMG Chrysalis Company
International Copyright Secured   All Rights Reserved
Used by Permission
Reprinted by permission of Hal Leonard Corporation and Range Road Music, Inc.

By My Side
from the Musical GODSPELL
Music by Peggy Gordon
Lyrics by Jay Hamburger
Copyright (c) 1971 by Range Road Music, Inc., Quartet Music and S & J Legacy Productions LLC
Copyright Renewed

Lyrics Permissions

Publishing and allied rights administered by Range Road Music, Inc.
c/o Carlin America, Inc. and Quartet Music c/o BUG Music, Inc., A
BMG Chrysalis Company
International Copyright Secured   All Rights Reserved
Used by Permission
Reprinted by permission of Hal Leonard Corporation and Range Road Music, Inc.

Day By Day
from the Musical GODSPELL
Music and New Lyrics by Stephen Schwartz
Original Lyrics by Richard of Chichester (1197-1253)
Copyright (c) 1971 by Range Road Music, Inc., Quartet Music and
S & J Legacy Productions LLC
Copyright Renewed
Publishing and allied rights administered by Range Road Music, Inc.
c/o Carlin America, Inc. and Quartet Music c/o BUG Music, Inc., A
BMG Chrysalis Company
International Copyright Secured   All Rights Reserved
Used by Permission
Reprinted by permission of Hal Leonard Corporation and Range Road Music, Inc.

All Good Gifts
from the Musical GODSPELL
Music and New Lyrics by Stephen Schwartz
Original Lyrics by Matthias Claudius (1782)
Translated by Jane M. Campbell (1861)
Copyright (c) 1971 by Range Road Music, Inc., Quartet Music and
S & J Legacy Productions LLC
Copyright Renewed
Publishing and allied rights administered by Range Road Music, Inc.
c/o Carlin America, Inc. and Quartet Music c/o BUG Music, Inc., A
BMG Chrysalis Company
International Copyright Secured   All Rights Reserved
Used by Permission
Reprinted by permission of Hal Leonard Corporation and Range Road Music, Inc.

Beautiful City
from GODSPELL
Music and Lyrics by Stephen Schwartz

The Godspell Experience

Copyright (c) 1972 (Renewed), 1973, 1993, 2012 Grey Dog Music and
S & J Legacy Productions LLC
Publishing and allied rights administered by Grey Dog Music
International Copyright Secured   All Rights Reserved
www.stephenschwartz.com
Reprinted by permission of Hal Leonard Corporation

Prologue (Tower Of Babble)
Learn Your Lessons Well
Light Of The World
Prepare Ye
All For The Best
from the Musical GODSPELL
Music and Lyrics by Stephen Schwartz
Copyright (c) 1971 by Range Road Music, Inc., Quartet Music and
S & J Legacy Productions LLC
Copyright Renewed
Publishing and allied rights administered by Range Road Music, Inc.
c/o Carlin America, Inc. and Quartet Music c/o BUG Music, Inc., A
BMG Chrysalis Company
International Copyright Secured   All Rights Reserved
Used by Permission
Reprinted by permission of Hal Leonard Corporation and Range Road Music, Inc.

Photography Credits

Many individuals contributed photographs and illustrations for this book. Below is an index of photos by photographer name, followed a list of photos from individuals. The page numbers refer to the print edition of the book.

Photographers from who photos have been acquired or who have given permission for their use:

Cole, Michael: 310, 311

Daniel, Jeremy: xiv, 200, 206, 248, 311, 312

de Giere, Terence: xiii, 14

de Giere, Carol: 68, 88, 242

Duncan, Kenn: (back of title page), 2, 103, 130, 182, 218, 384 (credit: Photo by Kenn Duncan/©The New York Public Library)

Freed, Sam: 124, 144, 212 (2 photos), 252

Parisella, Kami: 206

Phillips, Bill: 192

Randolph, William: 163 (Official credit: William "PoPsie" Randolph © 2008, Michael Randolph www.PoPsiePhotos.com PoPsie-photos@att.net)

Rosegg, Carol: 144 ©CarolRosegg

Schwartz, Stephen: sheet music 198-199

Swope, Martha 1, 100, 101, 104 (two photos), 200, 254 (credit: Photo by Martha Swope/©The New York Public Library).

Tsu, Susan: costume sketch 256

The remaining photographs are from the private collections of:

Michael Cole: 320 (two photos)

The Godspell Experience

Jesse Cutler: 103, 118, 164

Davenport Theatrical: 164 (cast album cover)

Nina Faso: 52

Gary Gunas: 102

Great Lakes Theater, page 52

Katie Hanley: 117 (bottom photo), 118, 301 (two photos), 302

Leon Katz: 52

Robin Lamont: vii, 68

Sherry Landrom and Rex Knowles: 276

Carla Meyer: 32, 33 (two photos), 150

Gilmer McCormick, 119

Nan Pearlman: 116

Bill Phillips: 31

George Salazar: 164

Don Scardino: 321

Stephen Schwartz: 13, 24

Susan Tsu: 51, 52, 224, 256

Trudy Tebelak Williams 12, 24, 52 (Photograph of Susan Tsu), 117 (photo of the Promenade) , 120, 121, 260, 261, 262, 276

While every effort has been made to trace copyright holders and obtain permission, we offer apologies for any instances in which this was not possible and for any inadvertent omissions. Any omissions brought to our attention will be remedied, and credit will be adjusted in future editions.

Index

Page numbers in italics refer to photographs.

A

A Chorus Line   138, 280
Aduba, Uzo   304, *311*
"Alas for You". *See* Songs (*Godspell* Vocal Score)
albums. *See* recordings: cast albums and soundtrack
Alford, Lamar   2, 74, 81, 83, 89, *101*, *104*, 110, *118*, 194, 213, *218*, 254
   death of   xii
   in Broadway production   268
"All for the Best". *See* Songs (*Godspell* Vocal Score)
"All Good Gifts". *See* Songs (*Godspell* Vocal Score)
Alterman, Charlie   305
Ari, Bob   45, 48, *52*, 126, 225
Arista   169
auditions   111
Australian productions   272–273
Aviks, Valda   *260*

B

Babel, Tower of   171
Bablon, Colette   17, 65
Bacharach, Burt   189
Baker, Word   23
band   86–87, 166, 223, 249
   at Café La MaMA   67
   at CMU   43

Barrowman, John   169
Bassey, Shirley   187
Baum, Rebecca   110
Bax, Clifford   225
Bayes, Sammy   273, 284, 287, 293
Bean, Shoshana   169
Beatitudes   100, 136, 141, 208
The Beatles   16, 18, 26
"Beautiful City". *See* Songs (*Godspell* Vocal Score)
Bell Records   108, *163*, 169
Berea Summer Theatre   9, 39
Berlin, Irving   208
Bernstein, Leonard   226, 231
Bernstein, Shirley   ix, 71
Beruh, Joseph ("Joe")   ix, xii, 65, 69–70, 87, 92, 96, 106, 107, 111, *118*, 223, 277
   as *Godspell* movie producer   281
Between Heaven and Mirth   153
Bible as source   x, 40, 76
Bible references
   Genesis 11:1-9   171
   Isaiah 40:3   179
   John 8:1-11   235
   John 8:3-11   100
   Leviticus 24:19-20   126
   Luke 10:25-37   99
   Luke 12:16-20   99, 203
   Luke 15:11-32   99
   Luke 16:19-31   100
   Luke 18:1-8   99
   Luke 18:10-14   99
   Malachi 3:1   179
   Matthew 3:3   179
   Matthew 5:11   208
   Matthew 5:12   208
   Matthew 5:13-16   219

Matthew 5:38-39   126
Matthew 6:22   62
Matthew 6:22-23   197
Matthew 7:12   154
Matthew 13:1-23   100
Matthew 18:21-35   99
Matthew 21:12   230
Matthew 23:13-37   126, 229
Matthew 23:15   229
Matthew 25:31-46   100
Blaemire, Nick   304, *311*
"Bless the Lord". *See* Songs (*Godspell* Vocal Score)
Bleu, Corbin   308
Bolick, Duane   43, 49, 59, 179, 213, 249
Boston production   109, 112, 113, 264
Bradley, Ian   270
Braha, Herb   ii, *1*, 55, 59, 60, 64, *68*, 93, *101*, *104*, 110, *118*, 122, *124*, 148, *218*, 219, *252*, *276*, 299
Braverman, Bart   *124*, *212*
Breaking the Fourth Wall   139-140
Brill, Tony and Margaret   7
Broadway productions. *See under Godspell* productions
Brodziak, Kenn   272
Brook, Peter   27, 28
"By my Side". *See* Songs (*Godspell* Vocal Score)
Byrd, David   75

C

Café La MaMa. *See Godspell* productions
Camera Three   264
Campbell, Jane Montgomery   214
Canada, Jimmy   57, *68*, 73
Candelight Dinner Theatre   129
Cannes Film Festival   296
Carnegie Mellon University   ix, 9, 11, *14*, 15-23, 70, 155. *See also Godspell* productions: Carnegie Mellon University
1960's spirit   15-16, 17, 21, 48
Carra, Lawrence ("Larry")   27, 40-41, 46, *51*, 65, 275
Carr, Jacquie-Ann   270
Chaplin, Charlie   127
characters   3, 38, 40, 42, 60, 61, 125-130, 155-156
  Gilmer   136, 193
  Herb   136, 219
  Jeffrey   136, 160
  Jesus   90, 125, 128, 131-133, 134, 135, 141-143, 145, 147, 153-155, 183, 207, 208-209, 253
  Joanne   83, 136, 203
  John/Judas   40, 47, 90, 136, 141-143, 180, 207, 208-209
  Lamar   136, 213, 214
  Peggy   129, 132, 134, 136, 238
  Robin   79, 132, 136, 187, 189
  Sonia   127, 136, 226
Cherry Lane Theatre   82-83, *88*, 89, 109. *See also Godspell* productions: Cherry Lane Theatre
Children of Eden   230
Chown, Avril   *260*
The Circle in the Square Theater   303, *312*
clowns in *Godspell*   38, 40, 42, 43, 44, 63, 83, 86, 89, 115, 125-130, 145-149, 155, 161, 291
Cole, Michael   316-319, *320*
Collins, Judy   187
Columbia Pictures   281, 296

community. *See Godspell* theme of community
costumes for *Godspell*   44–45, 47, 57, 64, 66, 67, 96. *See also* makeup
  movie costumes   291
Covington, Julie   270
Cox, Harvey   37, *118*, 152
crucifixion   295
Cutler, Jesse   87, *103*, *118*, *164*, 167, 249, 289

D

dance (choreography)   85–86, 210, *212*, 293
Danson, Randy   52
Davenport, Ken   137, 303–304
"Day by Day". *See* Songs (*Godspell* Vocal Score)
Day, Darren   169
de Giere, Carol   xi, xii
The Dick Cavett Show   106, 264
Duncan, Stuart   87, 115, 281

E

Eastwood, Jayne   260
Ebert, Roger   298
The Empty Space   28
Erat, Will   *144*, 169
Essex, David   *262*, 269–270

F

Faso, Laurie   *31*, 268
Faso, Nina   25, *52*, 63, 81, 91, 92, *118*, *119*, 158, 279
  as co-director (Los Angeles)   110
  as directing major   23
  as director   111, 114, 273
  as replacement cast member   105–106
  as Tebelak's associate at La MaMa   54, 57, 63, 64
  comments about Tebelak   18–19, 35, 36, 93, 155
  description of   18, 95
  script work   106
The Feast of Fools   37, 38, 128, 152
5th Dimension   187
Filichia, Peter   122, 308
"Finale". *See* Songs (*Godspell* Vocal Score)
finances   87, 277–280
Fitzwilliam, Neil   270
Foa, Barrett   *144*, 169
Foraker, Lois   268
Ford's Theatre production   *120*, 147
Forella, Michael   *117*

G

Garber, Victor   169, 268, 271, 285, 291, 296, 298, *301*, *302*
Garrett, Bob   113, *124*, 209, *252*, 268, *276*, 313
Garson, Barbara   26
Gattelli, Christopher   303, 309
Gerstein, Baillie   *150*
Gifford, Edwin and Michael   75, 107
Gister, Earle   22, 41, 56
Godspell title   38, 40, 73, 76
Godspell characters. *See* characters
Godspell Commune Company   277–280
Godspell Jr.   116, *206*
Godspell logo and poster   75, *76*, *164*
Godspell movie   219, 281–300
  songs for   257, 288–289
Godspell productions

357

Broadway   xiii, 268–269
Broadway revival   137, 194, 197, 220, *248*, 254, 303–310, *312*
Café La MaMa   xiii, 3
  casting   54–56
  music   59, 67
  opening and performances   65, 67
  rehearsals for   57–63
  State of the Show   65–68
Carnegie Mellon University   xiii, 3, 35–50
  opening   45–46
  rehearsals   42–45
  score   43–44
  State of the Show   47–50
Cherry Lane Theatre   xiii, 3, 99
  casting   73
  development of   69–76
  music   73
  opening   3, 97–98
  rehearsals at   xi, 82–86
  State of the Show   99–100
  Other   109–116, 263–275
Godspell publicity   107, 263–264, 264, 265
Godspell script   58, 77, 83, 106, 131
  adjustments   113, 115, 160–162
Godspell settings   129
Godspell theme of community   5, 37, 79, 123, 135–140, 145, 148, 155, 159, 172, 223, 238, 254, 308, 317
Golden Rule   154
Goldstein, Daniel ("Danny")   137, 146, 303, 304, 305–306, 307, 309, *311*
Good Samaritan. *See* Parables and Stories: Good Samaritan
Gordon, Peggy   60, 64, 67, *68*, 76, *104*, 110, *118*, 120, 136, 142, 149, *242*, 267
  as a singer   108, 220
  as composer of "By My Side"   21, 59, 170, 233–242
  as original cast member   *1*, 3, 81, 83, 84, 86, 89, *101*, *104*, 105, 107, *218*, *276*
  comments on Broadway revival   309
  comments on Joe Beruh   96, 278
  comments on Lamar   213
  comments on Tebelak   34, 58, 85, 95, 132, 134, 161, 171, 313
  description of   56
Grammy Awards   264
Grammy Awards ceremony   *163*, 264
Great Lakes Shakespeare Festival   27, 275
Greene, David   257, 282–286, 288–289, 292, 293, 300, *302*
Grotowski, Jerzy   23, 59, 114
Gunas, Gary   *102*, 112, 277

H

Haid, Charles   ix, 65, 71, 105
Hair (the musical)   19, 47, 110, 138
Hamburger, Jay   21, 25, 27, 29, 32, *242*
  as lyricist of "By My Side"   170, 233–242
  description of   233
Hamilton, Dan   *144*
Hanley, Katie   15, 109, 115, *117*, *118*, 169, 281, 284, 299, *301*, *302*
Hannum, Richard   53, 94
Harrison, George   189
Harris, Thrae   314

Haskell, David *ii*, 1, 44, *52*, 56, 58, 61, 84, 90, *101*, *104*, 109, 110, 127, 141, 180, *182*, *218*, *254*, 274, *276*, 296, *302*
  death of xii
Hayes, Helen 117
Head, Murray 269, 270
Heim, Alan 282
Heimann, Richard 282, 298, *301*
Heller, Randee 117
Henderson, Celisse 304, *311*
Henshall, Ruthie 169
Hewett, Colleen 187, 273
Hoffman, Abbie 48
Hoffman, Miranda 303
Holland, Michael 170, 202, 254, 305
Holmes, Prudence ("Tina") 56, 67, 73
Holmes, Tina 68
humor in *Godspell* 58, 61, 128, 152
Huntington Playhouse 25
Hutchison, Heather 146, 161
hymns, Episcopal xi, 78, 184, 203, 213–214, 215, 225

I

Ian, Janis 189
Improvisation (theater technique) 16, 28, 29, 45, 59, 62, 111, 114, 115
injuries during productions 267
intermission 223
Irons, Jeremy 270
An Italian Straw Hat 28–29
"I Want" song 184

J

Jackson, Merrell 285, *302*
Jacobs, Martha 52
James, Morgan 304, *311*
Jesus. *See under* characters
Jesus Christ Superstar 156–157, 269
John, Elton xi, 214
Jonas, Joanne 1, 2, 74, 79, 81, 83, 86, *101*, *104*, 117, *118*, 131, 138, 167, *218*, 268, 284, 299, 300, *302*
  as dancer 86, 293
  as singer 202
Judaism and *Godspell* 157–158, 180
Judas. *See under* characters

K

Kahan, Judy *124*, 252
Kalukango, Joaquina 304
Katz, Leon 19, 21, 28, 34, 36, 41, 46, *52*
Kazantzakis, Nikos 142
Kean, Peter *118*
Kimball, Chad 169
King, Stan *52*
Kleinsinger, George 9
Knowles, Rex 114, 152, 265, *276*
Korins, David 303
Krauss, Marvin 111
Kreppel, Paul 139, 215
Kritzer, Leslie 169
Krop, Eric Michael 304

L

La Bonte, Richard 87, *118*, 249, 289
Lacamoire, Alex 170
Laird, Paul 259
La MaMa (Café La MaMa) ix, xiii, 53, *68*. *See also Godspell*

productions
Lamont, Robin   5, 56, 58, 59, 67, 68, 79, 110, *118*, 126, *130*, 149, 159, 167, 219, 223, 267, 278, 295, *301*, *302*
  as CMU student and cast member   20, 22, 41–42, 46, 47, *52*
  as original cast member   *1*, 85, 95, *101*, *104*, 106, *218*
  comments on Schwartz   190
  description of   187, 225
  in Broadway production   268
  in *Godspell* movie   284, 292–293, 296
Lamp of the Body   197
Landrom, Sherry   152, 160, 265, *276*
Lange, Jeanne   109, 110, *124*, 141, *252*, 274, *276*, 283
Lansbury, Angela   69, 282
Lansbury, Edgar   ix, 65, 69–70, 81, 84, 87–88, 92, 106, 107, 111–110, *119*, 140, 277, 278, *302*
  and London production   269, 270
  as *Godspell* movie producer   281–282, 286, 297
  comments on Tebelak   133, 138
Last Supper   157, *252*, 257
The Last Temptation of Christ   142
Lathram, Elizabeth   *117*, *118*, *124*, *252*, 268
"Learn Your Lessons Well". *See* Songs (*Godspell* Vocal Score)
Lee, Bobby   268
Leung, Telly   170, 194, *200*, 304, 306, *311*

Levy, Eugene   *260*, 271
Lewis, David   250
licensing of *Godspell*   115–116
"Light of the World". *See* Songs (*Godspell* Vocal Score)
Limited in Company   25–33
The Living Theatre   34, 47
Lloyd Webber, Andrew   156, 264, 270
London production   269–271
Los Angeles production   109
Los Angeles revival   274

M

MacBird!   25–27, 30, 31, 39
Macgill, Moyna   281
Mach, Corey   304
Macintosh, Cameron   270
magic (illusions) & props   90, 136
The Magic Show   230
Maguire, Gregory   x
Makeup   145–149
The Mamas and the Papas   xi, 219
Manzano, Sonia   *1*, 20, 41, 43, 45, *52*, 56, 58, 60, 66, 74, *101*, *104*, 108, *117*, *118*, 127, *130*, *218*, 224, 225–226, 267
Marat/Sade   27, 39
Mariano, Patti   *276*
Marigold and Elkin   21, 233, 235, 237
Mark Taper Forum   110
Martin, Andrea   *260*, 271
Martin, Andrew   298
Martin, James (SJ)   153
Marx, Groucho   113
Mattison, Julia   304
Mazziotti, Mary   43, *52*
McCormick, Gilmer   2, 5, 22, 25, 55, 58, 59, 60, 63, *119*, 134, 161, 194, *200*, 219, 274, *276*,

278
and "By My Side" 234
as original cast member   1, 95, 101, 104, 105, 107, 218
in *Godspell* movie   284, 294, 302
Meldrum, Verity-Anne   270
Mendez, Lindsay   170, 202, 206, 304, 311
Meyer, Carla   26, 29, 30, 33, 150
Montgomery, James   203
Motown   18
Music Theatre International (MTI)   116
Mylett, Jeffrey   xi, 1, 25, 55, 59, 64, 67, 68, 84, 85, 101, 104, 110, 118, 218, 276
  as recorder player   214
  death of   xii
  description of   244
  in *Godspell* movie   285, 302

N

Nathan, Stephen   ii, 2, 25, 26, 29, 33, 54, 61–62, 62–63, 110, 118, 125, 130, 133, 135, 148, 157, 182, 183, 210, 276, 280, 314, 370
  as CMU student   14, 20
  as original cast member   1, 82, 84, 90, 91, 92, 101, 104, 218
  as singer   183
  comments on "Alas of You"   231
  comments on *Godspell* movie   285
New Zealand production   261
Nyro, Laura   xi, 74, 201–202

O

Ondrasik, John   170
"On the Willows". *See* Songs (*Godspell* Vocal Score)
Open Theater   34

P

Parables and Stories
  Good Samaritan   127, 160
  Good Seed   135, 213
  Prodigal Son   103, 128, 131, 132, 161, 219, 300
  Talents   97
Parkin, Deryk   270
Parrish, Hunter   304, 311
Paul Sills' Story Theatre   16
Pearlman, Nan   115, 116, 272
Pell, Reet   113, 118
Perez dé Tagle, Anna Maria   304, 306, 311
Peters, Tom   168
Phillips, Bill   8, 27, 30, 31, 34, 39, 41, 94, 114, 275
Pippin   x, 71, 72, 168
Pitchford, Dean   106, 109, 112, 117, 128, 147, 150, 153
  comments on Tebelak   162
Planner, Mark   117
Platt, Marc   259
"Prepare Ye". *See* Songs (*Godspell* Vocal Score)
Prodigal Son. *See* Parables and Stories: Prodigal Son
producers. *See* individual listings for Beruh, Duncan, and Lansbury
The Producer's Perspective   303
"Prologue". *See* Songs (*Godspell* Vocal Score)
Promenade Theatre   109–110, 117

Q

Quinn brothers   26, 67

361

R

Radner, Gilda   260, 271
recordings: cast albums and soundtrack   168–170
  1971 Original Off-Broadway Cast   108, 169
  1973 *Godspell* soundtrack   169, 289–291, 298
  1993 London Studio Cast   169
  2000 Off-Broadway Cast Recording   169
  2001 *Godspell* tour   169
  2011 40th anniversary album set   170
  2011 Broadway revival   *164*, 170
Reinhardt, Stephen   4, 74, 80–81, 84, 85, 87, 97, 114, *119*, 154, 166, 167, 273, 274, 319
  and soundtrack   289
  as singer   249
  comments on music   219, 245
Resurrection   158
reviews and reception   4, 98, 107, 110, 306–310
  challenges   265, 272
  religious response   5, 263
Rice, Tim   156, 264, 270
Richard of Chichester   188
Rohrer, Andy   23, 42, 45, 47, *51, 52*, 110, *118, 124, 144, 212, 229, 252, 254, 256*
Rolfing, Tom   268
Rossini, Gioacchino   208
Roundhouse   270

S

Saffery, Tom   270
Salazar, George   128, *164*, 220, 304, 310, *311*
Salsberg, Gerry   260
Sardi's restaurant   98, 105

Saturday Night Live   16, 271
"Save the People". *See* Songs (*Godspell* Vocal Score)
Scardino, Don   142, 148, *260*, 266, 271, 314–315, *321*
  in Broadway production   268
Schachner, Dan   169
Scheiner, Elliot   *164*, 166, 289
Schwartz, Carole   ix, 71, 86, *119*
Schwartz, Scott   275
Schwartz, Sheila (mother of Stephen)   9
Schwartz, Stanley (father of Stephen)   9
Schwartz, Stephen   ix, *xiv*, 3, 5, *13, 24*, 70–73, 74, *118, 119*, 127, 138, 140, 145, 149, *164, 311*
  as record producer   108, 289
  at CMU drama school   16, 25
  childhood of   9–11
  co-director (Los Angeles)   110
  collaboration with Tebelak   25, 77, 79, 84, 85, 92–96, 96
  comments on Broadway revival   304, 309
  comments on "By My Side"   238–239
  comments on casting   269
  comments on *Godspell* movie   286–287, 296, 297
  comments on intermission   223
  comments on Jesus   133, 154, 155, 159, 207, 208–209
  comments on Judas   142, 143, 207, 208–209
  description of   17, 77
  Godspell band. working with   86–87
  Jewish heritage of   78, 207
  musical influences   18, 189, 201–202, 208, 219, 226, 231, 244, 253

musical interests of   10, 214
musical staging by   93, 95
musical training   10
note to directors   130, 135, 162
passion for theater   10
pianos of   *xiii*, 71
RCA Records experience   ix, 71, 108
songwriting techniques   17, 78, 79, 80, 165–166, 171–172, 179–180, 187, 193, 201, 207–210, 229, 230–231, 243–248, 249, 253
script. *See Godspell* script
Sermon on the Mount   40, 100
Sesame Street   20
Set, Set Design, Lighting   3, 57, 63–64, 66–68, 75, 91, *101*, 181
  fence   3, 91, 253
  sawhorses and planks   63–64
The Seventh Seal   300
Shaffer, Paul   184, 188, 202, 272, 290
Shakespeare, William   125
Sherwood, Linda   *124*, 252
Short, Martin   146, *260*, 271
Shutter, Rick ("Ricky")   86–87, *103*, 289
Sills, Paul   16, 114
Simon and Garfunkel   18
Sims, Marley   *124*, 157, *252*, 268, 274, *276*
Smith, Wallace   143, 170, 304, *311*, 312
Songs (*Godspell* Vocal Score)   26, 78, 78–81, 78–80, 84, 165–170, 259
  "Alas for You"   80, 126, 229–232
  "All for the Best"   80, 86, 90, 141, 207–212, 288, 290, 294
  "All Good Gifts"   49, 81, 132, 136, 213–217, 300
  Arrangements   166–170
  "Beautiful City"   254, 257–259, 291
  "Bless the Lord"   1, 49, 79, 81, 85, 113, 201–205, 290
  "By My Side"   21, 59, 61, 67, 78, 97, 108, 132, 134, 233–242, 299
    song title   240
  "Day by Day"   4, 5, 49, 79, 81, 132, 140, 163, 187–191, 264, 273, 292
  "Finale"   80, 253–255
  "Learn Your Lessons Well"   97, 193–197
  "Light of the World"   219–223
  "On the Willows"   xi, 49, 249–251
  "Prepare Ye"   49, 142, 179–181, 254, 264
  "Prologue"   40, 80, 84, 171–178, 181, 288, 305
  "Save the People"   49, 132, 183–186, 254
  "Sermon on the Mount"   49
  "Turn Back, O Man"   49, 86, *224*, 225–228, 287, 299
  "We Beseech Thee"   90, *121*, 243–248, *248*, 257, 306
Songs (Other)
  "Eli's Comin'"   202
  "Fire and Rain"   214
  "Gemini Childe"   219
  "Lost in the Wilderness"   230
  "Marigold's Song"   59, 234, 236
  "My Sweet Lord"   189
  "No Good Deed"   230
  "Old Fashioned Wedding"   208
  "Save the Country"   202
  "The Raven and the Swan"   336
  "We Plow the Fields, and

Scatter" 214
"West End Avenue" 230
"What the World Needs Now" 189
"You Can't Hurry Love" 244
"You're Just in Love" 208
"Your Song" 214
Soper, Gay 270
soundtrack. *See* recordings: cast albums and soundtrack
South African productions 273
Spolin, Viola 16
Sponseller, Howard 39, 43, 113, *117*, 160, 271, 286, 291
Sroka, Jerry 113, *150*, 285, 293, *302*
Stevens, Clifford 278, 279
Stevens, James 52
Stewart, Ellen 3, 53
St. John the Divine Episcopal Cathedral 263, 273
Sucher, Sherrie 291
Superman shirt 44, *150*, *256*
The Supremes xi, 244

T

Taylor, James xi, 214
Tebelak, Genevieve (mother of John-Michael) 8, *12*, 35, 39
Tebelak, John (father of John-Michael) 8, *12*, 35
Tebelak, John-Michael vii, x, 3, 6, *12*, *24*, 53, 82, 89, *103*, *104*, *118*, *192*, *276*, 280, *302*
 and *Godspell* movie 286, 287, 288, 296
 as director 25–34, 57–60, 85, 93, 94, 114, 189, 229, 275
 at CMU 16, 18, 21, 25, 34, 35, 35–50, 97
 childhood of 7

collaboration with Schwartz 25, 77, 79, 84, 85, 92–96, 96
death of xii
description of 8, 18, 19, 27, 30, 72, 77, 93–94, 95, 105, 129, 275
influences on 23, 27, 34, 39
inspiration for *Godspell* 37, 125
passion for theater 8
spiritual inclinations of 35, 126
Theatre Maximus 115
Thigpen, Lynne 109, 110, 169, 284, 295, *302*
Thomas, Bill *124*, 214, 252, 266
Three Stooges 61, 128
The Today Show 5, 107, 264
Tolbert, Berlinda *150*
The Tonight Show 264
Toronto production *260*, 271
Tsu, Susan 44, *52*, 57, 67, 96, 98, 263, 291
 costume sketch by *256*
"Turn Back, O Man. *See* Songs (*Godspell* Vocal Score)

U

Utt, Kenny 282

V

Valando, Tommy 190
vaudeville 61, 207, 208, 226
Vereen, Ben 291
Viet Rock 34

W

Walker, Jewel 127
Webb, Marti 270
Webb, Rudy *260*
"We Beseech Thee". *See* Songs

(*Godspell* Vocal Score)
West, Mae   225
Whitney Players   *206*
Wicked   168, 230, 259, 303
Wilbur Theatre   112
Williams, Andy   187, 264
Williams, Trudy Tebelak   7, 8, *12*, 35–36, 40
Williams, Valerie   158, 268
The Wizard of Oz   180
World Trade Center   294
Wynn, Ed   84

Y

Yeats, William Butler   249
The Youngbloods   16

My *Godspell* Experience
(Write your own story!)

The Godspell Experience

Stephen Nathan as Jesus in the Cherry Lane Theatre production, June 1971. (Photo by Kenn Duncan/©The New York Public Library)

Made in the USA
Lexington, KY
17 March 2015